MW00387221

This day...I will bless you.
Haggai 2:19

We begin a New Year with a text from the Prophet Haggai. Consider the historical context. Centered in Jerusalem, the Kingdom of Judah was defeated by the Babylonians in 586 B.C. Babylon includes the modern nation of Iraq.

The Babylonian Empire fell to the Persian Empire in 539 B.C. The Persian Empire includes the modern nation of Iran. The leader of the Persians, Cyrus— called "the servant of the Lord" by the Prophet Isaiah— allowed the Jewish exiles to return home.

Like many of us who forget God's good fortune in our history when life is in the flow of success, so the former exiles took for granted God's gracious acts. God had instructed the people to rebuild their temple and renew their faith. Safely at home, procrastination set aside their spiritual duties. Negligence forestalled their promised commitments to the Lord.

The word of the Lord came to the people: Set your house in order. Set the right priorities in your life. Love God, love the members of your community, your family and neighbors as you love yourself. And make alive your center of worship, which presently you have forsaken. When you do this, in word and in action, God said: **"This day I will bless you."**

Eternal God, this day, the first day of a New Year, I reset my goals, priorities and purposes in life to your perfect will. Thy. Will. Be. Done. In Christ. Amen

Happy New Year!
Love, Mom
and Dad

Set my house in order,

*My soul is weary with sorrow; strengthen me according
to your word. I have chosen the way of faithfulness; I run in the path of your
commands for you have broadened my understanding. Psalm 119:28f
(Jesus said) "In this world you will have trouble.
But take heart! I have overcome the world." John 16:33*

Listen

L ord, at the beginning of this spiritual
journey, I sense my need for you.
Yet, I am not quite sure how to reach you.

I heard someone say, "Read your Bible."
But too often the words are like bullets
that ricochet off my brain.

I heard someone say, "Pray."
But my prayers, hurled heavenward, fall
back to the dusty earth like lifeless stones.

I heard someone say, "Meditate."
But my wandering mind was lost in a
desert of random thoughts.

Lord, *this day* speak to me through
prayer-listening and turn lifeless stones
to bread.

Lord, speak to the meditations of my
heart that I may see, hear, and feel your
presence, amid life's wilderness.
You are the way, the truth, and the life.
You are the Living Christ. Amen

We know that in all things
God works for the good of those who love him. Romans 8:28

On the entrance of a Christian mission in China I saw these words: "Thanks for what has been, 'Yes' to what shall be." The 'yes' at that moment looked like a failure of mission. The communist government had not dealt kindly with Christian missionaries. But the ones I met were not dismayed. They genuinely believed "that in all things," both good and bad, "God works for good." Sometimes we don't see how.

Failure is not bad. In fact learning from failure may be the only way to succeed with integrity.

Consider a history you have read or seen in a recent award-winning movie, the failures of Abraham Lincoln, America's greatest President in my opinion. 1816: his daddy lost the home in bankruptcy. 1818: his mother died. 1831: his first business failed. 1832: he lost an election for state legislature. 1832: he got a job but went bankrupt. He failed to get into law school. 1833: he started a business on a friend's loan, declared bankruptcy again, took 17 years to pay back the loan. 1835: engaged to be married, deeply in love, his fiancé died. 1836: mental illness struck Lincoln down, confined him to bed for six months. 1836: he won election, but rejected by peers as Speaker of the House. 1840: he sought election to the Electoral College, defeated by his own party. 1843: he ran for Congress and lost, was elected in 1846, and defeated in 1848. 1849: he was jobless and could not even get a government job. 1854: he lost his U.S. Senate race, and was defeated again in 1858.

Twenty-four months later, Lincoln was elected President of the U.S.A.

God moves in "strange and mysterious ways, his wonders to behold." In ALL things God works for the GOOD.

God, I confess my impatience and fear when failures surround me. I trust your deliverance. Amen

(Jesus said) "When you pray, go into your room, close the door and pray to your Father, who is unseen. Then your Father, who sees what is done in secret, will reward you. Matthew 6:6

Prayer clarifies the focus of two important quests in our human existence: the search for the true self, and the search for the true God. Let's be abundantly clear...our "search for God" is a euphemism, because God is not lost. God "searches the human heart." God is the subject and we are the objects of this disclosure. That is why "private prayer" is strongly emphasized by Jesus.

True prayer is a posture and perception of the inner most experience of our being. Prayer prepares us to be in the presence of the Grand Initiator, God. Christ does "stand at the door and knock" in the imagery drawn by the writer of Revelation (3:20); however, he is not passive. When Christ enters the locked doors of our hearts, every compartment of our lives will ultimately be infused with his vibrancy.

The late Dag Hammarskjöld, a global political leader, prayed this way: "Give me a pure heart—that I may see thee; a humble heart—that I may hear thee; a heart of love—that I may serve thee; a heart of faith—that I may abide in thee." St. Teresa of Avila (d.1582) said: "Let nothing dismay you, all things pass; God never changes. Patience attains all it strives for. One who has God lacks nothing. God alone suffices."

Our Father who art in Heaven, hallowed be Thy name. Thy kingdom come, Thy will be done, in my life, now, this day, and in all the days to come. In Christ I pray. Amen

I have seen you in the sanctuary and beheld
your power and glory. Your love is better than life. Psalm 63:3-4

Sometimes the shadows of magical experience fall across our wandering paths when we are least expecting it. Once walking the streets of Boston, I happened upon a bookstore with unorganized stacks of antique books, picking one whose aroma authenticated its date, mid-18th century, *Diaries and Letters of Reverend William Emerson, 1743—1776.* Enticing. Written during the years leading up to the American Revolution, I opened to January 2, 1775, and read this minister's "text for the sermon: To See thy Power and thy Glory." The pastor added at the end: "Training for the purpose of enlisting minute men was unsuccessful." However, on January 16, he noted, "50 to 60 Minute Men were enlisted." And from this entry forward, "Minute Men" was a proper noun. On the 29th day, the preacher wrote: "Weather benefitted warlike preparation… Proceeded with military maneuvers." For the minister, faith became action in the arena of current issues: "Who rules conscience—Government, Church Councils, or Christ? What should a faithful believer do in a time of revolution?" That day a new thought came to me, "When did the American Revolution really begin?" In the mind of Pastor Emerson, the idea of freedom had taken root years before 1776.

When did the revolution of faith in God's sovereign love and grace through Christ begin in my life? Was it when I was a boy, or, 2,000 years ago on a hill named Golgotha in Jerusalem, or before the creation of everything in the eternal heart of a loving God?

Lord of all, help me to have the wisdom to know your will in the complex web of life. This day I choose to have courage to do your will. In Christ. Amen

God said,"Let there be light." Genesis 1:3 Hear, O Israel:
The Lord our God, the Lord is one. Love the Lord with all your heart and
soul and strength. Deuteronomy 6:4

Our Lord is the God of the spoken Word. The first verb describing the original act of creation is the word "said." God spoke the cosmos into being. The key word of human faith and response to our kind of God is "hear." The summary statement of the Hebrew faith is called the "Shema," the Hebrew verb for "hear." This grand cosmos has come into being through a power that is to be heard, and the first movement in the symphony of belief is "hearing." Arthur Rubinstein said, "I'm passionately involved in life. To be able to speak, to see, to hear, to walk, to have music…it is all a miracle."

We cannot hear God when we are listening to the fear filled voices of the inner self, or when superficial material needs nag us for attention.

God has taught us through the hard experiences of life that "hearing" God comes first by silence. "Be still and know that I am God" is not only a suggestion. It is a mandate for the discipline of detachment…from everything that distracts us from God. Passive modes are not natural among the habits I learned that push me to win, achieve, and succeed. I confess.

Perhaps we may learn from the ebb and flow of nature. We gain vitality of spirit, in waiting, listening, resting, thinking about God whom we see in the person of Jesus.

Christ my Lord, I hear you speak. Your words carry across the canyons of human history like echoes gaining strength. I hear you say, "Follow me." I shall. Amen

(Jesus said) "Whoever has been forgiven little loves little."
Luke 7:47

The four Gospels depict eight occasions when our Lord Jesus accepted invitations to dinner. Three were normal social gatherings such as the wedding feast at Cana (which included an abnormal amount of fine wine, provided by Jesus). Five of the dinner stories about Jesus highlight the fact that Jesus defied the rules of social propriety. Luke relates the scene at a Pharisee's house, a highly respectable man. A "woman who lived a sinful life" heard that Jesus was there and came to the home with a present of perfume. She observed that Jesus' feet had not been washed by the host, the custom. So she falling to his feet in humble homage weeping, "began to wet his feet with her tears, wiped them with her hair, and poured perfume on them."

Imagine this scene. The Pharisee said that Jesus could not be a genuine prophet or he "would have known what kind of woman she is." The host recoiled at the self-revealing love shown in this interaction. Jesus accepted the woman without judgment. He pointed out to the Pharisee how the woman could love much because she had been forgiven much. The inflection of the closing sentence of the story is clearly directed to the Pharisee, and to any of us, who are quick to condemn and slow to forgive: "whoever has been forgiven little loves little."

C.S. Lewis wrote, "Prostitutes, outcasts, and society's selected sinners are in no danger of finding their present life so satisfactory that they cannot turn to God; the proud, the avaricious, and the self-righteous, are in danger."

God, thank you for showing us how your grace works for persons in the messy confluence of the humble and the proud, the strong and the weak, the bully and the victim, the advantaged and the destitute, the fortunate and the diseased. Amen

(Jesus said) "Where your treasure is,
there your heart will be also." Matthew 6:21

San Francisco Theological Sem-inary is not in San Francisco. It is settled in the beautiful Marin County hills, in San Anselmo, on the northern exposure of Mt. Tamalpais. This due, in part, to the wisdom saying of Jesus given from the Sermon on the Mount: "Where your treasure is, there your heart will be also." Robert Dollar treasured this place.

The location of the seminary was made possible from the gifts of Robert Dollar, a Scottish shipping magnate, philanthro-pist, and a Presbyterian. Some of the buildings look like old castles in Scotland.

As I listened to lectures from a pro-fessor who held the "Robert Dollar Chair of New Testament Theology," I admit succumbing to a wandering mind temp-tation enhanced by the sublime topogra-phy. The rocks used in constructing the first buildings of the seminary were from Scotland. They were brought to Ameri-ca, not for the purpose of a benefactor's gifts for buildings, but as ballast for the ships of the famous Robert Dollar, of whom, Governor James Rolph of Califor-nia said: "Dollar has done more to spread the American flag than any person in the world." With the ballast, ships could en-dure the Drake Passage around the Horn of South America (there was no Panama Canal). They returned to Europe laden with American products, but not before casting out the ballast.

How much of the old ballast in my life must be thrown out before the pur-pose-full leg of the journey of life begins? Destructive habits? Wrong career path? Wrong relationships? Self centered com-mitments? What is the treasure that mag-netizes my heart?

Thank you, God, for showing me what is good, true, just, and loving through Jesus Christ. Amen

*[Christ] made himself nothing, by taking the very nature of a servant,
being made in human likeness...he humbled himself by becoming obedient
to death—even death on a cross! Philippians 2:7-8*

Early one morning I received a nervous call from the director of a funeral home. Apologies began before any greeting, or lead ups. "Would you do a service today? I must say right off, three ministers have already said "no" (which are three reasons I was ready to say "yes.") A leader of a Hell's Angels motorcycle gang has been killed and the guys want to do the service and burial here," the director pleaded. "O.K.," I said.

In a short time I was visiting with the guys. These are the names as listed in the official Order of Service bulletin handed out at the funeral. It seems like a script for a cable television Indy movie: "Dirty Dave, Outsider Pete, Pig Pen, Centralia Ed, Robin, and Mike." Dirty Dave was the alpha gang member who carried forward our preparation conversations. He was direct. Well spoken. Not dirty. Dirty Dave asked a good question: "What can you, a Christian minister, say about the deceased? He was a murderer and he was killed by one."

"I cannot, will not, say much. Except, I believe Jesus Christ understands us better than we know ourselves. Christ will understand your friend. Christ died, on a cross, executed as a common criminal.

God is not surprised by any of us." Dirty Dave said, "Wow. Let's do the service."

God, thank you for Christ who was obedient to your love and never resorted to divine advantages but followed sacrificial love for all humanity to his death. May the Spirit that raised him from death, give us new life, this day and forever. Amen

*You will keep in perfect peace those whose minds
are steadfast, because they trust in you. Trust in the Lord forever,
for the Lord is the Rock eternal. Isaiah 26:3-4*

We thank God this day for his steadfastness. God's nature does not change according to the changing histories of the world. The scripture describes God's mercy that is from everlasting to everlasting. We follow an Eternal One whose creation brings order out of chaos, whose redemption delivers us from destruction, and whose leadership guides us out of captivity.

God trusts us to choose to put our trust in him. Fear is a universal emotion that permeates the development of our species. Fears rise up in our primitive brain. Fear invades our consciousness from the present complex environment. However, there is a grand boldness in trusting God that overshadows our quavering timidity. It is better to be with God in times of dreaded darkness, than to walk alone in the light. At times most of us have built habitats of false hopes on the beachfront of shifting sands. The energies of destructive habits, vain human relationships, and demons of materialism are churned by the "perfect storm" whose sea swallows our liberties.

In trust, we trust God who saves us from the vortex of death in our humanity, and gives us a chance to change the course of life. We hear today the word of Jesus from the hours before his crucifixion: "In me you may have peace. In the world you face tribulation. Take courage. I have conquered the world." (John 16:31)

Eternal God, not by our own wisdom, but with the gifts of faith, hope and love, we choose to place our life long trust in you. Amen

(Jesus to his disciples) "You stayed with me in my trials."
Luke 22:28

Shakespeare through one charac-ter says, "Debtor that I am, I am even poor in thanks." Numerous times I have felt that way. How many "passers of the past" have I failed to thank for their being there? Too many. In their absence, and before God, I try to recall from the cobwebbed chambers of my brain some of those great human beings.

Captain Charlie Plumb is a former Navy Fighter Pilot. On his 75th combat mission, he was shot down in Vietnam. He spent 2,103 days in horrid communist prisons, nearly six years, including days of vicious torture. He served as an un-derground "chaplain" in prison. After re-lease, and years later by a chance meeting in a restaurant, a man introduced himself saying, "You are Charlie Plumb, aren't you?" "Yes." "I was a sailor on the Kitty Hawk aircraft carrier. I used to pack your parachute."

A life-long friendship began. The 'safe' parachute was one reason Captain Plumb was alive. He was reminded of how many behind the scenes people are essen-tial to the ultimate success, and notoriety of any achiever. Henceforward, Plumb, a famous motivational speaker, would tell his audiences, "Remember who 'packed your parachute!"

In the final hours before his interro-gations, beatings and death by crucifix-ion, Jesus hosted the last meal and fellow-ship with his disciples. Many memories of the disciples are recorded, but not least among these, notation of Jesus expressing gratitude to others: "You stood by me in my trials."

This moment, Lord, I thank you for your gift of life through the presence, teaching, death and resurrection of Jesus. I thank you for these persons who 'packed my parachute' on this journey of life.... (each name the remembered ones). Amen

*Very early in the morning, while it was still dark, Jesus got up,
left the house and went off to a solitary place, where he prayed. Mark 1:35*

T. S. Eliot wrote: "Between the idea and the reality, falls the Shadow..." The thought underscores much of the drama of life. In seminary I had the privilege of meeting Dr. John Baillie, a notable theologian from Scotland. Dr. Baillie agreed to mentor me in the Ph.D. program at the University of Edinburgh. Between the idea and the reality of enrollment, the shadow

fell. Dr. Baillie died. The degree program remained on the agenda. Days after arriving in Scotland, Mrs. John Baillie graciously invited us to her home for dinner. She escorted us around Dr. Baillie's study where scores of great lectures, essays and books were created. Near a window looking over meadows and wheat fields one saw the soft rays of sunshine cast a Diarylide Yellow silhouette on a *prie-dieu*. The old kneeling bench had room for a few books and Bibles. The upholstery was worn out. That was the famous theologian's "solitary place, where he prayed." Impolitely I asked about when and how long he prayed, definitely an impetuous question, and with grace Mrs. Baillie just smiled.

Research science does not have an unequivocal answer to the question, "What effects does prayer have in a person's life, work, legacy and destiny?" Science can answer the question, "Who prays." Just about everyone.

My Lord and Savior, I do not know my future. I do not know what barriers and detours will change the partial road I see. I do not know what my condition of health shall be, how long my family and friends will live, or when my journey in this earthy mode shall stop. I do know you. I shall put my hand in yours. You know the way. Amen

Suffering produces perseverance; perseverance,
character; and character, hope. God's love has been poured out into
our hearts through the Holy Spirit. Romans 5:4-5

In our town, April 19 1995 was salted into our memories as a horrific crime that killed 165 persons and left hundreds maimed. The Oklahoma City Bombing is a historical benchmark of loss, valor, anger, love, perseverance and character. I listened intently to visiting Rabbi Harold Kushner, author of *When Bad Things Happen to Good People,* and a reporter asked him to reflect on, "What is God?" in the midst of this crisis. Kushner replied with empathy from the heart of one who knows the torture rack of pain from immeasurable loss. "I don't know 'what' God is. I can tell you how we experience God. Perhaps the right word is 'when' we know God is present." He said, "When someone forgives you, when someone is kind to you, when someone shares with you, when you share with someone else, when you heal."

After the Titanic had sunk and scores of people were striving for life in the cold, wind blown waves of the ocean, how could they hope that any would survive? Captain Rastron of the Carpathia heard an S.O.S. signal. He changed the course of the Carpathia, which was headed to the Mediterranean loaded with vacationers. He navigated at top speed through the dangerous ice field at night, for fifty-eight miles, to the site of the Titanic's demise. He instructed crew and passengers, some who were physicians, to transform the holiday cruise ship to a hospital ship. The Carpathia arrived at 4 a.m. to rescue survivors.

God's hope comes through the agents of mercy, people, who respond to the cries of others. Persons risk their lives to save life. "Character creates hope."

God's eternal hope came to us through a person, when Jesus Christ gave his life for us. William Cowper: "God moves in a mysterious way, His wonders to perform. He plants his footsteps in the sea, and rides upon the storm."

Thank you, God. You 'move in mysterious ways, your wonders to perform.' In Christ we hope and pray. Amen

(Jesus replied to Nicodemus, a Jewish ruler)
"No one can see the kingdom of God unless they are born again." John 3:3

A phrase from the classic play and film, "Green Pastures," rings true today: "Everything nailed down is comin' loose." Turmoil in families and major institutions seems overwhelming. The dark mood of society in Jesus' time was similar. One third of the population would fall to the Roman sword. Survivors of tyranny faced disease and starvation.

The center of Judaism, the Temple, and its priesthood, were destroyed within thirty years, never to be revived.

Nicodemus, a ruler and a teacher of Judaism, secretly admired Jesus. In the cover of night he met Jesus. He wanted to know about the true kingdom of God. How do the forces of God prevail over the chaotic world "where everything was comin' loose?"

Jesus offered an antidote: "Be born again." Start a completely new life. Paul Tillich taught this idea. We are first born into a world where others rule our lives, "heteronomy." We grow up. We become rebels against authoritarianism. This leads to self-rule, "autonomy." That does not work. Self centered lives self-destruct. We may try new absolutisms. These new rulers over our lives could be: drugs, political absolutisms, power, wealth, or prestige. Those fail. Our hope in finding the place where everything is not coming loose is a gift. Through faith in Christ, God rules within our selves by grace, "theonomy." Now we are ready for the new life in the house that God builds where everything good is nailed down.

Did Nicodemus accept this offer from Christ? Maybe. We don't know the rest of the story. We are responsible for our story.

Lord, I pray for the humility to let your Spirit rule in my life, through Christ. Amen

*Let us not love with words or speech
but with actions and in truth. I John 3:18*

Disraeli said, "Justice is love in action." After hearing all the words we speak, all the political orations, newscasts, podcasts, talk shows, sermons, and 4,000 advertisements per day, two things refresh my soul. One is silence. The other is witnessing love in action and that is the perfect validation of our faith. Love in action: watching a son feed his mother whose Parkinson's diseased trembling hands make it nearly impossible to eat. Does he remember his infancy and her feeding him?

Love in action: a high school athlete jumps between a gang and a beaten up kid with a bleeding nose and broken glasses. Love in action: a woman works two jobs, skips meals, walks to save gas, and pays for a child's tuition in a school where academic hope is alive. Love in action: a person trains to help isolated teenage girls by offering them financial and emotional support to make the right decisions in their lives about their pregnancies. There is a joy of seeing love in action: a group of people building a house on weekends to be given to a poor family who have been living in an old car.

See love in action: witness villagers in a poor nation receive fresh clean water brought by the gift of a simple PVC waterline from a mountain spring to their community. In that village you see love in the smiles of children whose grin is as wide as Africa. See the tears of love in action when a father, mother, wife, husband, brother or sister, welcome home a member of the family who was lost in anger, drugs, desperation, debt, or destructive relationships. That is love and truth in action.

God of love, I commit my faith in Christ to actions of love this day. Amen

In the church I would rather speak five intelligible words
to instruct others than ten thousand words in a tongue. I Corinthians 14:18

Paul writes to a little problem within the church at Corinth. This church is in a trade center, a crossroads of commerce with people of many nations. At the first Pentecost, after the resurrection of Jesus Christ, the Spirit of God inspired the disciples to speak the gospel in the tongues of the people of the "many nations" represented. The "ecstatic tongue" subject addressed by Paul was different. It required "interpreting what was 'ecstatically' uttered." Paul is blunt. "I speak in tongues more than all of you." He pleads for clear, concise and cogent words about the Living Word.

Recently I was waiting for a flight arrival of family that included grandsons Sam and Charlie Sandefer. On the same morning I had read I Corinthians 14. A concept stuck in my mind: the "five intelligible words" phrase of the Apostle. So I asked the young men, expecting brilliant answers from my 'perfectly precocious' grandchildren (we grand parents are excessively proud of our contribution to the Double Helix of DNA in our offspring—when it comes out well) if you had only "Five Intelligible Words" to say, what would they be?

Sam, ten years old at the time, said immediately: TEACH ME HOW TO WRITE.

Cogitating on that answer many times since, it's perfect.

(This prayer is by Sam Sandefer on his birthday.)

Dear God, thank you for answering all my prayers. You make me so comfortable after you answer a prayer. It fills me with joy when you do something spectacular like make a wonderful sunrise or sunset You are incredible and I thank you again. Amen

> *Know also that wisdom is like honey for you: If you find it,*
> *there is a future hope for you. And your hope will not be cut off.*
> *Proverbs 24:14*

Wise advice may be hard to follow. I recall an executive shouting at me over a policy debate, "You need a psychiatrist!" In retrospect, if she meant, "You need to know more about yourself," she was right. A sister, in her sixth decade of life, told me some years after her husband's death that the loss was assuaged by the experience of "learning more about myself."

According to a legend 2,500 years old, seekers of wisdom would visit the "Oracle of Delphi" in Ancient Greece to find the meaning of life. The inscription on the entrance read, "Gnothi Seauton." *Know Thyself.*

Mary Williams, an English-American author born in 1881 became internationally known for her children's book, *The Velveteen Rabbit.* In this story the Skin Horse, the oldest of the toys in the nursery, is asked by the Velveteen Rabbit, "How do you get real?" A good question for a toy, or a great question for a person. The Skin Horse replies: "It doesn't happen all at once. It takes a long time. That's why it doesn't often happen to people who break easily or have sharp edges, or who have to be carefully kept. Generally by the time you are Real, most of your hair has been loved off, and eyes drop out and you get loose in the joints and very shabby. But these things don't matter at all, because once you are Real you can't be ugly, except to people who don't understand..."

God and creator of all that is real, thank you for placing people in my life to teach me what is real. Most of all, thank you for your real love and grace in Jesus Christ. Amen

For God did not appoint us to suffer.
I Thessalonians 5:8-9

In the Roaring Twenties, Tommy Dorsey, and others, created a uniquely American tradition in music, blending Blues, Jazz and Gospel. In1932 Dorsey was scheduled for an important St. Louis concert. His pregnant wife Nettie insisted that he perform even as he worried about leaving their home in Chicago. During the St. Louis gig Dorsey received a heartbreaking telegram: "Your wife just died." His wife had a baby boy before she expired; hours later, the baby boy died.

Dorsey wrote: "I buried Nettie and our son in the same casket. Then I fell apart. I felt that God had done me an injustice. I didn't want to serve God any more, or write any more Gospel songs." Time passed, and one day Dorsey said, "I just sat down at a piano and my hands began to browse the keys...something happened. I felt as though I could reach out and touch God. I found myself playing a melody I had never heard and words came into my head." The words: "Precious Lord, take my hand, lead me on, let me stand, I am tired, I am worn. Through the storm, through the night, lead me on, to the Light; Take my hand, Precious Lord."

Dorsey wrote 400 Gospel songs after his wife's death. He said, "I learned that when we are in our deepest grief, when we feel farthest from God, this is when God is closest and when we are most open to that Restoring Power."

In the mystery of the suffering, we know that Light follows the darkest night.

God, you have seen me in the darkest hour of need. You have given Restoring Power through the Spirit of Christ to rise up in the Light of a new day. Thank you. Amen

I am not ashamed of the gospel,
because it is the power of God. Romans 1:16

Paul's letter to Christians in Rome demonstrates the essential core of our belief: God fully and freely accepts through Christ. By accepting this grace-gift, forgiveness, and new life begins. The Greek word Paul uses for "power" is "dunamis" which means "power, abundance, or might." The word "dynamite" is derived from "dunamis."

After attending a lecture at the University of Edinburgh, Scotland, by the famous Dr. Martin Niemoeller of Germany, I invited him to afternoon tea. Niemoeller accepted. My questions moved from his "heroic" U Boat experience in World War I, to his famous pastorate in Berlin during the days of the 'rise of the Third Reich' under Hitler, to his experiences in a concentration camp during WWII for his resistance to the Nazis. Memorably he said, "My worst days of suffering came after my release from five years of prison at the end of the war." Niemoeller described horrid nightmares that occurred nightly centering on a dream: "I dreamed I was in heaven, in an afterlife. Hitler was brought before God, and I was forced to look straight into the face of Hitler as God asked him, 'What do you have to say for yourself.' Hitler answered: 'I have never heard the gospel.' At that point of the dream I would wake up with a feverish scream. You see, the dream was about me. When I was arrested, Hitler, among others, interrogated me, wanting to know why I refused to support the new government. I argued on political and philosophical grounds. I did not give one word concerning the real basis of my resistance...my faith. And that was the nightmare from which I needed healing."

I confess to times when I did act 'ashamed' of the gospel. Have you had that experience?

God, thank you for the grace you demonstrate in Christ. Let me not be silent or shy to express through love this power from you in my life. Amen

Praise the Lord, my soul; all my inmost being praise
His holy name...He does not treat us as our sins deserve or repay us
according to our iniquities. Psalm 103:1, 10

Who is this God David knew so well? How do you define the character of God? David uses words like "loving, redeeming, healing, full of mercy." Since I was very young and forever since Psalm 103:10 was in my memory bank. I needed that. God "does not treat us as our sins deserve." As a boy in synagogue school Jesus would have memorized many of the Psalms. Do you think Jesus the Teacher, had this Psalm in mind when he told the story of the Prodigal Son? That story is really about the Waiting Father. It is a story of grace, forgiveness, and reconciliation. The theme of the home in the parable is sacrificial love.

This unrelenting forgiving love seems to make the father of the prodigal powerless to prevent the son from nearly destroying himself. He was waiting at the roadside when the son finally came home. Did the father go to that lookout place and longingly gaze as far as he could see down the long road day after sorrowful day, and prayerfully imagine his son coming home? I think so.

This is God's love. God chooses the way of the powerlessness of love that prevents him from stopping us from making bad choices. But it is the mystery of grace in his love that empowers us to return to him. The father in the parable gently, softly embraces his returning son, and "they celebrated with joy."

God, thank you for the homecoming we have returning to you, accepting forgiveness and your love. In Christ. Amen

It is good to praise the Lord and make music to
your name, O Most High, proclaiming your love in the morning and
your faithfulness at night. Psalm 92:1

With good fortune on occasions we witness such greatness in athletics, entertainment, or the performing arts that we are lost in sublimity without superlatives to describe our experience. Itzhak Perlman could transport me to that blissful state of being. To see the great violinist come on stage brings a silent sense of awe to the audience, because he suffered the disease of polio as a child, he can only move with heavy leg braces and walks with the aid of two crutches. After taking a chair, he readies himself for the concert, picks up his famous violin and nods to the maestro. Get ready to fly to heaven.

On November 18, 1995, the moment of realized expectation of joy came to a sudden stop. After the first few bars of music one of the strings of his violin broke with a "pop" of a small caliber pistol that could be heard across the Avery Fisher Hall at Lincoln Center in New York City. The conductor halted the orchestra. Each person in the audience imagined "what will happen now?" Perlman paused, eyes closed, then signaled the conductor to begin again. He played the entire piece of music with emotional furor, accuracy and beauty on the three strings. In his post concert interview he said: "It is the artist's task to find out how much music you can still make with what you have."

God of all the arts and sciences and expressions of love and joy, thank you for the gifts given to each of us, by whatever measure, to share with the community of life in Christ. Amen

We are justified by faith.
Romans 5:1

Is hope an illusion perpetuated by professional religionist leaders? In the 19th century, Freud said, "Yes" and proceeded to write "The Future of an Illusion." He discounted the validity of faith's hope, and yet, curiously argued that the "illusion" is better than not having hope at all. In 2013 George Packer wrote *The Unwinding: An Inner History of the New America.* His diagnosis? Americans are having "seizure shifts" and the "loss of social contact." America is a "Ponzi State." Between Freud and Packer hear W.B. Yeats (early 20th century): "Turning and turning in the widening gyre/ The falcon cannot hear the falconer. / Things fall apart; the center cannot hold; / Mere anarchy is loosed upon the world, / The blood-dimmed tide is loosed, and everywhere/ The ceremony of innocence is drowned;/ The best lack all conviction, while the worst/ Are full of passionate intensity." (from, *The Second Coming)*

These social conditions are not new. Ancient Greece told the story of Pandora's Box in which Zeus punished Prometheus for "loving mankind too much." Zeus took his revenge by sending the powers of evil on humankind to counterbalance the gift of fire given by Prometheus. Those extraordinary powers were released from "Pandora's Box" which gave away a multitude of powers but not the power of "hope."

The gospel is an alternative to the history of trenchant dismay. Through the life, teaching, death and resurrection of Jesus Christ, we freely receive the gifts of faith, hope and love. We accept these loving gifts with gratitude.

Spirit of the Living God, this day we live in the paradox of the world's dismay and your gift of hope. Let us love the world as Christ loved, in a way that the world cannot love itself, with faith, hope and love. Amen

*The kings of the Gentiles lord it over them; and those who
exercise authority over them call themselves Benefactors. But you are not to be
like that. Instead, the greatest among you should be like the youngest,
and the one who rules like the one who serves. Luke 22: 25-26*

The Greek word for "Gentiles" also means "the nations," as in "all the nations outside of Israel." In this case Jesus is speaking of the national leaders of the world, for even Israel did not rule itself. They were vassals to Rome. The doors to the Jewish Temple carried the Roman Eagle over the keystone, reminding Jews who was in charge.

Jesus spoke of the old world management style of top-down authority. What the manager gives is not an earned wage to valuable workers, it is doled out as a gift from a benefactor. The essence is clear. The manager owns you.

One day I heard Peter Drucker, one of the world's most famous teachers of the new management philosophy, speak to persons considered church leaders. His message did not vary from the business world. He said, "Ask yourselves these four questions: 1. What is your business? 2. Who is your customer? 3. What does your customer (church member) value in your product? 4. What mediocre program will you be stopping?"

Primarily Jesus, secondarily Paul, taught these principles. Read the New Testament. What business? The gospel. For whom? All people, slave-free, male-female, Gentile-Jew. What is valued? The redeeming, transforming love of Christ. What mediocrity will I stop? Probably a host of redundant, inane, time-consuming activities, and all that are clearly wrong.

Eternal God, thank you for meeting us in the Servant Lord Jesus Christ who communicated your love to us in word and deed. He is the Leader of all as Servant of all. We commit ourselves to follow Christ as servants and agents of reconciliation. Amen

*Put on the new self, which is being renewed
in knowledge in the image of its Creator. Colossians 3:10*

The Bible tells us that God created humankind in his "own image." The Imago Dei language of scripture has received not a few barbs from some of the best agnostics in all the ages since. Voltaire wrote, "The Bible says that God created man in his own image, and man returned the favor." What does it mean to be created in the image of God? We have the potential of partial discernment, love, joy, creativity, and mercy that we discover in God. How do we know the character of God? "The Son is the image of the invisible God," Paul wrote to the church at Colossae (Col. 1:15). I confess to our Father in Heaven, I see little of God in my own image. Can we deny, mar or obliterate the beautiful image of God in which we are created? Yes, yes, and yes. That is known as the "history of humanity."

Where do we turn to rediscover the true original image, of ourselves? Paul experienced this transformation, this metamorphosis in his own life. The very person he despised, Jesus, and followers of Jesus he tried to exterminate became the closest friends and loved ones. Paul's world was turned upside down when he encountered the Living God in Christ whose Spirit infused his life with a new being, a new reality. By grace through faith Paul was recreated as "Paul in the image of Christ." The "new Paul" turned hatred to love, regrets to joy, self-revulsion to self-acceptance, and anxiety to peace.

Thank you, God, for the gift of forgiveness, demonstrating your love in Christ, and transforming the "image" by which we see ourselves. We may now love others as ourselves and love you without reservation. Amen

God's gifts and his call are irrevocable
...to him be the glory forever! Romans 11:29, 36

If we are given a New Creation, in the image of Christ (see January 24 devotion), it follows as summer follows the springtime awakenings, we shall be given gifts and a "calling." Part of our life's sacred journey is to discover the passion of a true calling. We have many gifts with our individual "callings." God does not revoke his blessings. God is not capricious. Nor does God use gifts to manipulate us into a constrained relationship. We may lose a gift because we failed to use the gift, but that is from our choice of disciplines. That applies to everything from spiritual commitments in love to baseball practice. Use it or lose it. Trapped in a negative brain working overtime? Gratitude alone dispels negativity. Negativity blocks the joy that our callings and gifts open to us. Here are three ways to enhance the gratitude that opens doors to new rendezvous of creative life.

One: thank God for spiritual vision. Seeing begins with believing. Faith precedes knowledge, and as Augustine emphasized, that is reasonable. Knowledge is enhanced by faith, and faith is benefited by knowledge.

Two: thank God for the gift of "person-hood." We are not mechanical devices moving in a machine; we are not bits of protoplasm drifting in a cosmic soup of subatomic particles. We are persons created in the image of God living in a personal world where God is a Person whom we accept, love, trust, and enjoy.

Three: thank God for the future. We trust the future because our God is the Lord of the future. We participate with God as co-creators of the future.

God, help me accept the gifts and follow the calling you have given me. I thank you for the abundant life promised in this act of faith, through Christ. Amen

We put no stumbling block in anyone's path, so that our ministry will not be discredited. Rather, as servants of God we commend ourselves in every way in great endurance; in troubles, hardships and distresses; in beatings, imprisonments and riots; in hard work, sleepless nights and hunger, in purity, understanding, patience and kindness; in the Holy Spirit and in sincere love; in truthful speech and in the power of God...through glory and dishonor, bad report and good report; genuine, yet regarded as impostors...dying, and yet we live on; beaten, and yet not killed, sorrowful, yet always rejoicing; poor, yet making many rich; having nothing, and yet possessing everything. II Corinthians 6: 4ff

The Corinthians knew Paul. They knew he was a risk taker. All of us owe a mountain of gratitude to the forerunners of our faith and history. Risk takers gave us life, liberty, equality of opportunity, and freedom to practice what we believe. *National Geographic* magazine, in June 2013, published an essay outlining the achievements of several risk taker explorers. The Apostle Paul was a paradigm of such people. *NG's* story explained the neurobiological basis of great risk takers, driven by the dopamine system of the brain. Unlike "adrenaline junkies," a neurotransmitter activated to escape fear, the risk taker activates dopamine neurotransmitters that push the explorer through danger toward achievement of goals. Not all goals are equal, not all are honorable. Consider the risks Paul took and the quality of goals he sought to achieve: a community unlike any in history where men and women, slave and free, rich and poor would be as one. His highest goal was sharing the knowledge of the grace of God revealed in the life, teaching, death and resurrection of Christ as the single greatest truth of life. He would die likely by beheading in Rome, in 67 A.D. for taking this risk.

God, this day I do not take for granted the cost of my faith and life in Christ. I pause now to silently name the risk taking forerunners who blessed me...Amen

My heart is steadfast; I will sing and make music. Awake my soul!
For great is your love, reaching to the heavens; your faithfulness
reached to the skies. Psalm 57:7,10

Digital technology has changed our culture. One example is "additive manufacturing" or "3-D Printing." This power makes everyone capable of manufacturing everything from guns to couture clothing.

The 3-D printer works with materials of your choice: metals, plastics, ceramics, sandstone, cartilage, muscle tissue, bones, skin, or hair follicles. The 3-D printer produces thin layers, 150 microns, and layer upon layer are bonded in a process called sintering, until you have the shape, size, and color of the 3-D object you wanted.

From idea to design, to manufacturing, you have a shopping mall on your desk. Wake Forest Baptist Medical Center's Institute for Regenerative Medicine has printed muscle tissue, skin, kidneys, cartilage and bones. In 2013, Oxford Performance Materials in Connecticut used 3-D modeling and printing to produce a plastic implant for 75% of a patient's skull. Lotus Renault uses 3-D printing for parts on its Formula I racecar. One can make 98% of the parts for a 3-D printer on a 3-D printer.

Where does this lead us? I agree with Einstein that science without religion is blind, and religion without science is lame. C.S. Lewis wrote: "Increased knowledge without values, makes a more clever devil." Of course technology will be misused, but the same technology will save life. Knowledge is power. People have a choice to use scientific power to co-create life, or to destroy the creation.

(Today's prayer is by James Lee, my son-in-law, on his birthday.)

On this anniversary of Mozart's birth, let us listen to the wonder and gifts that surround us. To the life-affirming laughter of children, to the warm voices of friends and family, to the infinite variety of choirs in nature, to the wisdom in our souls. For all of these are His voice. Amen

(Jesus concludes the Sermon on the Mount, Matthew 5, 6, and 7)
"Therefore everyone who hears these words of mine and puts them into practice is like a wise man who built his house on the rock." Matthew 7:24

In the movie "Don Juan De Marco" Marlon Brando is a psychiatrist (Jack) treating a patient who believes he is "Don Juan," played by Johnny Depp. The psychiatrist succumbs to the illusion of his patient, and he too begins to believe Don Juan is real. Dr. Jack Mickler is married to Marilyn, played by Faye Dunaway. The psychiatrist has been masking his real love for his wife. Don Juan (Johnny Depp) becomes the counselor to the doctor and mentors him in the art of real human life and love. Don Juan asks Dr. Mickler four questions, questions worth our consideration: 1. What is sacred? 2.What is spiritual? 3.What is worth living for? 4.What is worth dying for? The dialogue leads to the same answer the New Testament gives. The answer to all four questions is love.

JamesOn Curry (sic) played basketball at Oklahoma State University. He came from a tough and problematic environment. He could easily have been one of the teenage statistics too common in America of death by gang violence, death by drug overdose, or life in prison. Before those disasters, he was chased down by God (some say he found God, but it is the other way around). JamesOn wore a tattoo on his arm, written in such a way that he could read it, not the ESPN audience: "You have made me see many troubles and calamities and you will revive me again from the depths and comfort me and I will honor you." (Psalm 71:20) JamesOn answered all four questions. To "love" he added "faith" as the answer.

Living Christ, thank you for showing me your grace and love through the Spirit of God. Amen

*It was now about noon, and darkness came
over the whole land...for the sun stopped shining. Luke 23:44*

In the heart of each person comes a time of 'darkness at noon.' Until this hour of despair passes, we have lost our vision of life. If a lyricist were writing words for the saddest music the earth has ever heard, the three hours in which Jesus was dying on the cross, she, or he, may use this scriptural text: "darkness came over the whole land." The true beginning of the gospel in our lives takes root in the depths of the human predicament of separation. We feel loneliness and fear. Alienation follows in the footsteps of fear. Will this unlighted world ever see the light of day again? Fully human, Jesus experienced the depths of our spiritual deaths.

God does not wait for us to come out of the fortress of darkness. God meets us at the utmost ends of our desolation. The hardest thing for us to do when the force of God breaks down the gates of the dark underworld in the human soul is summarized in a word— surrender. It is against our natural and nurtured instincts. We learn to stand strong, never give up or give in. Achieve. Jesus, the only truly fulfilled human life, sets the new course for bringing light to the dark noontide of life. "Into your hands, God, I commend my spirit," Jesus said as he surrendered his life on the cross.

"Not my will, but thy will be done," is not a surrender of defeat. It is the birth of the dawn of enlightenment.

Thank you, God, for the living Word of truth and grace in Christ Jesus who knows me and understands me and accepts me in the depths of my greatest need. Thy will be done. Amen

You are a mist that appears
for a little while and then vanishes. James 4:13-14

What is the essence of a person? In the view of some noted commentators on humanity the essential person has little value. Mark Twain said, "Man is the disease on the skin covering the earth." Albert Camus said that the 'real passion' of the time is 'servitude' in which we prefer 'security' to 'freedom.' Nihilism was born with our species. I recall a news report of a famous Edinburgh barrister arguing for the 'preservation of the established Church of Scotland' (read tax supported). He said, "While I do not believe in God, no one has a right to take away my established church."

On the other hand, notice the resilient words of Jurgen Moltmann, a first hand witness to Nazi nihilism. "Christian faith is not be understood as a handling on of something that has to be preserved. It is an event which summons the dead and godless to life." I cannot forget my Irish professor of homiletics. With arms waving and bushy eyebrows raised he shouted through his Gaelic tinged dialect, "What is preaching all about? You are charged by God to raise the dead, in twenty minutes!" Helmut Thielicke witnessed first hand the nihilism of Nazi dictatorship in Germany. "Anybody who has ever been snatched away from nihilism," he said, "knows that this does not happen by a harmless process of becoming; he knows that he has been laid hold of by a higher hand and drawn across the saving border. We live in this miracle or we vegetate." (Quoted by David Anderson, *The Tragic Protest*.)

Lord, we confess, at times, our feeling of nihilism, 'nothingness.' Thank you for filling this emptiness with your love and grace in Christ. Amen

> *If I have the gift of prophecy and can fathom all the mysteries*
> *and all knowledge, and if I have faith that can move mountains,*
> *but do not have love, I am nothing. Corinthians 13:2*

One of the joys of life is seeing the success and accomplishment of children. It assures us about the future that we often denigrate with cynicism. In the same manner we are deeply concerned about failure rates among some children. A research study with a longevity axis at the University of Maryland took on this subject of success/failure rates of school children. Carefully designed interviews were held with 200 children who lived in an environment of economic poverty and high crime rates. The interviewers were asked to give an opinion about what they projected for the respective students. The most common response, in a phrase, was 'this child has no future.'

Fifteen years later the research project was continued. The subjects were traced down where possible and follow up interviews were held. Of the now adult 'student' group found, the majority of the original 200, many were successful college graduates with good jobs and a sound life style. How did those who succeeded describe their own success? All the answers were the same. One teacher impressed each student with a view of self-worth, and motivation to be an agent of change starting with oneself. This happened because the original children of the study were in the same school and eventually passed through the grade level of one teacher who really loved the kids.

I know these results can be true. I have seen a teacher do it. Realized expectations happen when a teacher who "fathoms knowledge" also has "love."

With all the gifts you have given me, help me, dear Lord, to use the gift of love. Amen

My heart stands in awe of your words.
Psalm 119:161 NRSV

Lord of life, the paths of history behind me, and the highways to the future before me, cannot be compared to the place to stand you have put within me. In the exquisite architecture of the inner mind and soul, I experience the place you live and make me whole.

This day, this place, this now, this conscious thought is the fulcrum of faith by which you empower me with leverage to move the weight of life and the obstacles to love and serenity.

Today your kingdom comes into my midst. Now, you are meeting me with acceptance, meaning and friendship. To know you is the cultivation of awe and wonder. Work becomes a calling, fears are absorbed in love, nightmares are turned to dreams.

The mystery of the gift of faith enables me to believe and then to see. Knowledge may tell me I am an infinitesimal blob of protoplasm drifting at random in a finite space of an infinite universe. Small that I am, you call me by name, you give me a reason for the hope that is irrepressible, and you give me a spirit of courage.

You have even caused my questioning spirit to be the point guard of the pattern of discovery. Faith becomes the opposite side of the coin of doubt. Discovery is more joyous than dogma. Your complete love gives us a place to stand where we learn more from our questions than from our incomplete answers. I am standing, standing in awe of you, standing in the marvel of life.

Through the grace and power of Christ. Amen

For this reason I remind you to fan into flame the gift of God
...for the Spirit God gave us does not make us timid, but gives us power, love and
self-discipline. II Timothy 1:6-7

Great stories in literature have great heroes. Let us not forget one in our contemporary Christian history, Louis Zamperini. He was classified in the 1930's a "juvenile delinquent." He ran in the famous "Berlin Olympics" with Hitler in the stands and enlisted in the U.S. Army Air Corps. His plane was shot down in the Pacific. He survived for 47 days on a life raft, was picked from the violent ocean by the Japanese, imprisoned, endured horrendous torture.

Zamperini's epochal life does not reach the denouement after being freed by American forces. Zamperini was a war hero, but the real hero had not yet emerged from the chrysalis of life. In the postwar years he swung from being the noted speaker at banquets and popular guest of movie stars to another life as a prisoner, this time, the prisoner of abject alcoholism.

Those who knew Zamperini best, especially his wife, were steadfast in prayer and support waiting for the time he may discover a road to recovery. The young, not yet world famous Billy Graham, had a positive influence on Zamperini as Louis slammed to the bottom of the pit of life. His newly found experience in faith, surrendering his life to the "higher power" who is Jesus Christ, and days, months, years of recovery, all of these events, providentially created the real hero of faith, Louis Zamperini, a true veteran of cosmic and spiritual warfare between good and evil. Now for the 'rest of the story of a classic hero." Good prevails.

Eternal God, you have created me in a time and place to become a complete story. Let me be the person who becomes a true disciple of the One who inspires us, Jesus Christ. Amen

(This day's devotion is by Nicole Anderson Barr, my daughter, on her birthday.) But he said to me, "My grace is sufficient for you, for my power is made perfect in weakness." Therefore I will boast all the more gladly about my weaknesses, so that Christ's power may rest on me. That is why, for Christ's sake, I delight in weaknesses, in insults, in hardships, in persecutions, in difficulties. For when I am weak, then I am strong. II Corinthians 12:9-10 (In this unusual phrase "He said to me," Paul is citing internalized words of Christ concerning 'grace.')

Life does not always go according to our plans. In fact there are days when the mere idea of having any sense of control seems a somewhat ludicrous quest. Whether it is a divorce, loss of a dear family member, a life threatening illness, or trouble with a beloved child, life can bring us to our knees. However, it is at this point, on our knees, when we truly surrender our will and lives to God, we can finally realize the all encompassing never ceasing ferocious love of our Beloved Christ. Through this 'Love' not only comes immediate healing but also the swift immense 'Power' to do what only God can do.

During my darkest hours the flicker of the light of Faith has been restored time and time again.

Dear All Powerful Loving God: Thank you, dear God, for remaining a loving, faithful, and constant power in my life. In times of trouble help me to remember that suffering is temporary. Remind me to slow down and turn over my thoughts and will to you. Restore me through Christ Jesus as you see fit. In Jesus Name I pray. Amen

February 4

---

*I always thank my God for you because of his grace given
you in Christ Jesus. For in him you have been enriched in every way.*
I Corinthians 1:4-5

There are about sixty days in the annual cycle for persons living in the lush environs of the Puget Sound of the Pacific Northwest to say 'can't get better than this.' It was one such day when I was driving past Chambers Creek from University Place to officiate at a service at Mountain View Memorial Park. The 'mountain in view' is the *sine qua non* of such vistas, Mt. Rainier.

Then Murphy's Law kicked in, 'if any thing can go wrong, it will.' My car stalled. I noticed all traffic had ceased. Did not know this back road was just closed to traffic. I must get to the 11 a.m. funeral on time. I took the back roads to miss the traffic going to this affair, the memorial service for Edgar N. Eisenhower, brother of the late President Dwight Eisenhower. It was already 11 a.m. Heard a truck approaching, a work crew. Stopped to help. Begged for a quick ride in a three-ton gravel truck, crossed some lawns approaching the chapel on the back acreage of the cemetery estate. Crowds waiting. Mountain View staff sweating bullets. Leapt from the truck, robe and Bible in hand. 11:15 a.m. The first person to greet me was Milton Eisenhower, youngest brother of the deceased Edgar and late President Dwight. With the famous 'Eisenhower smile' he said: "I have no idea what happened, but Edgar wouldn't have it any other way."

With that gift of relaxing grace extended by a famous Kansan, the anxieties and *faux* excuses of a minister became unnecessary. The Risen Christ and his grace were noted in song and word. Gracious conversation presided at the graveside. The sun was still shining on Mt. Rainier.

Thank you, Eternal Christ, that we may be continually surprised by your grace. Amen

February 5

*(Jesus indicated the kind of death—crucifixion—by which
Peter would glorify God.) Then he said to him, "Follow me." John 21:19*

Once I walked in the shoes of the damned, literally. We entered the Cracow Poland Artists' Exhibit at the Edinburgh International Art Festival. At the entry of the exhibit hall were shoes, thousands of shoes—men, women and children's shoes—nailed closely together on the floor. The only way into the exhibit was to walk in the shoes. After you enter the greater hall you begin to see pictures, photos you have seen before. Photos that scar your neural pathways with memories you cannot mollify. You are seeing photos that the Nazis took of concentration camp victims. Then you see a very large picture of a stash of shoes and the shoeless, naked victims being marched in the 'next room,' the gas chamber. It is too late to turn back. You have entered the exhibit walking in the actual shoes of the damned.

Bad stuff in the world is created by truly 'bad guys.' Their atrocities seem to defy the limits of our darkest imaginations, but the worst evils in the world are committed by 'good guys' who do nothing. Jesus warned us in the parable of The Good Samaritan. The real evil done in the story is by 'good guys' doing nothing. Nazism became an unleashed wild demonic power when good people remained silent, until it was too late.

Peter learned this lesson. He would follow Christ, walk in his footsteps, footsteps of sacrificial love, the only love that can save our humanity.

Thank you, God, for the sacrificial love of Jesus whose life, death, and resurrection are my hope and truth. Amen

We are hard pressed on every side,
but not crushed; perplexed, but not in despair. II Corinthians 4:8

The early Christians were not soft-shelled patsies. They were tough as Vikings and adventurous as Homer's Argonauts. When they spread the revolutionary gospel among the nations of the Roman Empire their opponents in sophisticated centers such as Thessalonica referred to them as 'those people who turned the world upside down.'

Are Christians today so urbane and culturally contoured to blend into society that they are invisible, inaudible, and incapacitated? There are Christians today, like Paul, 'pressed on every side, perplexed, but not in despair.' There are revolutions of Christian encounters in societies beyond the 'old world' of Europe and America: China, Africa, South and Middle America. In fact, in the 200 decades since the resurrection of Christ, this last decade in the 21st century has the fastest growth of any time in the history.

We live on the cusp of a new renaissance that may be as startling as the series of events that began in the 15th century in Europe: the invention of the printing press which made possible the Renaissance, the Reformation, the Age of Enlightenment, the Scientific and Industrial Revolution and the birth of modern democracies. Is the social media the technology of the New Renaissance and New Reformation of faith? Possibly. In 2014 Gen Y and Millennials outnumbered Baby Boomers; 96% have joined a social network. To reach a 50 million users benchmark, it took radio 38 years, TV 13 years, Internet 4 years. Facebook added 100 million users in 9 months. Where is it going? I do not know the future. I do trust the Lord of the future. In some things we will be perplexed, however, in Christ we are not in despair, in fact we are 'more than conquerors through him who loves us.'

God of the future, I thank you for the verve and vivaciousness of faith, in Christ. Amen

> *Whether you turn to the right or to the left, your ears will hear*
> *a voice behind you, saying, "This is the way, walk in it." Isaiah 30:21*

We come to places in life where we are forced to make the right decision in the right time. It can be a life or death circumstance: this kind of surgery or chemotherapy, this risky military service or another career. How should we make tough decisions? First, know one self, "What is the purpose of my life?"

'Why' I exist changes 'How' and 'What' I do with my life. Americans live in a culture of overindulgence. I recently looked up "under-indulgence" in Dictionary.com: it doesn't exist, the answer, 'did you mean counter intelligence.' Nietzsche said if one has a 'Why' in life you can deal with any 'How.' Our grand freedoms are marvelous, however, if we have only used freedom for self-aggrandizement, we are suffering from the obesity of a self absorbed life. We become like the guy whose tombstone read: "Lived 89 years, Died at 31."

All know when they were born, few learn why they were born. Facing tough decisions may cause some moments of creative tension, but this is very healthy as we face the question, ultimately, who am I? If I truly answer, I am a child of God, a follower of Christ, then my quest may take this text in Isaiah to heart. We listen to all the voices. We hear all the advice. We study for objective evidence based data of science. We collaborate with trusted persons. Then, we are ready for the second step in making tough decisions: "Be silent, meditate, listen and observe with the sixth sense of the heart to the 'voice behind you,' the Voice of God. The third step has a 'serene' confidence. Lao Tzu (6th century B.C.) called it 'tranquil.' Decide and Do.

God, I live with imperfect knowledge and I accept your confident peace in making this decision: (each iterates his or her 'decide and do' act). In Christ. Amen

(This day's devotions are by Abigail Webb and Lucy Webb, my granddaughters, on their birthday, at age 7.) Be kind to one another, tenderhearted, forgiving one another, as God in Christ forgave you. Ephesians 4:32

Abigail said: "We learned this memory verse in Sunday School. I like to memorize Bible verses. It is fun to do. I think it is important to memorize Bible verses, because they help you do good things instead of bad things. It is good to be nice and to forgive people. And, when you do the good things that God tells you to do, you feel good inside."

Lucy wrote:

I know I am weak, but You are strong. Your hands are so big, they carry me.

She added: "Those are words from a song I like. Singing is a fun way to worship God. I like to sing. I also like thinking about God's big strong hands. He is strong, and He loves me. That makes me feel good."

Whenever you, or I, are stuck in the crabgrass of negative thinking just spend a little time listening to a child. Jesus said 'of such is the Kingdom of Heaven' for a good reason. A child is one of the Lord's promises that there is a future not to be mad about. A child is a reflection of guileless innocence, and we don't see much of that in the adult world reflected through our various media. A child reminds adults of the halcyon days of the 'child hidden' in adult memory banks. The uninhibited joy of a child reminds adults that real joy does not come from bottle of booze or a box of jewels. May we feel the 'big strong hands' of God,

the one's Lucy feels. Memorize Abigail's verse, 'it helps you do good things.'

Thank you, Jesus, for teaching us about learning from a child. Amen

*Trust in the Lord with all your heart and lean
not on your own understanding; in all your ways submit to him,
and he will make your paths straight. Proverbs 3:5-6*

Sometimes being ignorant of my unintended arrogance necessitates apologies and candid prayer saying, "forgive me my trespasses, please." Nikos Kazantzakis captures this remorseful posture through his protagonist in *Report of Greco* in this memorable paragraph. "Once, I remember, I had detached a chrysalis from the trunk of an olive tree and placed it in my palm... It was moving...the future, still-enslaved butterfly was waiting with silent tremors for the sacred hour when it would emerge into the sunlight. It was not in a hurry, but I was in a hurry. I began to blow my warm breath over the chrysalis...behold...a bright green butterfly appeared...it toiled in its own right to stretch, was unable to, and remained half unfolded and trembling...the maimed wings ceased to move and drooped down, as stiff and lifeless as stone. I felt sick at heart. Because of my hurry, because I had dared to transgress an eternal law, I had killed the butterfly. Years have passed, but that butterfly's weightless carcass has weighed heavily on my conscience ever since."

How did Judas feel, after the betrayal? How did Peter feel, after the denials? How did Paul, the "Pharisee of Pharisees" feel after his attempts to annihilate the followers of Jesus? Do I have remorse, regrets, self revulsion when I realize I have not been faithful to the high calling of Christ who said, "Follow me." We can all thank God that God knows our pitfalls before they happen, and God still offers us the gospel of forgiveness and accepts us as we are: sorrowful, forgiven, and filled with joy for the new life to come. I don't know, but maybe there will be a resurrection for Greco's butterfly too.

God, thank you for your gift of forgiveness, and redemption, in Christ. Amen

(This day's devotion is by Lolly Anderson, my wife, on her birthday.)
Take delight in the Lord and He will give you the desires of your heart. Commit
your way to the Lord; trust in Him and He will act. Psalm 37:4-5

Could this really be true? We can receive our heart's desires?

It took me many years to commit. I had to be on my knees—with the heavy rocks of fear burying me—fear of job loss, divorce, bankruptcy, social standing. It was at that moment, 3 a.m. in the morning, I finally said through tears, "God, I haven't done such a good job directing my life. I give up. I turn my life over to you to do your perfect will. What would you have me do today?"

That was the turning point in my life. My surrender started me on a new path. And it's not that I was free of stress or trauma afterward. But I had a new center: a rich, limitless center tapping into a universal reservoir. Good things started happening at a level I never thought myself worthy or capable of.

Previously I thought if I surrendered to God completely I would be restricted to dull clothes and no makeup living a circumscribed life without excitement. How wrong I was. Once I committed to the ultimate paradox, my life became richer, more colorful, more exciting, and filled with more love than I ever imagined. Is my life perfect? Of course not.

My earthly journey has become a five-star adventure, a top-drawer experience, a glorious ride in and out of the spiritual realm touching down on earth when needed. If I switch the equation and take the rocky road in and out of the earthly realm touching the spiritual only

when needed....that's when I can't even trust myself, much less God.

Please, God, help me to always commit my ways to you first. Amen

Blessed is the nation whose God is the Lord.
Psalm 33:12

We approach Lincoln's birthday, February 12, and Presidents' Day later in the month. Consider the statements of faith and beliefs of a few of the founding leaders of the United States. The Commander-in-Chief in the American Revolution, First President of the United States said: "It is the duty of all nations to acknowledge the providence of Almighty God, to obey His will, to be grateful for His benefits, and humbly to implore His protection and favor." John Adams, signer of the Declaration of Independence and the Bill of Rights, and the second President of the U.S., wrote: "We have no government armed with power capable of contending with human passions unbridled by morality and religion. Our Constitution was made only for a moral and religious people. It is wholly inadequate to the government of any other."

James Madison was the fourth President of the U.S. He said, "Before any man can be considered as a member of civil society, he must be considered as a subject of the Governor of the Universe." One of my teachers said, "All questions are comments." Two questions raised by the sixth President of the U.S., John Quincy Adams, imply his comments: "Is it not that the Declaration of Independence first organized the social compact on the foundation of the Redeemer's mission upon earth? That it laid the cornerstone of human government upon the first precepts of Christianity?"

The discussion on faith and culture, faith and one's nation, is a minefield full of explosive opinions. For a Christian, one rule is always immutable. Christ alone is sovereign in matters of faith and life. Speak the truth in love, live the truth in faith and hope.

Thank you, God, for the freedom to exercise faith in you. Help us to be faithful. Amen

(This day's devotion is by Laura Sandefer,
my daughter, on her birthday.) Be still and know that I am God.
Psalm 46:10

The earthly seasons reflect my search for you, my God. How tangible You are when the green of new life bursts forth on every branch and the wildflowers spread their glory. When the air feels warm and the scent of honeysuckle brings sweet memories of childhood joy, I sense with clarity Your enveloping Love for me.

But today the earth looks dead. The branches are barren. The ground is cold. My world is gray and brown. I am alone and You are not answering my prayers. Where are You? Why are you so quiet? I am asking for a sign and You give me nothing. I wait. Then a rumbling deep in my soul begins to rise. It is a restlessness that feels familiar.

This visual dormancy disguises the truth. There is a new life brewing deep in this cold, hard ground. In me, even. This season of Winter must happen for new life to sprout forth. What in me must die today? What must I shed and bury?

You have been so clear, Lord. Today, You surprise me with your stillness. I have been slow to hear You in death, in the gray, in the cold, in the quiet. Forgive my impatience. My fear. Father, I trust Spring will come. I trust You. You are faithful. You are quiet. I will rest in these cold, quiet days in the trust that You are bringing me New Life. Let my old self die. Let the dark soil of my soul regenerate. Help me let go and be still with You. Amen

> *Do you not know that your bodies are temples*
> *of the Holy Spirit, who is in you, whom you have received from God? You are not*
> *your own; you were bought at a price. Therefore honor God with your bodies.*
> *I Corinthians 6:19-20*

John Wooden, The Wizard of Westwood, coached basketball at UCLA. His teams won ten National Championships in twelve years, and had four undefeated seasons (never accomplished by any other coach). Most of all, Wooden was a man devoted to God, his wife and family, and the perpetual need to be a learner.

Wooden lived 99 meaningful years of inspired life. He said: "Things turn out for the best for the people who make the best of the way things turn out." So, how did he do that? Hear the coach answer: "Be true to yourself, help others, make each day your masterpiece, make friendships a fine art, drink deeply from good books—especially the Bible, build a shelter against a rainy day, give thanks for your blessings, and pray for guidance every day."

There was strength in the humility of Wooden that surpassed the brash brilliance of many notable persons in the sports world of fame, money and popularity. He loved to coach, read, write, and recite poetry, enjoy his family and cultivate his friendships. Surrounded by famous Hollywood "Names" and superstar athletes in one of the greatest media centers of the world, the coach had this humble thought: "Talent is God given, be careful. Fame is man-given, be grateful. Conceit is self-given, be careful."

Consider this moment a 'time out' in the game of life, and we are gathered around Coach Wooden listening, learning, and ready to honor our body, mind, and soul where the Holy Spirit of God dwells. Game on!

Thank you, God, for your gift of mentors who coach us and teach us about faith and perseverance on this journey of life, through Christ. Amen

*I pray that you, being rooted and established in love, may
have power...to grasp how wide and long and high and deep is the love of Christ,
and to know this love that surpasses knowledge. Ephesians 3:17*

What is my attitude when I read the Bible? Am I using the Bible as a place to find a collection of answers to questions? Or, as theologian Karl Barth put it: "The Bible is a place where God questions us. To hear the Word of God is to hear the question from God. Thus when the All Mighty God asks us questions He does not render us speechless, but He renders us answerable."

Through the text from Paul, I do hear the question from the All Mighty God. Do I have any grasp of the greatness of God's love for me? Is there an experience of this love that 'surpasses knowledge?'

One of the spiritual exercises necessary for me is to step out of the snake pit of judgments. In the church community we sometimes fall into the judgment pit naming others as players and spectators, lovers and haters, participators and dissemblers of our perceived truths. I know the ensnarling spirit of judgmental negativism diminishes me. How often have we loosed this deadly toxin in our own homes and contaminated the person closest to us?

The question God asks me today as I read the Bible, "Can you love like Jesus and judge without passing judgment?" Mahatma Gandhi read Leo Tolstoy's book, *The Kingdom of God is Within You.* The movie, "Gandhi," has a scene where

Gandhi is reminding a Presbyterian clergyperson that being nonjudgmental like Jesus takes great courage: "I suspect Jesus meant you must show courage...I have seen it work."

Teach me, Lord, to love as Christ loves us, without judgment. Thank you for your love. Amen

Do not conform to the pattern of this world,
but be transformed by the renewing of your mind. Romans 12: 2

In the 6th century before Christ, Judah, the 'Southern Kingdom' of Israel, fell to Babylon. While the Israelites were in Babylonian Captivity the rest of the world was in a transformative era. Gautama Buddha founded a way of life followed by millions. Confucius brought an enlightened philosophy to China. Persia (modern Iran) became the greatest Empire of the period bringing commercial inventions used to this day, such as a postal service. The Greek theater became a mass media communication's tool. Rome formed a Republic. Aesop wrote fables told to this day. Indian surgeon Susrata successfully performed cataract operations. Public libraries opened in Greece.

In this time of change, Lao Tzsu of China wrote: "After a time of decay comes the turning point. The powerful light that has been banished returns. There is movement, but it is not brought about by force. Transformation of the old becomes easy. The old is discarded and the new is introduced."

Joseph Schumpeter, economist-philosopher, said: "Transformation comes through gales of creative destruction."

When I consider major change in my life, and others, I believe the convergence of our scripture text, Lao Tzu, and Schumpeter make a perfect circle. God works the miracle of transformative change in our lives by our encounter with the gospel of Christ. Frequently, we are not ready to abandon our self-made philosophy until a time of chaos and crisis prepares us. When we finally acknowledge the power of forgiveness, accept God's act of grace in Christ, and receive his Spirit in the depths of our being, we experience transformation, peace, and happiness of the New Mind and New Life.

God of all existence, I finally can say, not my will but thy will be done. I thank you for transforming my life through Christ. Amen

(Jesus said) "Remain in me, as I also remain in you. No branch can bear fruit by itself; it must remain in the vine. Neither can you bear fruit unless you remain in me." John 15:4 "What life have you, if you have not life together? There is no life that is not in community, and there is no community not lived in praise of God." T.S. Eliot, "The Rock"

Eternal God, as I listen to the songs in the hearts of others, and in my own, many are sad. There is a deep yearning in the human community to belong to one whose power is greater than our own. Saint Augustine cried out, "Our hearts are restless until they rest in Thee." We are groundless until we belong to you. We are not ultimately comfortable when we are isolated from others. We need to experience the vitality of life that is connected in love to you and to others. Like marble in the master sculptor's hand crying out for shape and refinement, so my life calls out for the contours and forms of your creative influence.

When I belong to you, I am released from my captivity to the dark and destructive powers. I am not free to be until I am willing to belong.

Not one follower of your truth can walk in the truth alone. Thank you for the sinews of faith that bind us together. Together we experience the Spirit; the surprising variety of modes of love, arise from the unlikely, the unexpected, and uncommon persons of your world.

Today I promise to reach out to someone who desires to belong but feels shunned, rejected, or disconnected from others.

Today, I thank you for coming into my life and giving me the assurance of belonging to the companions of the Way who is Jesus Christ. Amen

February 17

(This day's devotion is by Michelle Webb, my daughter, on her birthday.) Have I not commanded you? Be strong and courageous. Do not be afraid; do not be discouraged, for the Lord your God will be with you wherever you go? Joshua 1:9

I read this verse after a F5 tornado swept through Moore, Oklahoma devastating an entire community. Many lost lives. Many lost homes. Many lost their most precious belongings. The storm swept through in forty-five minutes taking away everything in its path. It happened fast, in minutes everything is changed. From the vista of our home we could see the terrifying twister coming toward Moore, just before we entered our cellar shelter.

It is at times like this that our faith is tested. It is easy to be strong and brave when things are going well. But whether it is a natural disaster such as a tornado, or a life struggle that seems to be destroying our inner most self, God is commanding us. He is not hinting or suggesting. He is 'commanding' us to be strong and brave. Do not be terrified. Do not lose hope. For He is with us everywhere we go. God expects us to obey His commands. In return He fulfills His promises. He will be with us, and He will give us perfect peace.

You will keep in perfect peace all who trust in You, whose thoughts are fixed on You. Isaiah 26:3

I will put my trust in the Lord. Regardless of my circumstances, I will be strong and brave. I will not be terrified or lose hope. I will keep my thoughts focused on my Lord. He will keep me in perfect peace.

Dear God, thank You for your commands. Thank You for your promises. Thank You for your steadfast love. In Jesus' Name. Amen

(Jesus said) "Do not suppose that I have come to bring peace to the earth. I did not come to bring peace, but a sword." Matthew 10:34 "Put your sword back in its place," Jesus said to him, "for all who draw the sword will die by the sword." Matthew 26:52ff (Jesus' words to Peter, according to Gospel writer John, on the night before the crucifixion.)

The words of Jesus comprise a perfect paradox. Should a follower of Christ resort to violence or love to achieve justice?

Once I had the opportunity of visiting with Lady Epstein about her famous sculptor husband the late Sir Jacob Epstein. We talked about sculptures at the exhibit where we met. One that stood out for me was entitled "Ecce Homo!" ("Behold, the man!" Pilate's words when he released Jesus to the religious rulers for crucifixion.) The sculpture began with a two-ton chunk of while marble. She said, "Sir Jacob was a devout Jew who studied carefully the New Testament." The pathos in "Ecce Homo!" reveals the heavy sorrow of God suffering for the sins of the world. "My husband made a heavy rock look heavier."

Sir Jacob also sculpted the Archangel Gabriel in the victory scene from the book of Revelation when Christ triumphs over Satan's empire of evil. The archangel holds the sword of death, but paradoxically, has a look of compassion on his face.

I think Epstein understood the New Testament. God has the power in Christ to annihilate the world and all its evils. The paradox is this: all that power reaches us through sacrificial love in Jesus Christ.

Thank you, Christ, for the costly gift of forgiveness and grace. Amen

Then, because so many people were coming and going that they did not even have a chance to eat, he said to them, "Come with me by yourselves to a quiet place and get us rest." Mark 6:31-32

Is it possible that we may suffer from compassion fatigue? Was Jesus, who according to both Scripture and Nicene creed was "fully man," ever suffer from compassion fatigue? Numerous times in the records of the four gospels, we witness Jesus moving out of the maelstrom of the masses to the quiet place for prayer and restitution of mind and spirit seeking the perfect will of God. Of course this strategic withdrawal took place in the climax of the gospel's narrative, the night before the crucifixion in the quiet olive tree scented Garden, where Jesus prayed, "Not my will but Thy will be done."

George Smiley, a character John le Carre's novel, *Tinker, Taylor, Soldier, Spy* confesses: "I have a theory which I suspect is rather immoral. Each of us has only a quantum of compassion. That if we lavish our concern on every stray cat, we never get to the center of things." Jesus, not an immoral teacher, led his disciples to know the limitations of human compassion. Times of detachment and renewal are essential to vitality.

Entering my study for a place and time of reflection, I pass this sign with the words of Michel de Montaigne (1533-1592), a French Enlightenment Era writer who had extraordinary influence on the thinking of American Founding Fathers. "We must reserve a back shop all our own, entirely free, in which to establish our real liberty and our principal retreat and solitude."

God of life, action, innovation, motion, light, you are the God of silence, darkness, hibernation, stillness, quietness, and tranquility. Thank you for times in which time ceases and new birth arises from you, Father, Son and Holy Spirit. Amen

*I walk about in freedom, for I have sought out your precepts
...Remember your word to your servant for you have given me hope.
Psalm 119:45, 49-50*

Why Do Clocks Run Clockwise? is the title of a fun science book by David Feldman. The answer to the question is probably because we had sundials before clocks. Clocks were invented by persons living in the Northern hemisphere where the shadows on the sundial rotated in what we call a "clockwise" direction. The practical reality of the clock's motion is based on the greater reality behind it. Sundials' shadow motions are caused by the heliocentric solar system where we exist.

I suggest that the Bible is true and dependable in our lives for exactly the same practical reason. Its words are about the "Living Word," God, who is the great reality behind the words of the persons who wrote the Bible. Simply and personally stated, when I seek truth about God, life and my identity, the Bible speaks to me. Many others testify to the same experience. The greater reality—beyond others, myself, written records—is God.

French philosopher Emil Clay, well known to his contemporaries, was a leading writer in the 'anticlerical movement' in France. He wrote a book entitled, *The Book that Understands Me*, in an attempt to explain 'human existence.' Reading his own book he decided he knew nothing of human existence. His wife gave him a Bible, which he had never read. Upon reading it he said, "Lo and behold, as I read through the Bible, the One of whom it spoke came alive to me. Suddenly the realization dawned upon me, this is the book that understands me."

God of all, give me a willing mind and humble heart to let your Living Word meet me in the words of scripture. Thank you for a Bible that understands me. Amen

The fool says in his heart, "There is no God." Psalm 14:1
You make known to me the path of life; you fill me with joy in your presence,
with eternal pleasures at your right hand. Psalm 16:11

The *London Observer* carried a comely story about a family of mice who lived in a great piano. They loved the music of their piano world that filled the dark spaces of their lives. They were impressed, comforted, and filled with wonder from the belief that an unseen "Someone" made music from beyond them, yet close to them. One day a rebellious mouse began to question, "Is there really an unseen Someone?" He began his investigation looking for empirical evidence and found it: 'strings of steel' he disclosed, which vibrate at the same time the music is heard. There is 'no unseen Someone; that is a myth of the older mice.' Later, an even younger rebellious mouse questioned the 'vibrating string theory.' She discovered the music was made by hammers striking the strings, ergo, 'the mouse world's music is a mechanical and mathematical world proved by measured lengths of strings and observable forces of hammers.'

But the Unseen Pianist continued to compose and play music that would melt the hearts of the appreciative mice that lived in the world of the Great Piano.

The Musician, the Psalmist, said: "Fools say in their hearts, 'There is no God.'"

I pray whenever my critically trained brain wanders into the matrix of doubt and dissembling profundities: God, help me to doubt my doubts and believe my beliefs, without fear of encountering either the hard questions or the surprising answers.

This day Lord, I thank you for giving me freedom to question without the experience of divine disapproval. Infinitely greater is the gift of faith, hope and love, in you, and from you, through Jesus Christ. Amen

When He, the Spirit of truth, comes,
He will guide you into all the truth. John 16:13

John Wooden, referred to earlier in *This Day* said: "Failing to prepare is preparing to fail." The word of Jesus in our text comes from the "private discourses" of our Lord to the eleven disciples, during the last days of his earthly mission. He is preparing his disciples not to fail. If they are receptive, they shall be given a Spirit who resides within their minds and hearts and shall guide them on paths avoiding disaster, give them mind sets that cause the mission to succeed. Their mission is to take the good news of God's saving grace to a godless, graceless world. Preparation for this mission is paramount. The need for empowerment is palpable. By their own wits, will, and wealth the disciples that Jesus chose are a motley crew. No religious hierarchy, no Roman authority, no person of wealth should ever suspect that these persons could get two donkeys into the barn before a storm hit, let alone threaten power structures of the world. But one cannot over estimate the power of Spirit in the life of ordinary people.

Robert Louis Stevenson in *Kidnapped* places the protagonist, Balfour, on a deserted island as a castaway. All means of rescue fail. All the wit and will of Balfour cannot save him from what seems to be his death. Suddenly (was it by chance?) Balfour aimlessly wanders around the island and beholds a saving phenomenon. The unusual low tide has revealed a berm of bedrock (hidden under the surface of the water) from the island to the mainland. Balfour can walk home.

Jesus has prepared us to receive an astonishing opportunity of rescue. Are we ready to accept the Spirit of God?

Lord, I believe the word of Christ. This day I receive with thanks the Spirit. Amen

*We are therefore Christ's ambassadors, as though
God were making His appeal through us. II Corinthians 5:19*

There are three identity quests on our personal journeys. What is real about God, what does it mean to be 'human,' and what does it mean for me to be real. Paul taught the Christians to be 'ambassadors of Christ.' We can do this only to the measure of being 'real' and not being a counterfeit personality.

One of the chief learning opportunities for mortals like me is the model and mentor I see in other people. If we were little gods running around earth we could expect some divine revelations. We are humans who learn best through humans. We have the innate gift of choice, meaning we choose what quality of mentor we wish to teach us. I think the great thing about university experience is choice. Choose an academy that has some real mentor scholars from whom we learn. The basic word itself, 'school,' comes from the Golden Age of Greece where groups of students, called a 'school,' followed a great mentor. If we are fortunate in our birthright, we have great mentors in our own family, and the learning/mentoring starts even before birth.

We are well advised to look for mentor-ships in all three areas of our identity quests.

The three 'identity quests' meet in one person, the man Jesus. He shows the identity of God: 'if you have seen me you have seen the Father.' He mirrors one's self to one's self, both strengths and weaknesses. Thirdly, in the community of others, the identity quest shapes our lives: 'as much as you loved the least of persons in the human community, you loved me.'

Lord, it is time that I get real: to know you through Christ, to love others in all the human community, and to know more fully myself. I pray in Jesus' name. Amen

How long, Lord? Will you forget me forever? How long will you hide your face from me? How long must I wrestle with my thoughts and day after day have sorrow in my heart? How long will my enemy triumph over me?...But I trust in your unfailing love; my heart rejoices in your salvation. I will sing the Lord's praise, for he has been good to me. Psalm 13:1ff

In the throes of The Great Depression and the beginning of another World War, in 1939, a Princess (Elizabeth) handed a poem to her father, King George VI of England, to read on BBC as part of his "King's Speech at Christmas." Minnie Louise Haskins' poem was read again when The Queen Mother died, 2002, and twice again on BBC broadcasts December 19 and 25, 2010. Minnie Haskins' poem, "God Knows," excerpt below, became known as "The Gate of the Year:"

"And I said to the man who stood at the gate of the year:
'Give me a light that I may tread safely into the unknown."
And he replied: 'Go out into the darkness and put your hand into the Hand of God.
That shall be to you better than light and safer than a known way.'
So I went forth, and finding the Hand of God, trod gladly into the night.
And He led me towards the hills and the breaking of day in the lone East.
God knows. His will
Is best. The stretch of years
Which wind ahead, so dim
To our imperfect vision,
Are clear to God. Our fears
Are premature; In Him,
All time hath full provision."

In the beginning of the shadow hours of crisis we may fear the impending darkness to come. Then and there we take hold of God's strong hand. He leads us to the light.

Thank you, God, for meeting us, leading us, sustaining us in the hours of crisis. Amen

*For I do not do the good I want to do, but the evil I do
not want to do—this I keep doing. Romans 7:19*

Paul, in this text, describes his mature Christian life's struggle, not his early life as the antagonist in the Christian narrative. It is important to know that as followers of Christ, we do not feel fulfilled, surrounded by serenity '24/7.' Henri Nouwen, a profound leader of Christian spiritual formation spoke of the 'partial' taste of the grace of God that renews our life: "Just as a whole world of beauty can be discovered in one flower, so the great grace of God can be tasted in one small moment." As a youth reading Goethe, a polymath devotee of Christ, I was shocked to read his self-revealing comment on 'happiness.' I thought this kind of guy should basically be happy all the time. Goethe said, "Of all the years of my life, I think the times of real happiness would add up to about one month."

Much older, I now see what the Apostle meant when he wrote, "We see through a glass darkly, but the day will come when we see face to face."

As we grow older we begin to realize the significance of even one sacred moment when truth was crystal clear. We recall that time and place where God's presence was formidably near. We never forget the instance of perfect joy.

One such moment is worth more than decades of aimless apathy. Good life is not measured in a succession of years, but the success of one moment in the Real Presence of the Eternal Lord. Paul answered the dilemma of his partial apprehension of God's will: "Who will rescue me from this body that is subject to death? Thanks be to God who delivers me through Jesus Christ our Lord."

Amen!

Nobody has ever heard of opening the eyes of a man born blind.
If this man were not from God, he could do nothing. John 9: 32-33

Eternal God, in the mist of the early dawn I begin to see partial outlines and shapes of realities. You remind me of two truths: all my sight-based knowledge is limited. All my deepest yearning draws me toward you. I am caught lovingly in the soft web of paradox. There is the desire for reasonable truth, and there is a deeper yearning for the ultimate truth. You are beyond the space and time that creates the shadows and reflections of all things that live and move and have being. Nevertheless, I believe you, and I believe in you.

With physical sight I see the four kinds of entities that make up the whole universe: the inanimate natural objects like the clouds picking up the pinks and blues of the morning sky, the living organisms like the ivy plants growing on the gazebo, the constructed artifacts like the quaint gazebo itself, and all the sentient beings from the great blue heron at the water's edge to humankind.

You have also given me spiritual sight to see the consciousness of your presence with the eyes of the heart. That I should know you and believe in you, I acknowledge, has no more to do with my own initiative than I had to do with causing my own birth. You are the initiator of both our physical birth and our spiritual rebirth.

This day I thank you for the startling gift of faiths. You have given me the boldness to walk by faith, not by sight, onto the unknown terrain of the future. This faith is not blind. It is a new way of seeing. I am like the man the Apostle John described: "Once I was blind, but now I see, now I believe." Amen

Now Peter was sitting in the courtyard, and a servant
girl came to him, "You were with Jesus of Galilee," she said. Matthew 26:69

Rembrandt was the signature artist of the Golden Age of Dutch painting. An assiduous student of the Bible, he brought his artist skills and Christian faith to the biblical themes of many masterpieces. I am not an art expert but when one beholds another person's talent that is the *sine qua non* in an arena of human expression, one does not need to be an acknowledged expert to appreciate greatness.

The astonishing painting by Rembrandt depicting the poignant scene of Peter's Denial at the House of Caiaphas, the high priest, minutes after the arrest of Jesus and the night before his crucifixion reveals the artist's genius. The painting caused a stand-still moment of meditative reflection for me. It gave me a new understanding of the character and motivation of the 'servant girl' described in scripture.

Until I saw this painting I had always cast the servant girl in the role of a 'little snitch,' or at best, a whistle-blower. The quintessential use of light and shadow was Rembrandt's way of creating a provocative question. The light is focused on the servant girl's out reached hand and gesture. It is not, in his painting, a finger pointed at Peter like a prosecutor's expecting an indictment. Her hand is open, and beseeching Peter, and you feel her saying: "Weren't you one of his followers? I went to meet Jesus. Would you..." and she is interrupted by fear based Peter and his vehement denial of Jesus.

Am I not like Rembrandt's servant girl, yearning to meet Jesus? Direct, person-to-person, no mediators of doctrine, dogma or theologies. Yes, I am.

Thank you, God, for those who interpret to us the wonder of your truth and grace in the person of Jesus Christ. Amen

For now we see only a reflection as in a mirror;
then we shall see face to face. Now I know in part; then I shall know fully,
even as I am fully known. I Corinthians 13: 12

As a seminary student I attended illustrated lectures by Charles M. Schulz, creator of "Peanuts." A Christian, Schulz commented that many of his ideas were 'memoir' based on family and faith. Here is an example and exposition of our text.

Lucy in one of her trademark loquacious diatribes exams Charlie: "You know what I don't understand? I don't understand love." Charlie: "Who does?" "Explain love to me Charlie Brown!" "I can't. I can recommend a book…" "Well, try, Charlie Brown, try!"

"Well, say I see this beautiful, cute little girl walk by—." "Hold it Charlie, why does she have to be CUTE…maybe she has a big nose." Charlie tries again, "Let's say I see this girl walk by with this great big nose…" "I didn't say GREAT BIG NOSE!" Charlie sighs: "You not only can't explain love, you can't even talk about it."

The Bible does. God so loved the world that he sent his only Son, Jesus Christ, to be divine love in action. The Bible explains and extols the way God's love works.

Because love is God's *modus operandi*, we mere mortals question 'who is in charge down here, who runs history?' Reinhold Niebuhr said, "Either there is no pattern of history at all (in which sense cosmic caprice will finally destroy every sense of the meaning of life) or, there is a pattern but it is beyond our comprehension, and under a Sovereignty which we can only dimly discern." Back to the Bible, "we see only a reflection, as in a mirror." True of love, and of life.

Thank you for faith, God, that your love is the Way, Truth, and Life in Christ. Amen

Paul and Timothy, servants of Christ Jesus, to all the saints in Christ Jesus who are in Philippi, with bishops and deacons: Grace to you and peace from God our Father and the Lord Jesus Christ. Philippians 1: 1-2 NRSV

Who is a saint? Simone Weil said, "We live in an age which is quite without precedent: today there is nothing in being a saint. We need a saintliness proper to the present moment, a new saintliness, which is also without precedent. The world needs saints of genius, just as a city stricken by the plague needs doctors. Where there is a need there is an obligation. A new type of saintliness is an uprising, a discovery. It is almost the same as a new revelation of the universe and of the human destiny."

I wish we could go back to the original meaning conveyed by the Greek text of the New Testament. Look at all those 'common' (not capitalized) nouns in Paul's greeting to Christians in Philippi: "saints, bishops, deacons, servants." Do you long for the day of yore when the church was humble? It took three centuries of Christendom for those words to get "caps," to become 'proper nouns' according to formal syntax. Originally, the church people were not "Orthodox" "Catholic" or "Protestant." Paul called the 'followers of Jesus' by a simple common noun term, "saints in Christ." The Greek word's meaning? "Called out ones, separated by a calling." Jesus said, "I called you, you did not call me." One who believes knows who initiated belief. Faith is a gift from God. Your spouse, doctor, lawyer or closest friend may not call you a 'saint.' If you believe Christ, you are a saint. (Probably not talk about it.)

Thank you for the calling to follow you, Christ Jesus, my Mentor, Guide, and Friend. Amen

March 1

Taste and see that the Lord is good;
blessed is the one who takes refuge in him. Psalm 34: 8

Lord and God, the creator of savory things, you said, "Taste and see that the Lord is good." You, Christ, invite us to taste life. Taste brings sacred memories: the last meal we shared with a loved one departed, or with a child who moved on to begin a new home.

Why must I 'taste life' in order to see your holy presence? Must I existentially surrender physical senses to experience your Presence in the here and now of daily agenda? No. I taste, and feel your attendance in common duties when my 'mind is set on thee.' Forgive me for the times of indifference, ignorance, and indolence when I refused to 'taste and see' the extraordinary in the ordinary milieu of life. Let me escape the prison of unfeeling. Wonder and awe are real.

You are beyond finding out like a paradox concealed in an enigma surrounded by mystery. And yet, you can be experienced. I want to 'taste and see' that you are unmitigated Goodness and Holy Presence.

God, let me not be a fatalist who thinks all things are desperately controlled by an unseen force. Let me not be trapped in the narrow and dark valley of the positivist who believes that there is no One to believe.

When I am exhausted from fleeing your call, thirsty after tasting all the polluted waters of the world, you offer me the spring of water welling up to life. How could I experience this truth unless I am indeed thirsty, and willing to 'taste and see?'

Thank you, God, for memories of taste: mother's apple pie, dad's homemade candy, hot chocolate after skating on the frozen lake, après-baseball ice cream at the ballpark. Thank you for quenching the deep thirst in our souls. Amen

> *We live by faith, not by sight.*
> *Corinthians 13:2*

Early in life, perhaps the death of a grandparent, a child will ask the question, "How long will I live?" It may be in the springtime of our life span, or in adult years that we ask the more profound question, "What is the quality of my life?" Some never get to the second question. Consider *Waiting for Godot* by Samuel Beckett: "We have time to grow old. The air is full of our cries. But habit is a great deadener. At me too someone is looking, of me too someone is saying, 'He is sleeping, he knows nothing, let him sleep on.'"

We may be tempted to view life superficially, sort of the human value equivalent of 'quantitative easing,' to use an economic term. If I can add years to my life I have made it more worthwhile.

Marcus McCutchen, science editor of *Omni* magazine, gave us these 2008 data points for an average life: Start with 76 years, if male, subtract 2, if female, add 4; if an urbanite, subtract 2; if a smoker, subtract 7; work at a desk job, subtract 3; physically demanding job, add 3; exercise 5 times weekly, add 4; sleep 10 hours or more a day, subtract 4; have a pet, add 1 (did not mention pet rhinoceros); overweight by 10 pounds, subtract 4; by 50 subtract 15. (Do your own math.)

Now the qualitative value added: if you have an active faith expressing love of God and others, add 15 years to your life. The 'quants' data get our attention. The quality of life is more important.

Thank you, God, for awakening me from a life-long sleep. Your Spirit alerts me to receive and give your love. You have shown me in Christ, it is not 'how long I live,' but 'what through love I give.' Your love is my Spring of Joy. Amen

Pride goes before destruction, a haughty spirit before a fall.
Whoever gives heed to instruction prospers, and blessed is the one
who trusts in the Lord. Proverbs 16:18, 20

The Bible recounts epic stores of "how the mighty have fallen," a phrase describing Saul's reign as King of Israel. With the color commentary of Dr. Seuss, in *Yertle the Turtle*, we see the truth of our text from Proverbs. "I'm ruler of all that I can see. But I don't see enough. That's the trouble with me," said the 'pond King.' He was toppled from power by a tiny turtle, squeezed under his ponderous body, who wiggled and wiggled and toppled Yertle. Now: "The great Yertle, the marvelous he, is King of the Mud. That is all he can see."

Let us not be mistaken, the text applies to all of us. We don't have to be a magnate of banking or industry, or a rich celebrity, to succumb to pride. Focus on 'self' as the epicenter of the universe is a universal temptation. If we don't know it in advance, we are slapped in the face with the truth of the text, "Pride goes before destruction." Every time.

After the 'fall' of our self-centered creation, we look for help. We could be, but don't need to be, like the person described by Edith Wharton, *In the Fullness of Life*. We are living in a "Great House full of rooms (so many we have not entered most of them)...and in the innermost room, the holy of holiness, the soul sits alone, and waits for a footstep that never comes."

Thank you, God, that we can hear the footstep of One who comes to the door of our heart. Christ knocks, He enters, He encounters us in the heart of our fear and loneliness. Lonely, we are not alone. You are here. Amen

March 4

*I lift up my eyes to the mountain—where does my help
come from? My help comes from the Lord, the Maker of heaven and earth.
Psalm 121: 1-2*

Crashing Through is a story by Robert Kurson (2007) about one of life's heroic personalities, Mike May. May was blinded at age three from an accident. He defied even the most optimistic expectations of family and friends: setting a record for speed in downhill skiing, winning three medals in the Paralympics in skiing, employment with the C.I.A., inventor of a GPS for vision impaired persons. He married, and with his wife raised a great family. In 2000 he underwent an innovative surgery for cornea transplants that involved a stem cell procedure, with mixed results. He can 'see' but cannot make out three- dimensional objects, cannot distinguish individual identity by sight alone, including his own family members. Visual impairment researchers say, causes the occipital lobe of the brain to lose its sensitivity. This impairs the brain to process spatial objects.

Research also shows that the brain functions for sight depend on regular visual input. For example, if one were not using the optic nerves and brain signals determining spatial subjects for a period of time, that ability is lost. Mike May had not 'exercised' the visual inputs for 43 years. What we learn: Mike May courageously continued life without sight. Science is very valuable but always is a 'work in progress' and is always researching for new paradigms and casting out old ones. Most of all we learn about transcendent love in May's family. Dostoevsky underlined this simple, evidenced based truth: "One who desires to see the living God face to face should not seek Him in the empty firmament of one's mind, but in human love."

Thank you, God, for the help that comes from you, thank you for the gifts that we perceive with the eyes of our hearts, faith, hope, and love. Amen

A word was secretly brought to me, my ears caught a whisper of it.
Amid disquieting dreams in the night, when deep sleep falls on people,
fear and trembling seized me and made my bones shake. Job 4:12

Did poor old Job have a seizure? Do people really have seismic dreams that change faith's topography of their lives? Well, yes to the second question. I don't know about Job. Dreams and visions certainly continue through the New Testament times. Peter preached: "Your sons and daughters will prophesy, your young men will see visions, your old men will dream dreams." Dreams and visions continue through the ages with scientists, thinkers, movie directors and almost all of us. Some dreams are the precursors of careers, innovation, and inventions.

Teilhard de Chardin, a leading scientist in the field of paleontology and a profound philosopher, documented a vision that he could never forget. He was a medic serving French troops in the worst war in the history of conflagrations, World War I. What he saw in his dream-vision was based on a visual fact, a beautiful church in the middle of a battlefield. It was still smoldering after being bombed. Dead and dying soldiers lay about. Nothing was left standing in the burning rubble except a portion of the east wall containing a stained glass window depicting the Risen Christ. He was inspired for life. The beatific vision of Christ's resurrection is the only hope standing amid the bloody ruins of human destruction.

"Nullius in Verba," is the motto of the Royal Society, the oldest scientific society in the world, founded by an Anglican Bishop of the Church of England. It translates, roughly, "Take no one's word for it."

Dream your own dream.

God, I pray that you guide my dreams and visions through prayer, in Christ. Amen

March 6

You have been raised with Christ,
set your hearts on things above, where Christ is. Colossians 3:1

If I tell a critic of the faith that I believe in the resurrection of Christ as the central point of my belief, the critic may respond, "Of course, you are paid to believe that." Granted. Many ministers are paid. Also, many of the critics of faith hold jobs where their environment rewards the criticism. As Upton Sinclair noted: "It is difficult to get a man to understand something when his salary depends on not understanding it."

I would like to call an independent, pro bono witness, who is among the world's greatest novelists, John Updike. From *Seven Stanzas at Easter*: "Let us not mock God with metaphor, analogy, side-stepping transcendence; making of the event (of resurrection) a parable, a sign painted in the faded credulity of earlier ages; let us walk through the door. The stone is rolled back, not papier-mâché, not a stone in a story, but the vast rock of materiality that in the slow grinding of time will eclipse for each of us the wide light of day...Let us not seek to make it less monstrous, for our own convenience, our own sense of beauty, lest awakened in one unthinkable hour, we are embarrassed by the miracle."

Paul said to the Colossians 'you have been raised' with Christ. Sorry to be technical here, that verb is in "past aorist tense" in Greek and it means 'an action completed in the past and continuing.'

By faith we experience now the power of the Risen Christ. We sing to the music of Beethoven's *Ode to Joy* "Christ is risen! Hush in wonder: All creation is amazed. Drink the wine of resurrection. Jesus is our strong companion, Joy and peace shall never end."

Amen!

*Have you not heard? Those who hope in the Lord will renew
their strength.They will soar on wings like eagles, they will run and not grow
weary, they will walk and not be faint. Isaiah 40: 29ff*

The 14th century was indeed a time of disorder and new order. Europe was wrapped in the scourge of the Black Plague, which killed one third of the population. The 'Holy Roman Empire' of Catholic Church-Monarchies axis of power was beginning to collapse. Not necessarily in this order, came the winds of change: printing press, Renaissance, Reformation, 'nation-states,' exponential growth of universities-academies-schools.

One Sunday, a few years ago, in an underground church in Pakistan near the border of Afghanistan, each of us arrived for the service per instruction one or two at a time. The Lord's Prayer was whispered. So advised, a hymn was sung, as a whisper. The hymn by Isaac Watts, composed in 1707, whispered in Pakistan in the 21st century: "When I survey the wondrous cross, on which the Prince of glory died, my richest gain I count but loss, and pour contempt on all my pride." Watts had turned down a free education in 17th century England because he would not pledge a loyalty oath to the established church, which would also establish a clergy career with remuneration. From age 17 he suffered poor health, poverty, and public derision for his "Methodist" faith. In America his music found voice. Today, his Christian music is sung worldwide.

Ten thousand miles from home, I heard a Christian woman wearing a hijab singing Watts, music born in the crucible of political upheaval four hundred years ago: "Love so amazing, so divine, Demands my soul, my life, my all." I could imagine the wafting of air in the sky above and visualize the Great Eagle.

God, thank you for music to sing for the celebration of our faith, in the Name of the Father, Son and Holy Spirit, Amen.

During the days of Jesus' life on earth, He offered up prayers with fervent cries and tears to the one who could save him from death. Son (of God) though He was, He learned obedience from what He suffered, and became the source of eternal salvation for all who obey Him. Hebrews 5:8ff

Rejection may be the answer, not the problem in life. In the course of serving on an oversight commission for the National Institutes of Health, I had the opportunity of getting to know Dr. Harold Varmus, Director of N.I.H. and winner of the Nobel Prize in medicine. Among other interesting things about this famous person, I learned that he was twice rejected by Harvard Medical School, where a dean said 'enlist in the army.'

Because of that volunteer work with N.I.H. I also met Meredith Vieira. She interviewed Warren Buffet who recounted to her that he had been rejected by his choice of schools, Harvard Business School. Rejection, the carom on life's pathway, made his successful career. Other note worthy rejections: Scott McNealy, co-founder of Sun Microsystems, Ted Turner, media magnate, and Tom Brokaw of broadcast journalism. Meredith Vieira allowed that she, too, had been turned down by Harvard, and bouncing off to Tufts, new contacts created her sparkling career. The punch line here is not, 'if you want to succeed get dissed by Harvard.'

Faith and culture have this in common. We may learn more from failure than success; rejection may be positive. It may be a 'brilliant move' we only ascertain in retrospective analysis. Many examples of rejections-become-positives are in the Bible. Move to The Top Story: Jesus rejected by the people; God rejected his plea to escape suffering; Jesus became the Source of Salvation for billions of people.

Thank you, God, in retrospect for the times (each names events in the past) of rejection that have led to redemption. Amen

> *There is a time for everything, and a season*
> *for every activity under the heavens.*
> Ecclesiastes 3:1

In the days of our lives we learn that the timing of events is inexorable. Certain things cannot happen until the time is right.

Christians began to practice liberty and freedom for all in the earliest congregations saying: 'there is neither Jew nor Gentile, slave nor free, male nor female in the church, but all are one.' In reality, disparities continued in culture and church for centuries. At the time of the foundation of the U.S., abolition of slavery became a clarion call in some churches, in some nations.

Meet William Wilberforce, 1759-1833. Englishman, born into wealth, Wilberforce thought he would enter the priesthood to effect the abolition of slavery. Friends dissuaded Wilberforce from the priesthood with the admonition: enter politics. Through Parliament 'you may get laws passed to end slavery.' One political friend in London was a former slave trader named John Newton. After his conversion, he wrote a song known around the world today, "Amazing Grace," memoir for Newton.

Wilberforce was successful in elections, but unsuccessful in passage of bills for abolition. Disillusioned, he had a final visit with an old dying friend and mentor about his decision to leave politics, none other than John Wesley, founder of the Methodist Church. His extant letter to Wilberforce reads: "Unless God has raised you up for this very thing, you will be worn out by the opposition of men and devils. But if God be for you, who can be against you? Are all of them stronger than God?"

Six days later Wesley died, 1791. Wilberforce struggled for forty-two more years on the issue. In 1833, the Parliament of England passed the Emancipation of Slavery Act. Three days after the victory, William Wilberforce died. The good deed was done.

God of grace, forgive us for not saying, "The Time is Now" for demonstrating your love in the world. In Christ. Amen

March 10

I will remove from them their heart of stone and
give them a heart of flesh. They will be my people and I will be their God.
Ezekiel 11: 19

I hope every one has at least one chance to see the phenomenon of a 'totally changed person.' Superlatives are in abundance in our language but I like the simple 'word picture' used in this story by the prophet concerning a miraculous heart transplant: remove 'the heart of stone' then transplant a real 'heart of flesh.'

Scientific American magazine in 2007 carried a story about "Unfreezing a Frog." Certain cold-blooded creatures have evolved with a physiology that permits them to endure extremely cold environments. The wood fog 'freezes solid' in each winter of its life. Concealed under leaves near banks of lakes it freezes and exists in 'suspended animation' requiring neither nutrition nor oxygen, and its heart stops beating. The frogs' livers convert glycogen to glucose, which acts like antifreeze saving the vital organs, in a process called 'super-cooling.' How to thaw out? With M.R.I. technology scientists learned that the frog thaws, beginning with the heart, and from the inside out.

The analogy of this 'thawing process' is almost too obvious to overlook for a preacher searching for new material. Let's not be proud, I like this natural process of life, and I like the idea that when we discover that we have a new "heart for God" that our lives are warmed up and changed, and this spiritual transformation starts from the inner life of the Spirit. The new heart is willing to accept God's forgiveness, grace, and transformative love.

Yes, I saw a person with a "heart of stone" transformed to a new person with a real, warm heart of flesh. Everything in that person's world changed for good, from the inside—out.

Thank you, God, for taking out our hearts of stone, and giving us hearts for love. Amen.

God the Creator of the heavens, who stretches
them out, who spreads out the earth with all that springs from it,
(you) give life to those who walk on it. Isaiah 42:5-6

Who are we? What does it mean to be human? Science, philosophy, psychology, anthropology, and theology…all of the disciplines of the arts and sciences ask these two questions.

Oscar Wilde said, "The final mystery is oneself. Who can calculate the orbit of his own soul?" (from *De Profundis*)

We could take a cosmological view of things and say, well, we cannot be much, as far as we know. Only four percent of the universe is made of stuff you and I know anything about, things like all the planets, all the stars, all the galaxies, all the living and inanimate things, and 96% of the 'out there' is dark matter and dark energy. It has a 'there-ness' of which we know nothing, bosonic string theory notwithstanding.

Jane Goodall thinks about this quest in *A Reason for Hope: A Spiritual Journey*. This great scientist and explorer of thought wrote: "Science does not have appropriate tools for the dissection of the spirit. How sad it would be, I thought, if we humans ultimately were to lose all sense of mystery, all sense of awe, if our left brains were utterly to dominate the right so that logic and reason triumphed over intuition and alienated us absolutely from our innermost being, from our hearts, from our souls."

This day, let us pray intuitively with a few evocative suggestions leading us…

God of all that is: Am I known by you? Will your Spirit stir the embers to flame in the hearth of my soul? Will I see 'evidence of things hoped for' because of my faith in you? Will you ever take Christ's grace from me? Can I be loved, and give love? Amen

*Let us run with perseverance the race marked out for us
fixing our eyes on Jesus, the pioneer and perfecter of faith. For the joy set
before him, he endured the cross. Hebrews 12: 2*

"Define yourself radically, as one beloved by God," John Eagan said, "for this is the true self. Every other identity is an illusion." If we have an identity based in the love from God, we are ready for the next step, living a life of purpose. To paraphrase Nietzsche: 'the right word' is like a 'raft when we are adrift in a sea of meaninglessness.' The right word is our "God-given purpose" in life.

George Bernard Shaw (1856—1950), an Irish playwright who received the Nobel Prize in Literature, gave us one of the greatest 'purpose statements' of all time:

"This is the true joy in life—the being used for a purpose recognized by yourself as a mighty one; the being a force of nature, instead of a feverish, selfish little clod of ailments and grievances, complaining that the world will not devote itself to making you happy. I want to be thoroughly used up when I die, for the harder I work, the more I live. Life is no brief candle to me; it's a sort of splendid torch which I've got to hold up for the moment, and I want to make it burn as brightly as possible before handing it on to future generations." (from *Man and Superman)*

Jesus lived with unabated purpose for the mission of giving God's grace to the world. His purpose, passion, and joy are given to all who follow him.

God, whose purpose is to love the world in a way the world cannot love itself, with forgiveness: thank you for the 'true joy' of being used for your purpose, as agents of reconciliation. Amen

The Word became flesh and lived among us full of grace and truth.
John 1:14

Soren Kierkegaard, Danish existentialist philosopher, has had substantial influence on culture and faith for many generations. S.K. developed a philosophy with a strong emphasis on Uncertainty and Despair in human life. The idea that God would become incarnate, human, is intellectually absurd. This absurdity can be bridged, Kierkegaard said, by a 'Leap of Faith' as if leaping over '70 thousand fathoms of the deep.'

This leap, S.K. took, and wrote about it: "The Absurd is that the eternal truth has come to exist, that God has come to exist, is born, has grown up and so on, and has become just like a person, impossible to tell apart from another person." (from *Concluding Unscientific Postscript*)

Kierkegaard's reflections were written in the context of the same events in which Marx wrote *Das Capital* and *The Communist Manifesto*. Both S.K. and Marx reacted against the master plan of Hegel's dialectic idealism in which "humanity" is lost in a small paragraph of inconsequence. Political turmoil and revolutions for democracy in Europe colored the scene. Marx took the route of dialectic materialism. Marx rejected Christ. S.K. took the dialectic analysis route through Christian faith. S.K. accepted Christ.

Today I looked into eyes of a mom in Moore Oklahoma, holding her 5-year-old son's hand as they stood on a cement slab that marked the place on earth that was their home. She has lost everything, except her son, destroyed in an EF 5 tornado, 307 mph winds. Death, destruction, despair, everywhere. She had taken the leap of faith. I did not ask her, she said it: "Jesus is with us. He understands. He will help us overcome even this."

By the leap of faith we meet the One who meets us, where we are, how we are, now.

God, thank you for your Word that became flesh, in Jesus. I gratefully accept your gift. Amen

Made alive in Christ, we are saved
by grace through faith...this is a gift of God. Ephesians 2: 5ff

Faith is not unlike being on a runaway horse. If you take seriously the love of God to be the ultimate motivating power, not just of your life, but of the world, it 'takes' you. You are not in control. But you trust that this wild expression of faith gives you something that is greater than false illusions of your security systems of the past.

Prince, my very dependable horse, over whom I assumed that I, the rider, was always in control of the ride, well, Prince changed my mind. We were caught in a blinding thunder and lightening storm. Soon I was riding a runaway horse. Nothing I knew or tried would bring my good horse back under my control. The story had a good ending. Prince brought me home.

Using a title of a sermon by Martin Luther, 500 years ago, spells out the truth in unmistakable clarity: "Let go. Let God." Malcolm Muggeridge was for years a darling among the littérateurs of Europe and America. Then, later in life, he converted his loyalties when he took the Kierkegaardian 'leap of faith,' in Christ. Many of his former friends of the intelligentsia voiced opinions about Muggeridge losing his mind. He knew the difference of the territory of his new realm in faith and mentioned a hazard all Christians may heed: "The only ultimate disaster that can befall us is to feel ourselves to be at home here on earth. As long as we are aliens we cannot forget our true homeland which is the Kingdom (Christ) proclaimed."

Eternal God, our Father, we have prayed 'thy kingdom' come. Let us be faithful citizens in the New Kingdom of Christ and accept the new life experiences that come with the ferocious ride of faith with Christ in control. Amen

> *Therefore I tell you, do not worry about your life...The Father
> knows your needs...Seek first his kingdom and his righteousness
> and all these things will be given to you. Matthew 6:25ff*

Why do bad things happen to good people? All of us have wondered at times about the balance of power between good and evil. Why, we wonder, when we are trying our best, it is not good enough. We witness horrendous unjustified suffering and question God. Is God good enough? Archibald MacLeish, author of *Job,* based on the biblical Job, has a refrain raising the question of omnipotence and omni-benevolence of God: "If God is Good, He is not God. If God is God, he is not Good."

Oliver Wendell Holmes viewed this through a limerick: "God's plan had a hopeful beginning/ But mankind ruined it by imaginative sinning./ We trust the story/ Will end in glory,/ But at present, the other side's winning."

I don't have a logical answer that can explain the question why bad things happen to good people. I can turn to two sources: Augustine and Paul.

Augustine said, "God can permit evil only insofar as he can transform it to good." Paul complemented this faith perspective saying: "In all things (that is both good and bad) God works for good." (Romans 8:28) This is a believer's text; it does not make sense on the humanistic level. If one takes giant leaps through history, it is evident that good prevails... in the long run. Hitler, Stalin, Mao, Pol Pot, don't win. The primary truth of both Augustine and Paul's faith is Christ. On Thursday and Friday of Passion week, evil prevailed, but not forever. Forever God's goodness and grace in Christ prevails.

God, please give me the eyes of faith to see present circumstances in the perspective of the timeless grace and presence of Jesus Christ. Amen

*Now faith is confidence in what we hope for
and the assurance about what we do not see. Hebrews 11:1*

"Humpty Dumpty sat on the wall. Humpty Dumpty had a great fall. All the king's horses and all the king's men, could not put Humpty together again."

I heard a woman tell this story. "I was raised to believe that nothing but my own fear could deter my success. I wanted to be a lawyer, tort law, and succeed like no woman had succeeded before in Los Angeles. Nothing was going to stop me. I came at that change point in American society where women were being admitted to law schools, a few at a time in each new class. Stanford treated me just fine. A coveted position in a large San Francisco law firm followed. I loved my work, litigation, and my work loved me. I handled the defense of a Hollywood 'Name.' The success in this case brought more prestige and financial rewards grew beyond anything I had imagined. I was not fearful of anything, 'only my own fears could ever deter my success.'

What I did not know is that mere simple 'substance' could bring my downfall. The innocuous phrase 'substance abuse' explains my Humpty Dumpty experience. I successfully climbed a great wall, a wall few women before my time successfully conquered. I did not fear addiction, because I denied the disease's existence. I got high on Humpty Dumpty's Wall. I am Humpty Dumpty, and I, Humpty, had a great fall. I am a witness now before the court of the general public appeal. Neither I, nor all the people I could hire, could put me back together again.

But 'The King' did. King Jesus, and the royal Virtue of all virtues, Agape-Love, unconditional, grace laced, free, unrelenting Love of God. This Humpty needed to surrender to that higher power and begin a life of faith. That is my story. Watch me, and see if it is true."

Thank you, Christ, for being the one to whom I surrendered and found life. Amen

The Lord is my shepherd, I lack nothing...He leads me...He refreshes my soul...He guides me even in through the darkest valley...You are with me...You prepare a table for me...Your love will follow me...forever. Psalm 23:1ff

Sheep can act really dumb. I hope I am not offending anyone. Watch how they behave in a storm, compared to cattle, coyotes, or collies. They don't know what to do. Sheep need a shepherd. The Psalmist knew the metaphor of God, "My Shepherd," would communicate to his agrarian audience. We are told that the shepherd, in the steep hill country of Judea, would take rocks and make a small dam to slow down the fast streams so the sheep could drink, or, cup his hands to give it water. The shepherd leads, guides, protects and feeds them. Come to think of it, I'm not so smart. This Shepherd Lord, I need.

There is likely not one single person who has not at sometime, somewhere, experienced 'The Darkest Valley' in the rough terrain of life. The Divine Shepherd guides us there too. Remember the Gaelic prayer: "As the rain hides the stars, as the autumn mist hides the hills, as the clouds veil the blue of the sky, so the dark happenings of my lot hide the shining of thy face from me. Yet, if I may hold thy Hand in the darkness, it is enough. Since I know that though I may stumble in my going, thou dost not fall."

Note the syntax change in Psalm 23 from the distant God as 'third person' to the 'second person' pronoun, "You." Now my faith is personal. "You" are with me in the presence of evil. "You" prepare me for the presence of enemies. "Your" love follows me forever.

Thank you, Blessed God, for being the good shepherd in my life. Amen

I am the resurrection and the life. The one who
believes in me will live, even though they die...Do you believe this?
John 11:25

Lord of life, death, and eternal life, I meditate on the meaning of dying. Sometimes dying seems natural like harmonic balance...the old elephant walking over the last horizon, alone...the golden retriever's knowing eyes looking into my own as he accepts the end-time of an abundant life...the wind blown Cyprus tree defeated and uprooted on a beach after a perfect storm from the sea...the beloved family member who sustained the clan with wisdom and love to end.

Lord God, how can it be that I should learn about life from the experiences of death? The paradox of painfulness and illumination of love are mixed. Desperate isolation brings me to closer participation with you. You give me a glimpse of the 'joy of Christ' set before him in his death. I cannot explain the dichotomy of life and death, and yet, I believe in the experience of the resurrection. Is dying a prelude to living, as crucifixion precedes resurrection? "The seed put into the ground first dies and then grows a hundred fold." Dying to powers of destruction in my life, help me Lord, to discover the undying transformation of your eternal love.

You teach me, Lord, that not all dying is necessary or acceptable...horrific careless accidents, death camps, killing fields, deadly passions and deadly diseases. Experiencing more and more of the vicissitudes and ambiguities of living, I am sensitized to participate with you, God, in the devilish deviations of the world where your 'kingdom comes as it is in heaven,' beyond the veil of tears, beyond the dying, in the serenity that passes understanding. Amen

There was a man who had two sons.
The younger one said to his father, "Father, give me my share of the estate."
... He squandered his wealth in wild living. Luke 15:11ff

This parable of Jesus has been mis titled "The Parable of the Prodigal Son." Jesus did not give 'titles' to his stories, publishers did, and I doubt that Jesus would come close to agreeing with this title. I think the Lord would say, "You missed the point of the story. It is not about the son. It is not about being judgmental about human folly, that's too easy. The parable is about the 'waiting father' who represents forgiveness and grace from God. All people are prodigals in some way, no one really needs to be reminded of that. What we forget, deny or don't know, is that God's grace is sovereign, relentless, patient, and primed to be received by anyone who is ready to accept. That's the story, and the headlines should point to the extraordinary quality of love we meet in God.

Neither Google nor I could find the author of *Melody in F (The Prodigal Son)*:

"Feeling footloose and frisky, a featherbrained fellow forced his fond father to fork over the farthings. And flew far to foreign fields and frittered his fortune feasting fabulously with faithless friends.

Fleeced by his fellows in folly, and facing famine, he found himself a feed-flinger in a filthy farmyard. Fairly famished, he fain would have filled his frame with foraged food from fodder fragments. 'Fooey, my father's flunkies fare far finer,' the frazzled fugitive forlornly fumbled, frankly facing facts. Frustrated by failure, and filled with foreboding, he fled forthwith to his family.

Falling at his father's feet, he forlornly fumbled, 'Father, I've flunked, and fruitlessly forfeited family fellowship and favor.' The far-sighted father, forestalling further flinching, frantically flagged the flunkies to fetch a fat-ling from the flock and fix a feast."

God of grace, I return to you this day. I humbly accept your feast of love and forgiveness. Amen

(Continuing Jesus' parable on the Waiting Father and the Lost Son)
The son said, "Father, I have sinned...I am no longer worthy to be called your son."
But the father said, "Quick! Bring the best robe and put it on him. Let's have a feast
and celebrate. For this son of mine was dead and is alive again." Luke 15:21-22

How do we respond to Jesus' teaching about God's amazing grace? God accepts us as we are. When one lives in the light of forgiveness, walks the walk in grace, everything changes.

First, we change our understanding of ourselves. Scriptures teach us to love others 'as ourselves.' Now we began the right kind of love of self, and can begin the second step, the right kind of love of others.

Do we believe the Good News of grace revealed in this story, or, deflect it? Ours is a sophisticated species adept in deflecting the astounding truth. Here are a few deflections in the story of a person lost in a self-defeating pattern of life, the prodigal son:

A subjective person: "Oh, I feel for you." An objective person: "You are suffering the logical consequences of your choices." A religious ideologue: "Only bad guys get into this much trouble, it's your fault, pay for it." The news reporter: "I hope we get exclusive rights to this story." The bureaucrat: "Did he pay taxes on the inheritance?" The environmentalist: "Were the pigs living in proper 'green' conditions?" *Saturday Night Live*, "Church Lady:" "Oh my, never heard of such a thing, and the father, what was he doing with that 'feast' thing?" Self-pitying listener, interrupting Jesus' story: "Let me tell you what happened to me..."

Jesus responded: "Come to me, all of you with heavy burdens. You are forgiven. Now walk in the light of God's love."

God, thank you for giving me forgiveness, the foundation of my future. Amen

When Jesus came to the region of Caesarea Philippi,
he asked his disciples, 'Who do people say the Son of Man is?'..."But what about you?
he asked. 'Who do you say I am?' Matthew 16:13-1

That is the key question of Christian faith. "Who do I think Jesus is?" Often times, when we don't know a person close up, we can be shocked, negatively or positively, about our discoveries of *"Who is this guy, really?"*

I dribbled my way into the ministry, literally. My sole reason for attending Whitworth University was its basketball schedule. My high school coach Jud Heathcote, later coach at Michigan State, confirmed this choice. So, I chose a place for a college education because of a basketball schedule, and scholarship. *Prima facie* not good thinking!

Unexpectedly, academic experiences under the mentoring of three professors in diverse fields played a major role in the way God works, sending us a 'calling,' for me, the ministry. In those days, our school played a great Jesuit institution, the University of San Francisco. USF had a player that was so remarkable, coaches, players, sports writers simply ran out of bounds looking for superlatives to describe his influence on a game. He not only changed every game he was in, he changed the history of basketball including the NBA, *"Who is this guy, really?"* It was William Felton "Bill" Russell: a five-time winner of the NBA Most Valuable Player award, twelve-time NBA All-Star, the 'centerpiece' of the Celtics' eleven NBA Championships during his thirteen-year career in Boston.

How do you identify a person who in retrospect of your meeting changes history? Think of how people honestly saw Jesus, "Jeremiah returned from the dead," or "John the Baptist returned from the grave," beheaded, now alive "preaching and healing." Once a non-believer, the Christian historian H. G. Wells said, *"This penniless preacher from Nazareth is irresistibly the center of history."*

Who do you say he is?

Thank you for faith to answer you, Living Christ; you are the Living Word of God in my heart and life. Amen

Christ...who, being in very nature God, did not consider equality
with God something to be used to his own advantage; rather, he made himself
nothing by taking the very nature of a servant." Philippians 2:6-7

If daily media are correct, this day is the time to consider world power. Who are the greatest powers on earth today: America, China, India, Russia, Japan? What makes a nation a great power: economic, political, social, or military strengths?

Reflecting on Paul's letter written from the center of the greatest power the world had known, Rome, it is more than a little ironic that Paul is a powerless prisoner while writing about the greatest power on earth, that of his Servant Lord. The power of the Servant Lord is mystifying. Denied, rejected, disbelieved, abused and killed, the Servant Lord is still to this day the greatest power on earth. How can that be?

The Greek word for the translation "he made himself nothing" is *kenosis*. It means "self-emptying." This Servant Lord had no army, no friends in high courts, no magical powers, no superior technology, no financial resources, no special charm or cleverness in his personality. He was a penniless Nazarene, from a poor province of no consequence in the grand scheme of the empire. Yet, this 1st century itinerate Jewish rabbi turned the world upside down. The Roman empire has been gone for sixteen centuries. Today, the name of the Servant Lord commands more interest, attention, loyalty, service discipline, and benefit for human life than all other powers combined.

May the power of God's love in Christ be with you. The force is with you!

O God, as I leave this quiet place, give me a sense of your serene strength and glory in Christ Jesus. May I walk in the light and force of Jesus' humble might. Amen

*When I look at your heavens, the work of your fingers, the moon and the stars
that you have established; what are human beings that you are mindful of them?
You have made them a little lower than God. Psalm 8:3ff NRSV*

Life is stranger than fiction. I guess that is why some people prefer fiction. They can believe it.

As we behold the headline news on our smartphones several times a day we may develop a jaundice view of the human species. Nothing in all the media coverage about people around the world comes close to the Psalmist's declaration: "Discovery: Humans are Created a Little Lower than God." I think the NRSV Bible is the right translation of the Hebrew word used here: "Elohim." It is the same word used for God scores of times in the Hebrew Scriptures. It can be rendered "divine beings."

How do you view human nature? Are we so many carbon and hydrogen atoms configured in a particular way in a material cosmos? Is the human nature you perceive only created for a material world for material functions? Or, do you conceive of a human being portrayed in the conceptual world of the scriptures, a multifaceted being of body, mind and spirit? The "measure of personhood" in the Bible is Jesus Christ. He reveals to us the depths and heights of our humanity. We are a paradox wrapped in mystery. We can be demonic, and we can be godly. There is no one dimensional flat earth simplification of humanity in our scriptures: our loves and hates may be god-like, or devil-like, and this is why 'life is stranger than fiction.'

Thank you, God, for your creation and for revealing the depths and heights of our humanity in Jesus Christ, in whose name we pray. Amen

Whoever believes in me, as Scripture has said,
rivers of living water will flow from within them. John 7:38

In the Palouse Country of Southeast Washington State, my granddad's ranch provided the stage of many memorable events from boyhood and youth. Recently I was reviewing the film-tape of the mind about one of those days. There was a fresh-water spring that gushed from a particular hill about a mile from the ranch house. Both my horse and I enjoyed this repeated ride. Prince could stop and drink from the cool fresh spring water. It was a beautiful secluded nook in which we could ponder the meaning of life, or the other stuff boys and horses think about. Time passed, a different year, same journey, different experience. I was shocked to learn that the spring was deformed to a torpid swamp filled with weeds and stagnant water. My horse did not stop to drink. None of the usual wild life presented itself. Looking around, one could see that a landslide had taken place and the little spring's passage was blocked. Fresh water had not come into the pool for months; stagnation and stench were unabated.

Our lives may emulate this country scene. We are created to be a channel for the fresh spiritual water of God that refreshes our inner life. From the great Source we may become 'rivers of living water' to nourish the thirsty world around us. The desert dry souls of humanity thirst for the Living Water of Christ's love. We are the channels for the rivers of living water to flow, not from us, but through us. New Life starts with these springs of love. Only spiritual stagnation can prevent the miracle happening.

God of the Living Waters, you have called us to be channels of your refreshing spirit, not stagnate pools of malcontents. We accept this day the Source of the renewing water of life, in Jesus Christ. Amen

Those who hope in the Lord will renew their strength.
They will soar on wings like eagles; they will run and not grow weary,
they will walk and not be faint. Isaiah 40:31

First permit me to do a quick hand-off to another metaphor in motion, altering from an eagle to a goose. I grew up with a phrase you have heard, "If you had the sense of a goose, you wouldn't have done that." True. Geese are rather intelligent beings.

You may recognize these data: 1. Geese fly in a "V" formation that creates 'uplift' for each following bird, increasing speed and distance for the formation over a solo flight. 2. Geese rotate the most strenuous lead position, just like a NASCAR team. 3. Two geese join a wounded goose forced to fall out of formation, and 'care' for the casualty until the goose can fly again. 4. Geese in the back of the "V" formation do the 'honking' to encourage the leaders.

The lesson a spiritually discerning community learns from geese is invaluable: have a mission goal, fly together in a strategic formation, encourage leaders, care for those in need.

Perhaps faith communities fail by not knowing from 'whence strength comes.' It comes from the Lord, "Those who wait upon the Lord will renew their strength." Secondly, failure comes when we forget that we are a community with a common mission from Christ. Why act like a confederacy of dunces? We are the body of Christ supporting weak members and sharing strength from strong members.

The group that can do these four objectives can have a transformative effect on the world. In fact this group can "soar on wings like eagles!" (Yes, we changed back to the scriptural metaphor.)

Eternal Christ, we commit ourselves to the mission for which you called us, in the strength of your love and grace. Amen

God said to Moses, "So now go, I am sending you
to Pharaoh to bring my people the Israelites out of Egypt....But Moses said,
"Pardon your servant, Lord. Please send someone else." Exodus 3:10ff

Moses was a reluctant leader who ran out of excuses not to lead. The stammering hesitancy of Moses, one of the greatest leaders in history, is also a story about our discipleship as Christians. Each person has this question brought to our deepest consciousness when we meditate in the presence of God: "When will I stop making excuses and start obeying the higher call of Christ to personal morality, responsibility, and service to Christ?" In a sense, each of us is called to be a moral and spiritual leader in the realm of life we inhabit: home, profession, relationships, and communities.

Victor Hugo said that "greater than the marching of armies is an idea whose time has come." In the New Testament faith, that idea whose time has come is Christ's universal call to spiritual leadership. For all believers it is said: "You are a chosen people, a royal priesthood, that you may declare the praises of him who called you out of darkness into his wonderful light." These words (I Peter 2:9) come from the writing of the New Testament's most reluctant leader, the Apostle Peter. Like Moses, he came kicking and screaming to the role of moral leadership.

The unrelenting grace of Christ pursues all believers. God wants all of us to be moral and spiritual leaders in this broken world. Hedonistic relativism is rampant in the free societies of the world. Like a snake eating its own tail, the pleasures may seem temporarily satisfying, but soon the law of diminishing returns sets in. Now is the time for spiritual leadership.

God, for freedom you have set us free in Christ. Let us use our freedom gracefully in obedience to your good will and purpose in the world. Amen

The time for my departure is near.
I have fought the good fight, I have finished the race,
I have kept the faith. II Timothy 4:6-7

Long before the end comes, we may write an epitaph representing a projected retrospective of our life. Paul's athletic metaphor on his life is a perfect description of discipleship. But note, Paul could not have written this thought as a young man. His mid-life crisis and radical transformation are well documented. That is one of the wonderful attributes of God's grace. We have a chance to finish the race of life a champion, a champion over the forces of destruction.

Darryl Strawberry is such an example: selected as Number 1 draft pick by the New York Mets in 1980, 1983 Rookie of the Year, won four World Series titles, eight All-Star Game appearances. At 21 years of age he was introduced to cocaine, nightclub life, celebrity coddling, and lots of money, a volatile cocktail for any one. Then the race of life went off the track: trouble with the law, personal relationships, finances, and health—colon cancer twice.

At the perigee in his orbit around existence, Christ met the 'has been' great athlete. Darryl Strawberry, like the Apostle Paul, in mid-life crisis, surrendered his self-willed life to Christ. The road to recovery began. In all aspects of his being—body, mind and spirit—

Strawberry was transformed through the painful process of claiming his place on the inside lane of the racetrack of life.

Now he is running a good race, and knows the Lord he meets at the finish line.

Strawberry's epitaph will be interesting to read. I would like to nominate him to the 'Sports Hall of Fame for Athletes who Suffered, Battled, and with God's Grace Recovered from Addiction.'

Ad majorem Dei gloriam: To the greater glory of God.

Thank you, Lord, for meeting us in our greatest need. We accept your grace, love, and hope through faith in Christ. Amen.

Very early in the morning, while it was still dark, Jesus got up,
left the house and went off to a solitary place, where he prayed. Mark 1:35

If prayer was quintessential to Jesus, is that not a signal to us, if we sincerely seek to know and do the perfect will of God? Augustine said, "Without God we cannot, without us God will not." Prayer is the way we experience the love of God.

A new word was entered into the Oxford English Dictionary in its 2005 edition. The word is *neophilia*, a "lover of what's new," and the word *neologist* is "one who makes new words."

Sometime after the first writings of New Testament began to be read in the Greco-Roman empire, after 50 A.D., the Greek speaking world must have been surprised about a key 'new word.' This word defined God, described the mission of God, and was commanded to all Christ followers. The word was "Love." Not any love, not *eros* not *philia* and not *storge*. The *neophiliac* would have known the new word was *agape*, "love that is sacrificial, serves the best needs of others, the character that is Christ-like." Classical Greek had faintly heard of it, but the Christian definitions were entirely new. Also, in the history of human belief, no one had heard this definitive proposition: "God is love." Even the idea that God in Christ could express sacrificial love for his created beings, humanity, was complete foolishness to Greeks, and a scandal to Jews.

Can we step back and gain the perspective of time and appreciate the radically new and refreshing truth that God's grace encounters us in the here and now?

Lord God, thank you for the overwhelming stupendous love we have received from you, this day, in this place, in this emergence of spiritual presence and peace. Amen

For me to live is Christ, to die is gain.
Philippians 1:21

For Christ followers, death is a somber fact before a glorious destiny.

Believing in the resurrection of Christ should not create flippancy in attitudes about death. If you have been separated by death from a beloved person who radiantly reflected the joy of life every day of your life, you know that death has fangs that tear away the sinews of your core being. A believer in Christ understands the pathos of Robert Frost's subdued poem:

Nature's first green is gold, Then leaf subsides to leaf,

Her hardest hue to hold. So Eden sank to grief,

Her early leaf's a flower; So dawn goes down to day.

But only so an hour. Nothing gold can stay.

Paul could grieve for a loved one lost, even as Jesus wept at the grave of his friend Lazarus. In the grief and through the sorrow a comforting mystery arises like a golden sunrise in the break from a foreboding dark night. We say it, and then we discover the poet's meaning: (Tagore) "Death is not the extinguishing of the light, it is putting out the candle when the dawn has come."

What is to be gained from death? More and infinitely transformed life. Thomas Wolfe, in *Home Coming*, captured the Apostle's elliptical truth, to live is Christ, to die is gain. "Something has spoken to me in the night, burning of the waning year; something has spoken in the night, I shall die, I know not where. Saying: to lose the earth you know, for greater knowing, to lose the life you have, for greater life; to leave the friends you loved, for greater loving; to find a land, more kind than home, more large than Earth."

God, I accept your gift of life that leads from my birth, through death, to you and all eternity, through Christ. Amen

(This day's devotion is by Anna Webb, my granddaughter, on her birthday—at age 13.) Love must be sincere. Be joyful in hope, patient in affliction, faithful in prayer. Do not repay evil for evil. As far as it depends on you, live at peace with everyone. Romans 12:9ff

A poem with wise advice from Mother Teresa: "Because It was Never Between You and Them:"

"People are often unreasonable, illogical, and self-centered; forgive them anyway.

If you are kind, people may accuse you of selfish ulterior motives; be kind anyway.

If you are successful, you will win some false friends and some true enemies; succeed anyway.

If you are honest and frank, people may cheat you; be honest and frank anyway.

What you spend years building, someone could destroy overnight. Build anyway.

If you find serenity and happiness, they may be jealous; be happy anyway.

The good you do today, people will often forget tomorrow; do good anyway.

Give the world the best you have, and it may never be enough; give the best you have anyway.

You see, in the final analysis it is between you and God; it was never between you and them anyway."

Anna writes: "To me, this poem is a reminder to always be kind and good. No matter how negative a person is to you, show kindness. People can ruin good and happy things in your life easily. But we need to be nice to them anyway. It doesn't matter what others think of you. What matters is if your heart is right with God. People may be jealous of things you have or did, but our job is to be kind to them anyway. Always remember that our attitudes should reflect our relationship with God, not with those who hurt us.

Dear God, thank you for the teaching of Jesus, 'to do unto others as you have them do to you.' Thank you for showing us the kindness and patience of Jesus, in His Name. Amen

I call with all my heart; answer me, Lord, and I will obey
your decrees. I rise before dawn and cry for help; I have put my hope
in your word. Psalm 119:145

Prayers have been like mountains marking my journey through the landscapes of life. My mother at the age of eighty-two told me she had 'dedicated' me to God for 'ministry' before I was born. She had twin babies, my sisters, and one or more miscarriages before my birth. The 'dedication' was part of her negotiations with God to give her beloved husband a son. I cannot guess God's mind in the matter, but wisely, my mother never told me this story until I had served decades in the ministry. She understood rebellion from parental dominance was more than skin deep in her son.

Prayers were a natural part of my dad's life. He was a superintendent of schools. Without prejudicial assumptions he would pray for the youth he knew were in serious trouble, as if they were part of the family, and in the larger sense, they were. I considered my dad a friend, so I never had to reject the positive prayer experiences as a form of revolution against the ruling party, which is a common in our species in the transition of growing up.

In the community of faith, prayer with people in crises provided a rock-like foundation where an anxious soul could stand and face the circumstance that could not be changed. Prayer helped them change attitudes how to respond to immutable harsh realities. I saw this happen with families suffering from the Oklahoma City Bombing. (1995) Prayer is not something we "do." Prayer allows the communion of Christ to happen. Prayer's power is what God does.

Eternal God, through prayer you have made your presence of hope, peace, and joy real in our time-bound lives. Forgive our trespasses, and renew our love for you. In the Spirit of Christ, we pray. Amen

People were also bringing babies to Jesus for him to place his hands on them. When the disciples saw this, they rebuked them. But Jesus called the children to him and said, "Let the little children come to me, and do not hinder them, for the kingdom of God belongs to such as these." Luke 18:15ff

The child becomes a paragon of faith because the child accepts unfettered joy. Once upon a time, most adults had this ability. We may be scared like the Eugene O'Neill character who said: "You are born into the bright light of life which begins to be covered with shadows of ambiguity, dark evil, and ultimately comes to an endless night." (*A Long Day's Journey Into the Night*)

Seismic change comes back into the adult world when we accept the power of acceptance. God invites us to the family of faith; we accept the invitation. We are surprised by joy with the banquet feast that follows. John Irving's humble character, Owen Meaning, lets his kindly insightful stream of consciousness flow gently over the scene of humanity: "I find that Holy Week is draining; no matter how many times I have lived through his crucifixion, my anxiety about his resurrection is undiminished—I am terrified that this year, the resurrection won't happen. Anyone can be sentimental about nativity; any fool can feel like a Christian at Christmas. But Easter is the main event: if you don't believe in resurrection, you're not a Christian believer." (*A Prayer for Owen Meany*)

God of compassion and grace, let me never again choose a road of unbelief. Not accepting your infinite grace and ubiquitous presence leads me to the cynical and dark side of existence that separates me from the Spirit. I find that my own horizons crumple in upon my soul. Thank you for shaking the foundations of my complacent world. You have rattled me out of the cocoon of indecision and ignorance. I accept your indescribable love. Amen

In your anger do not sin,
Do not let the sun go down while you are still angry.
Ephesians 4:26

Jackie McMullen has a worldwide audience as an ESPN sports commentator on the famous "Around the Horn" daily show. She is a reporter for the *Boston Globe* where she wrote about the 'real story within the story' the day after the sensational New York Giants win over the New England Patriots in the 2008 Super Bowl. This happened before the game on media day:

"A boy no more than eight or nine years old was handed a microphone… and he made a beeline toward Giants' coach Tom Coughlin, who, spotting the junior inquisitor, leaned over in an almost grandfatherly fashion and tenderly attended to what he thought would be a question. 'I hear you've been a lot nicer this year,' said the child. 'Who put you up to that?' asked the coach to gales of laughter."

After going 8-8 in the 2007 season, Coughlin met with his veteran players. They told him he yelled too much, communicated too little, and listened barely at all. Veteran player Michael Strahan called the change, "a transformation, sometimes I barely recognize him." (*Boston Globe*, January 30, 2008)

Nice guys don't finish last; the nice guy here looks good with a Super Bowl ring.

When Mickey Mantle was in a batting slump, on occasions after striking out, he would kick the water cooler out to the playing field stopping the game. His manager Casey Stengel made an acute observation, "Mantle, it ain't the water cooler that's getting' you out!"

How often is our anger misdirected guilt or shame that we cannot admit? The Apostle Paul's sage advice: 'think the situation over, this day, don't let the sun go down on your anger, don't sleep on it. Don't be too proud to give forgiveness, and ask for forgiveness.' Nice guys do win.

God, please forgive my anger this day, and I forgive others who offended me. Amen

The Lord is good to all; he has compassion on all he has made.
All your works praise you, Lord: your faithful people extol you. Psalm 145:9-12

About a dozen years ago I chaired a symposium entitled, "The Human Frontier: DNA, Genes and Molecular Biology." James Watson, Nobel prize winner and co-founder of the architecture of DNA, was one of the eight distinguished scientists who presented at this event. At an after-event dinner, I was asked in various ways, why a minister would be interested in genetics and biology, and if I found this an assault on my beliefs. It turned out that more than half of the scientists in the group were active members in some church, and four of the eight taught Sunday school classes. This did not surprise me.

Scientists are not dissimilar from the culture we share, some believe, some do not. We do have a common objective, truth about reality. Science seeks evidence based answers on What is real, and How it works. Theology asks questions of Who, and Why.

In the years since our symposium, scientists have deciphered the genetic architecture of many species of living things. There is a wonderful commonality in creation. For example, a person may not look like Vitis vinifera, but we share 24% of our genes with this species (wine grapes), 65% of our genes with Gallus gallus (a chicken), and 85% of our genes are shared with Bos taurus (a cow).

The mystery in the midst of the creation remains to be viewed, as Einstein said, "with a sense of awe." We continue to be students of 'How' the universe works even as we are students of 'Who' the creator is. For the Christian, we encounter God in the Word made flesh, Jesus Christ.

Lord, all your works praise you. Thank you for disclosures of knowledge of your creation. Increase our devotion to truth spoken with love, in Christ. Amen

The Lord said to me, 'My grace is sufficient for you,
for my power is made perfect in weakness.' II Corinthians 12:9

John Calvin was a 27-year-old lawyer when he begin to be known for writings that were pivotal to history through the Protestant Reformation and transformative thought in developing democracies. The opening words of his magnum opus: "Well-nigh the whole sum of our wisdom consists in two parts, the knowledge of God and of ourselves." Among his thoughts about humanity is the concept of the universality of 'missing the mark.'

No one is perfect, none are completely fulfilled, all have 'missed the mark' of the goal of humanity. One of many words for 'sin' in the scripture is *hamartia* (ham-ar-tee-ah). This word is used as a metaphor in the picture of an archer aiming at a target and 'missing the mark.' Who among has not had that experience? Calvin said we are the creature who universally 'misses the mark.' For this reason the church and all bodies of governance must be so designed that there is a balance of power for human decision because all people 'miss the mark.' Good intentions never have totally satisfactory fruitions.

Paul understood this. To paraphrase his thought, "I am content with my inability to personally accomplish the great goals of life; why? because when I admit my weakness, I can affirm Christ's strength. When I am weak, he is strong." God's grace is sufficient. Therefore, ultimate power and authority should never be lodged in a single person, body politic, council, pope or kings, because all persons sin, 'miss the mark' of good intentions. The 'protestant' concept of Calvin clearly stated that only God is the ultimate ruler of conscience. Governance can only be just when there is a balance of powers among the imperfect brokers of power. Then, God's grace is sufficient.

God, you are the sovereign Lord of all nations and persons. Thank you, for your all sufficient grace complementing our persistent weakness. Amen

The pride of your heart has deceived you; you who live in the clefts of the rocks and make your home on the heights; you who say to yourself, "Who can bring me down to the ground?" Obadiah 1:3ff

M.I.T. professor Dan Ariely said: "Why do bankers lose sight of the economy?" People behave in a predictably irrational manner. "We are beings with qualities that can be destroyed by the introduction of economic gains." All of us can name examples. We may look into our hearts. Ariely's comments came in 2009 as the largest bankers in America were pleading for government 'stimulus funds.' One of the reasons that having more money creates the need for more money (it does not matter if we earn it or it comes as a subsidy) is an internal fault line that runs through the human soul. Aristotle explained: "It is the nature of desire never to be satisfied."

What mid-course correction can we make on our flight through life? We do not have to accept fate, or incapacities as an excuse. Nor do I agree with baseball player Ted Williams who said, "If you don't think too good, don't think too much." I would opt for Yogi Berra who said, "Ninety per-cent of winning is half mental."

Wake up from the brainless absorption of pride. Take on the danger of curiosity and hang fearlessly to the cliffs of faith. When we have goodly 'gains' is a time to make new challenging moral commitments. The first question for a Christian to ask in days of increasing prosperity is, "How may I increase my charity?" Faith's answer is clear: "Sincerely follow the perfect will of God." Do that now, before the Great Depression of Pride takes place. In the words of John Wayne, get going, 'you're burning daylight, pilgrim.' (Movie: "The Man Who Shot Liberty Valance" 1962)

Lord, give me a gracious dissatisfaction with new wealth without new wisdom. Amen

God of all comfort, (you) comfort us in all our troubles,
so that we can comfort those in any trouble with the comfort we ourselves
receive from (you). II Corinthians 1: 3ff

In American, European, African, and Asian churches I have seen The Fourteen Stations of the Cross represented by indigenous artists. In all cultures there is a poignant experience in our common humanity that is, in the words of the gospel, like "a sword in your soul." That is the Fourth Station of the Cross, where Jesus, minutes before the crucifixion, meets his mother Mary.

Can you imagine? Mary knows the most painful privilege of being a parent, when a son or daughter precedes the parent in death, in this case, a horrific, unjustifiable death. Mary was between 12 to 15 years of age when Jesus was born; she was 42 to 45 years old when he died. She was the only person present at both his birth and death. Percy Shelley writes:

When the lamp is shattered
The light in the dust lies dead,
When the cloud is scattered,
The rainbow's glory is shed.
When the lute is broken,
Sweet tones are remembered not,
When the lips have spoken,
Loved accents are soon forgot.

The passion will rock thee
As the storms rock the ravens on high;
Bright reason will mock thee
Like the sun from a wintry sky.
From thy nest every rafter
Will rot, and thine eagle home
Leave thee naked to laughter,
When leaves fall and cold winds come.

The gospel story packs a rib breaking punch to the complacent body of religious traditions and practices. The truth in Christ strikes deep in the sinews of body, mind, emotions, and spirit of our human lives.

Lord, continue to bring your comfort to persons suffering unspeakable loss, in Christ. Amen

May our Lord Jesus Christ himself and God our Father, who loved us, and by his grace gave us eternal encouragement and good hope, encourage your hearts and strengthen you in every good deed and word. II Thessalonians 2: 16-17.

From ancient Greek mythology we learn a story repeated in plays and film to our 21st century. Pygmalion was a sculptor living in Amathus, a little seashore town on the southern coast of Cyprus. He could fashion from the crudest marble beautiful statues, some used in temples of worship. He was wealthy, famous, and lonely. He had no one to love.

Upon a time, he fashioned a beautiful statue to love for himself. Her hair was so perfect he could image it moved in the breeze flowing over the casements of his window opened to the sea.

One day he heard a great parade on the street below. The people were dancing, laughing, singing, and following a statue of a beautiful goddess, a sculpture he created. He followed the procession that went to the temple where the statue became the center of attention. Pygmalion returned more disconsolate to his home. His personal trophy was gone! Disheartened, he began to cry, then he heard a voice behind him. It was a beautiful woman, a real person, and her hair moved with the breeze from the sea. They fell in love, married, and living happy in love ever after; the artist discovered what each of us must learn: an authentic person cannot fashion love. Love is a gift of God. Love fashions us.

You will recognize G.B. Shaw's play, "Pygmalion," which Churchill saw, liked, and didn't want to say so; the great Broadway play, and film, "My Fair Lady," in which Audrey Hepburn as Eliza Doolittle is "fashioned" to be a lovely person by Professor Higgins (Rex Harrison). The 'fashioner' becomes the one fashioned.

Spirit of the Living God, take us, mold us, fill us, use us, in Christ's love. Amen

*Start children off on the way they should go,
and even when they are old they will not turn from it. Proverbs 22:6*

Due to long standing law, there can never be a building in Washington D.C. greater in height than the Washington Monument. This monument is under repair due to the April 23, 2012 earthquake. The workers at the top of the scaffolding can see two words on the aluminum cap: *"Laus Deo."* (Praise be to God!) This grand obelisk was begun in 1848. 1848: U.S. acquires Texas, New Mexico, California, Utah, Nevada, Arizona, Wyoming, and parts of Colorado from Mexico in return for a large indemnity treaty; Revolution in Vienna, Emperor Ferdinand I abdicates; Revolt in Rome and the Pope flees to Gaeta for safety; Marx and Engels publish *The Communist Manifesto;* and J.S. Mill publishes *Principles of Political Economy.*

Back to the monument: 898 steps, 50 landings; on the 12th landing is a prayer offered by the City of Baltimore, on the 20th is a memorial presented by Chinese Christians, and on the 24th a statement by Sunday school children from New York City and Philadelphia quoting Proverbs (above) and Luke. The cornerstone of the Washington Monument was laid on July 4th, 1848, and its depository contained, *inter alia*, a Bible.

What monuments to the future should you and I leave to history's long, long memory? We shall conclude with parts of George Washington's prayer for America:

"Almighty God; We make our earnest prayer that Thou wilt keep the United States in Thy Holy protection...And that Thou wilt most graciously be pleased to dispose us all to do justice, to love mercy, and to demean ourselves with that charity, humility, and pacific temper of mind which were the characteristics of the Divine Author of our religion, through Jesus Christ our Lord, Amen."

I am the way and the truth and the life.
John 14:6

Roads signs are important. We need them in crucial instances of life: strange city, you are on the Interstate, your wife is about to give birth in the car, must find a hospital in a hurry; just returned from Afghanistan on military duty, attending a wedding in a town you have never seen, no time to waste, 'get me to the church on time' and you're the groom! Road signs are lifesavers sometimes.

It is 1944, World War II, this took place as the Allied forces were moving from France toward Germany on a major offensive across the frontline. A 'great bulge' in the weakened front line was caused by the German counter-offensive. Will "The Battle of the Bulge" be won by the Germans? The Germans cleverly dispatched soldiers across the lines. They were dressed in U.S. Army uniforms and drove U.S. Army jeeps. They took down or changed hundreds of road signs. The ploy worked. The ensuing confusion left Allied battalions misdirected. Directions are crucial.

Remember the childhood story of *Alice's Adventurers in Wonderland*. Alice is lost and asked the Cheshire Cat for help: "Would you tell me, please, which way I ought to go from here?" Cheshire Cat said: "That depends a good deal on where you want to go." Alice: "I don't much care where I go." Cat: "Then it doesn't matter which way you go." Alice: "I just want to go somewhere." Cat: "Oh, you are sure to do that if you only walk far enough."

We need a good map, the Bible. We need to know the right way. Jesus said, "I am the way, the truth and the life; follow me."

Thank you, God, for the road map of scriptures, and the leadership of Jesus Christ. Amen.

> *Then Absalom sent secret messengers throughout*
> *the tribes of Israel to say, "As soon as you hear the sound of the trumpets,*
> *then say,' Absalom is King.'" II Samuel 15:10*

The tragedy of betrayal is that a good person suffers immensely and sometimes dies. Absalom was King David's son. David loved Absalom with all his heart. Absalom had the charisma of his father. He was a popular war hero and carried the favor of the people. Duplicitous behavior marked his inglorious means to achieve power.

Betrayal tragedies in the Bible are prescient indicators of human nature's dark side. Delilah betrayed Samson to the Philistines (Judges 16: 16-21). Sex, addictions, greed, power, and self-aggrandizement punctuate these biblical stories. The servants of King Joash, a "good king" among a bunch of terrible rascals according to the scriptures, betrayed him and mercilessly dispatched their act of regicide (II Kings 12:20-21). The four gospels of the New Testament recount the treacherous act of Judas Iscariot who betrayed Jesus with a kiss.

In all the betrayal stories, the sovereign will and love is undeterred in its direction and purpose of redemption. After each of these despicable acts, the kind, true, and just power of God's grace is irresistible. Human aggression, arrogance, superciliousness, conceit, and haughtiness are mere hot coals poured into the cool, clear, sea of God's mercy.

The sovereign power of God's grace is indefatigable. Joseph's brothers did shameless acts of betrayal and evil against Joseph. In retrospect, Joseph said to his brothers: "You intended to harm me, but God intended it for good." In the cosmic war of demonic and evil forces, ultimately the sovereign grace of God prevails. We therefore know the outcome of the human drama, because we know the beginning and the end of the narrative, the Alpha and Omega, Jesus Christ.

Thank you, Lord, for the unfaltering force of your grace in Jesus Christ. Amen

In this world you will have trouble. But take heart!
I have overcome the world. John 16:33

This prediction and promise of our Lord's teaching is validated by experience. Prediction: 'in this world you will have trouble.' Promise: stay with Jesus, 'I have overcome the world.' Jesus' own experience proved the prediction and promise are true. Soon his disciples found it to be true. You and I may find this prediction and promise true.

Irina Ratushinskaya described her Soviet imprisonment in the book, *Gray is the Color of Hope*. The Russians considered Irina and her prison associates as very dangerous because they believed radical ideas, what we call the Bill of Rights. These 'dangerous' women were put in the "Small Zone" of the Siberian gulag, a small space for a large number of prisoners. Soviet sociologists believed such confinement led to dissension, havoc, even death. Experience in other gulags proved the idea worked. Not with the group around Irina.

"We used an unusual force, I call it unselfish love," Irina wrote. It works silently and cannot be silenced. It works internally, and cannot be suppressed. It is the unselfish love Jesus defined. Irina and her Christian friends survived because they put this faith into action.

Joan Benny, daughter of Jack Benny, talked about her beloved dad's weekly family routine. "Let's get in the car and go for a ride." Everyone on board, Jack would feign starting the car without fully engaging the ignition, then say, leaning over to his little daughter, "Honey, this thing just won't start until you give me a kiss." Joan said for years she believed there was a connection between the kiss and the car starting. There was; it is called 'unselfish love.'

The unloved world is a place of trouble. Take courage. Practice the Love of Christ.

Thank you, God, for the gift of the forceful presence of Christ-like love. Amen

> *Now Peter was sitting out in the courtyard, and a servant girl came to him, "You also were with Jesus of Galilee," she said. Matthew 26:69ff*

Let's consider Peter's Denial of Jesus, actually 'denials,' from a new perspective. What was the effect on Jesus? His disciples abandoned him; the world of power brokers turned against him. If Jesus was only a man like most of us, could he not have succumbed to despair and retreat during his hellish week before the crucifixion?

Consider the case of George Fredrick Handel. Early in life he became popular, had a successful career, favored by the royal court. Then cultural moods changed in England toward Italian arts and drama, on which Handel had built his career. Handel became *persona non grata*, could not find work for his skills, became a debtor, slid into abject depression, had a stroke, and friends abandoned him.

We know very little about the internal moods of Jesus. He did plead in a tense prayer with God that he would not have to face the trial for his life. But, at the point of complete abandonment, something happened in the lives of Jesus and Handel that changed despair to joy.

In the case of Handel, an associate, in the middle of the night handed the composer a manuscript of words that needed music. Handel read them aloud: "Comfort ye, comfort ye, my people, saith your God, and the glory of the Lord shall be revealed." The music-making miracle began to unfold. The greatest oratorio ever composed was finished in twenty-two days and nights as music poured forth from his heart and pen. You have sung it: Handel's "Messiah."

Jesus turned his night of potential despair and defeat into triumph too, with the words, "Not my will but thine be done."

In spite of negative circumstances in the dark hours of life, follow the God-given mission. On the wings of the morning, gladness comes.

God, I pray, not my will, but your will be done. Amen

The great crowd that had come for the festival heard that Jesus was on his way to Jerusalem. They took palm branches and went out to meet him, shouting, "Hosanna! Blessed is he who comes in the name of the Lord! Blessed is the king of Israel! So the Pharisees said to one another, "Look how the whole world has gone after him." John 12: 12ff

The pleasure of popularity may end abruptly. "Pleasure like the poppies spread, you seize the flower and the bloom is shed; like snow that falls on the river, it's a moment white, then gone forever." (Robert Burns) Christ was not seduced by the tangential nature of the pleasure of popularity.

Can I see myself along the palm strewn road watching Jesus pass as crowds are cheering him, "Superstar, World's Greatest, Better than Anyone, President of the Universe," and, "we hope his miraculous powers will help us." Are there not times I have put Jesus in the category of 'The King of Helping Me with a quick fix?'

When I follow Jesus on the day he is celebrated as royalty, am I willing to follow all the steps of my Lord in the five days succeeding this brief pleasured moment of success? Some time soon Mozart's "Requiem" will resound in my brain, and I shall hear those haunting words cry out: "Remember, merciful Jesus, that I am the cause of your journey." Yes, all the journey, step by step to the cross.

In the movie "The Last Emperor," the emperor of China, encumbered with immeasurable luxury, is asked by his brother, "What happens when you do wrong?" "When I do wrong, someone is punished, publicly."

Jesus reversed the ancient pattern of power. When we do wrong, the "king" suffers, in love, for us. That is the grace of Christ.

God, be with me as I follow the footsteps of Jesus this day, this week, in Christ. Amen

On reaching Jerusalem, Jesus entered the temple courts and began driving out those who were buying and selling there. He overturned the tables of money changers... He said, "Is it not written: 'My house will be called a house of prayer for all nations?' But you have made it a den of robbers." Mark 11:15ff

There goes the image of 'sweet Jesus, meek and mild,' if you ever had that picture stored in your mind. It is in this person that God reveals his extraordinary love. Have we misunderstood love? Jesus knows how people of power can misuse common people of faith. This is a classic case of the conflict between the lovers of power and the power of love. The civil and religious rulers were an axis of power that suppressed the people robbing them of money and freedom. Worse still, they did it in the name of God, in the temple of God. Jesus fully anticipated the results of his actions. "The chief priests began looking for a way to kill him, for they feared him, because the whole crowd was amazed at this teaching."

Can we not see religion misused in our world by tyrants, terrorists, and perfidious teachers of hate? Many suffer from tyrannical absolutism, but especially the poor. Those kinds of despots function in the poorest communities of humanity. Make no mistake about it. Jesus had the courage of a hero and savior willing to make a stand for love and justice; justice on God's terms is love in action.

As we follow the footsteps through Passion Week, we learn that his passion comes from the heart of God. Jesus had great courage and a heart for God's will, an omnipotent combination of forces. There cannot be a more 'passionate' event in the history of humanity than God's costly love loosed in a love-forsaken world.

God, all-powerful, full of love, help me to see the truth of redemption through the grace of Christ. Amen

The Pharisees went out and laid plans to trap (Jesus) in his words: "Teacher, tell us what is your opinion? Is it right to pay the imperial tax to Caesar or not?" Jesus knowing their evil intent said, "You hypocrites, why are you trying to trap me? Show me the coin...whose image is on it?" "Caesar's," they replied. He said, "So give back to Caesar what is Caesar's, and to God what is God's." Matthew 22:15ff

This story in Matthew is part of the 'set-up' in his gospel that leads to the climatic crucifixion and the finale, resurrection. What can be missed in reading this episode on 'Caesar and taxes' is the sharp humor of Jesus, in which he likely drew applause from the common folk. When Jesus asked for a Roman coin, the truly religious leader should have said, "I don't have Roman denarii, I have only the Hebrew shekel, the proper coin used in the temple area." The very fact that he had a Roman coin exposed his hypocrisy. Deeply religious Jews objected to the Roman coin because with the emperor's image, it represented the idolatry of "emperor worship." And it is true that some Caesars referred to themselves as 'god.' In this simple exchange Jesus unearths a huge issue in politics and theology. The religious rulers were in such collusion with the political overlords they even forgot to cover up their duplicity.

The religious leaders were right on one thing. The penniless rabbi from Galilee was a threat to their spurious political and religious authority. How far can one let the Light of Truth shine once the beacon is turned on?

When my heart is Christ's home, the bright light of his grace and truth shines in all the rooms, all the compartments, everywhere: personal life, social life, politics, economics, and relationships.

Lord God, you invaded this world in the Word and with Spirit, in Jesus. Give me a willing heart and open mind to see this miracle and experience the joy. Amen

Jerusalem, Jerusalem, you who kill the prophets and stone those sent to you. How often I have longed to gather your children together, as a hen gathers her chicks under her wings, and you were not willing. Look, your house is left to you desolate. Matthew 23:37ff

Jesus is about to leave the city of Jerusalem. Only a couple days ago he came to the city crowning the highest hill in Judea in a triumphal procession. It is a moment of deep reflection upon the mission he chose before he began his ministry of teaching the good news of the Kingdom of God. Everything in his life proceeded from that choice.

The choice about our calling is given to each of us. The choice we make defines our future. Will I become what God wants me to be?

Consider the opposite poles on this spectrum of choices. Existence is only about a material world without morality or god. Or, existence is about a God who creates and loves the world.

Three centuries before Jesus taught, Epicurus said: "The purpose of living is to enjoy life. We are not the children of a benevolent God, but stepchildren of an indifferent nature. Life is an accident in a mechanical universe." Some may choose this philosophy today.

On the other end of the spectrum of choice: in the words of the 1647 Westminster Catechism, "What is the chief purpose of human life? To glorify God and enjoy God forever."

We have this spectrum of divergent views of life from which to choose. When we make this choice, we predict our behavior and our future. There is a note of sadness in Jesus' thought about the 'city of faith' where religious leaders chose not the way of God's grace.

This day, eternal God, I choose to glorify you with my faith, and enjoy this choice forever. Amen

I have eagerly desired to eat this Passover with you before I suffer... He took bread, gave thanks, and broke it, and gave it to them..."This is my body given for you; do this in remembrance of me." Luke 22:19ff

The Lord's Supper, Holy Communion, the Eucharist, the Mass: Christians celebrate the "sacrament of the Lord's Last Supper with his disciples" somewhere, every day of the year around the world. It is the chief sacrament for Christians. A sacrament is a visible sign with an invisible meaning. I will use four poignant verbs used by Jesus in that Last Supper before the arrest, trial and crucifixion as four movements of a grand symphony of faith.

Jesus "Took the Bread." You and I are chosen for this mission of faith in life. We did not invent faith, we did not call ourselves out of darkness into the light. We are chosen. God is the grand initiator of faith. It is a gift.

Jesus "Blessed the Bread." Paul wrote Christians that God's love for them existed in the heart of God before the "foundations of the universe" were laid. God, the artist, the innovator, and the creator, intended to show goodness and blessing for his creation before the beginning of time and place.

Jesus "Broke the Bread." This is the hard part of faith. "Not my will, but thy will be done." If EGO stands for 'easing God out,' God finds another way back into our hearts. Often God comes when we are, in the circumstances of life, run over by the Humble Express train. On our knees, we learn to stand tall in faith. The word is surrender.

The fourth verb: "Gave the Bread." We truly are exhilarated and filled with joy when we are giving all we have to the highest purpose and love of our lives.

Each life may be a sacrament, a visible expression of an invisible meaning and faith.

Christ, you are the Bread of Life. Thank you for nourishing my soul. Amen

Father, forgive them, for they do not know what they are doing.
Luke 23:34

At Good Friday services I am most breathless— silenced by one of The Seven Last Words of Christ from the cross. "Forgive them…" Jesus is putting into action the hardest words from his own teachings. "Love your enemy." I don't think anyone in the history of philosophy or religion had uttered that proposition. Now, in the midst of the horror of crucifixion, Jesus acts on this stupendous truth. If one did not know why we sing "Amazing Grace" this is the reason. Nothing is more revealing of the heart of Christ's character than this astounding utterance. The great scientist Edward Teller, and the even greater Albert Einstein, spoke of the nature of truth as being 'that which is the ultimately simple reality.' The simple truth is Christ forgives us.

This day, think of the ways that God's forgiveness affected your life. Pause and visualize the event.

Forgiveness means being released. We may forgive another who does not, will not, or cannot accept it. This act releases us from the chains of resentment, anger, and impossible retribution.

Good things happen when forgiveness is given and received. Miracles of new life take place: families come together, churches heal from the disease of partisanship, individuals recover from addictions, young and old alike find renewed life, purpose and health—all from the humble action of forgiveness.

The Coventry Cathedral was completely destroyed by German bombing during WWII. When the new Cathedral was built, a decision was made to exhibit forgiveness. A large bronze art piece for all to read and pray says: "The hatred which divides nation from nation, race from race, class from class—Father forgive. The pride which leads to trust in ourselves and not in God—Father forgive."

Lord, this day I remember Christ's costly forgiveness of me. Amen

*My God, my God, why have you forsaken me? Christ descended to the
lower earthy regions...in order to fill the whole universe. Psalm 22; Ephesians 4*

Saturday, following Crucifixion Friday, is symbolically the darkest day in the history of time. Psalm 22 was quoted by Jesus from the cross. Ephesians 4 is an oblique reference used by the early church theologians who summarized a statement of faith in the Apostle's Creed. The creed argues that the whole universe is the domain of the grace of Christ; hence, we cite, "... he descended into hell..." Saying the creed we believe that God took the outreach of his grace to the spiritual depths of the universe. The church considered this magisterial presence happening in that time for which the gospels are simply blank, Saturday of Passion Week.

Hell is a state of being, total separation from God. What is that like? The closest description I have heard came from a student in the 1960's Age of Disruption. "Greg" came from nowhere to join a Bible study group on a campus. He told me, "I am a total loser, was even unsuccessful in a suicide attempt." He described the state of being in hell, the total absence of God. Psalm 22:1, he said, was like a mantra. Greg did come to that turning point of discovering the sovereign grace and surprising presence of Christ.

By the providence of coincidence I ran across Greg again, 13 years later.

When we revisited his spiritual memoir he said, "I never told you exactly why I was unsuccessful in suicide. I was going to ram my car at 100 mph into an overpass buttress, make it look like an accident, people would feel sorry for me. The plan didn't work. Got to 100 mph. The car ran out of gas."

Lord Christ, we thank you for the surprise of your presence and the grace of your acceptance. Amen

I know you are looking for Jesus, who was crucified.
He is not here; he is risen, just as he said. Matthew 28:5-6

The gospel writers are candid about the role players in the narrative about the resurrection. The disciples were "terrified." When they heard "words of resurrection" they said, "This is an idle tale." They had doubts about their own confidence in Jesus, saying, "We had hoped that Jesus would redeem Israel." When news of the resurrection came to them, they were "behind locked doors because of their fear." Coming closer to accepting the reality of the resurrection they "saw the risen Jesus and thought he was an apparition." When they begin to feel the good emotions, the gospels note, "in their joy they were disbelieving."

Is it not good that something can be "too good to be true" and we find it is true? That Jesus was raised from the dead is a fact of history that was not created out of the willful projection of the disciples' mind-set. If we depended on a human source for this event we would all be atheists. This glorious truth of resurrection comes through the horrific suffering and death of Jesus. W.B. Yeats put it right: "Odor of blood where Christ was slain/ Made all platonic tolerance vain."

Thomas doubted the risen Lord; Luke said, "all doubted." Doubt is the opposite side of the coin of faith. God accepts hard questions. Disciplined minds question doubts. Jesus questioned God. Eventually we doubt our doubts and believe our beliefs. When Thomas questioned Christ,

Christ answered Thomas. Thomas firmly responded, "My Lord and my God." Thomas became one of the greatest missionary Apostles of Christ. He took the gospel of the life, teaching, death and resurrection to India where the church bearing his name thrives today.

This day, Christ is risen.

Risen Christ, I am surprised by joy in the power of God over death. Hallelujah! Amen!

Then their eyes were opened and they recognized him...Were not our hearts burning within us while he talked with us on the road and opened the Scriptures to us?" Luke 24:31ff

Millions of pilgrims have "had their eyes opened" to the Risen Christ on 'Emmaus' road experiences such as the story told by Luke. In the 13th century St. Mechthild, a German mystic who descended from a noble family in Saxony, gave up her privileged life to follow the Risen Christ. She writes, with God speaking: "I, God, am your play-mate! I will lead the child in you in wonderful ways for I have chosen you."

In the dark hours of WWII in France, Simone Weil, who died at age 34, spoke of her new life in Christ: "Joy fixes us to eternity and pain fixes us to time. But desire and fear hold us in bondage to time, and detachment breaks the bond." Do I trust the Bible, speaking of Jesus, "For the joy set before him he endured the cross and despised its shame"?

Professor Roberta Bondi, wrote *Memories of God*, depicting her experience of a great 'void' which had 'no meaning.' She prayed for help asking God: "Show me what I have missed about Christianity!" Some time later she woke up in the middle of the night and heard her own voice repeating the words of the Easter Prayer: "The joy of the Resurrection renews the whole world." She said, "Every cell in my body heard these words and I knew for the first time they were absolutely true...my heart filled up with a joy so fierce that it spilled out and ran through the whole of my body...Jesus did not die to bring death to the world, but to establish the life God intended for us from the beginning...not death, but joy."

God awaken me today, tonight, now, with this fierce prayer: "The joy of the Resurrection renews the whole world." Amen

Our Father in heaven...your will be done...
forgive us our debts, as we also have forgiven our debtors. Matthew 6:9ff

Not to forgive is not to live. Jesus put a 'rider clause,' a contingency addendum in the (now famous) Lord's Prayer: "forgive our debts, as we also have forgiven our debtors." Christian faith is always triangular in the geometry of its theology. Our relationship to God is not bilateral; it is trilateral. We may love God, and neighbors as ourselves. We may be forgiven as we forgive. Notice Jesus' prayer, our act of forgiveness, is in the past tense, therefore it is a contingency agreement. When we have forgiven, we may receive forgiveness.

Virginia Woolf was a brilliant writer who, as she said, lived in "a great lake of melancholy, a wedge-shaped core of darkness." Her last act of life was suicide. I wish she had been gifted with the ability to give and receive forgiveness.

Emily Dickinson was also a brilliant writer. Her quatrain: "They might not need me, they might!/ I'll let my light shine just in sight/ This tiny beam of mine might be/ Precisely their necessity."

St. John of the Cross, a Spaniard, tried to bring the gospel of grace, forgiveness, and reformation within the church during Reformation. He was banished by powerful Catholic clerics and died at age 49. In 1926, 675 years later, he was declared "Doctor of the Church." St. John wrote: "The soul of one who loves God always swims in joy, always keeps holiday, and is always in the mood for singing."

"Praise God from whom all blessings flow; Praise Him, all creatures here below; Praise Him above, ye heavenly host; Praise Father, Son and Holy Ghost."

(The most common "Doxology" sung in the 21st century is from the *Geneva Psalter* 1551, 'The Old Hundredth." Is that tune playing in your mind now? It is mine.)

We praise you God, we praise you Christ, we praise you Holy Spirit, from whom all blessings flow, forevermore. Amen

In the past God spoke to our ancestors through the prophets at many times and in various ways, but in these last days he has spoken to us by his Son...who is the radiance of God's glory and the exact representation of his being. Hebrews 1:1-3

If we do not have an ultimate value, we shall likely succumb to one or several of the false gods: worship of wealth, focus on sex, slave to an addiction, hand-cuffed with fear. Faith leads us to one who is the representation of God. Before we accept this gift, we may stumble along with an idol, a false-god. The Hebrew word for idol means 'no god.' George Eliot (pen name for Mary Ann Evans) constructed a perfectly balanced novella, *Silas Marner*. Silas is a case study for the 21st century.

Unjustly accused of a crime, Silas escaped from the accusatory village to the refuge of a country hermitage. Alone for 15 years, living with smoldering resentments and neurotic regrets, his life became the gold he horded. Night by night he would sit by firelight and count his wealth; then it was stolen. Misery was added to misery.

In a winter storm a mother and child were stranded. The mother died, the little girl, Eppie, found refuge in Silas' cottage in the middle of night. He did not awake; she laid down by the fire and went to sleep. In the dark early morning he came to stir the embers of fire. He saw a golden object on the hearth, "Someone has returned my stolen gold!" He lunged and grabbed the gold. It was the long beautiful hair of Eppie. The story unfolds in rapid steps of redemption and renewal. Silas no longer focused on money, but on a person he loved as a family he never had. The miracle happened. Eppie's love transformed his life.

Christ, radiance of the glory of God, transform my life with grace and truth. Amen

Saul spent several days with the disciples in Damascus. He began to preach in the synagogues that Jesus is the Son of God. Those who heard him were astonished and asked, "Isn't he the man who raised havoc in Jerusalem among those who call on this name? Yet Saul grew more and more powerful and baffled the Jews living in Damascus by proving that Jesus is the Messiah. Acts 9:19ff

Saul, his Hebrew name, who became Paul, his Roman and Christian name, is the prototype convert to the Christian faith. He is an example how the grace of God in Christ became a worldwide phenomena. This faith upsets the status quo of empires and gains the allegiance of believers in every nation of the world for the past twenty-one centuries. Paul's conversion is centered on the experience of meeting the Risen Christ.

The Easter story is not about what people think. It is about what God does.

God in Jesus overcame death through the resurrection of Christ. Saul was a "Pharisee among Pharisees," highly trained in religion. After the resurrection, he became a humble witness to the reality of the resurrection. The open door of the tomb of the crucified Jesus became the open door to Paul's new life.

John Polkinghorne is the former Cambridge University (England) Professor of Mathematical Physics and President of Queens' College, Cambridge. Dr. Polkinghorne is a leading scientist and witness to the Christian faith. He wrote: "The miracle of the resurrection also makes sense as the sign of deeper insight into the nature of God than is afforded by everyday religious experience, and as the anticipation of a destiny awaiting all humanity beyond death."

Can you think of a person who changed from unbelief to belief in Jesus Christ? What changes in character do you see?

Lord God, thank you for the mystical experience of knowing the Risen Christ. Amen

For God, who said, "Let light shine out of darkness", made his light shine in our hearts to give us the light of the knowledge of God's glory displayed in the face of Christ." II Corinthians 4:6. In the beginning God created the heavens and the earth. Now the earth was formless and empty, darkness was over the surface of the deep, and the Spirit of God was hovering over the waters. And God said, "Let there be light," and there was light. God saw that the light was good. Genesis 1:1ff

Almighty God whose mystery lies beyond the reach of all imaginations of humankind, I thank you for reflecting your image in "the face of Jesus."

You are the eternal source of all life. You care for us as a Good Shepherd, a wise mentor, the model of beauty, and a teacher of truth. The best of our arts and sciences seek the profound creativity of your patterns of life.

When I am reflecting upon your revealing light, I acknowledge that my incompleteness, brokenness, and sorrow are often the places you illuminate with soft rays of hope and courage. Sometimes your love is carried by a friend or beloved member of the family. There are times a stranger, as an angel in disguise, is the messenger of loving light.

Lord, I am a pilgrim on a journey that evolves before me. I have a sense of destiny that I do not perfectly see. You are reflecting the light of guidance as a "lamp for my feet," one step at a time, one day at a time. You have given the gift of optimism that this road I travel is not destined to oblivion. It leads to you, the Creator and Redeemer of life, the Source-Light of the world. Amen

The light of the gospel that displays the glory of Christ,
who is the image of God... displayed in the face of Christ.
II Corinthians 4:4ff

This text repeats the April 25th text to cast more thought on the phrase "the image of God...in the face of Christ." Jesus summarized the astounding truth of the incarnation: "If you have seen me, you have seen the Father."

There is a beautiful legend in the Roman Catholic tradition about the Sixth Station of the Cross, the picture of Veronica as she wipes the face of Jesus, who is carrying the cross up the Via Dolorosa. The street is named from Christian tradition; "Via Dolorosa" means "the way of suffering." Jesus is on the way to Golgotha, the place of execution. According to this ancient story, Veronica was one of the women who took compassion on the suffering and condemned Jesus. Veronica emerged from the jeering crowd, took her head cover, and wiped the blood, sweat, and tears from the face of Christ.

Later, she became 'sainted.' The denouement of the story revealed that 'the very image of the face of Christ' remained on the fabric of that head cover, hence, the name given to the nameless woman from the crowd, "Veronica," from *verte icon*—the "very image" of the face of Christ.

Totally blind, how did Helen Keller "see" this glorious imagery? She said,

"It's wonderful to climb the liquid mountains of the sky. Behind me and before me is God and I have no fears." Keller "saw" as you and I may see, with the eyes of the heart and soul.

This day, meditate for a moment on this thought: "If the only face of Christ that someone around me can 'see' is the *verte icon* of Christ *reflected from me*, who, what do they really see?"

God, I humbly ask, help me reflect the love and joy of Christ, this day. Amen

You are witness of these things.
Luke 24:48

"Witness" comes from the Greek word *martus (mar-toos)*. A witness can give a first hand account of a person or event. It is also the root of our English word for "martyr." We are called to "witness" the "Good News" of Christ.

Elie Wiesel, Romanian born author of 57 best seller books, recipient of the Nobel Prize for Peace in 1986, and survivor of one of Hitler's utterly contemptuous death camps Auschwitz, is perhaps the best "witness" I have ever heard. At the invitation of the Oklahoma Bar Association he was a witness to the "power of the story." This is one of the "stories" he told. I shall paraphrase:

Many years ago a great rabbi saw misfortune threatening the Jews. He went to a special place in the forest to pray, lighted a fire, said a special prayer, and the miracle of averting disaster occurred. Later, a disciple of the celebrated rabbi had another occasion to intercede for the Jews. He went to the same place in the wood, did not know how to light the fire, prayed the special prayer. And the miracle of averting disaster was done.

Another generation passed, another rabbi in succession, another threat, the rabbi went to the forest, and said, "I do not know how to light the fire, I do not know the special prayer, I know the place, and this must be sufficient." The miracle was done.

Still another generation, another rabbi, another impending disaster, and the rabbi prayed, "Lord, I do not know the place in the wood, nor how to light the fire, nor I do know the special prayer. I can tell the story." He did, it was sufficient, and the miracle was done. In Wiesel's words, "God made humankind because he loves stories."

Spirit of God, teach me to be a witness to the Good News Story of Christ and his love. Amen

Therefore, since we are surrounded by such a great cloud of witnesses, let us throw off everything that hinders and the sin that so easily entangles. And let us run with perseverance the race marked out for us, fixing our eyes on Jesus, the pioneer and perfecter of faith. Hebrews 12: 1-2

Paul and the author of Hebrews use sports metaphors in their letters. Sports were as much a major part of the Greco-Roman culture as they are in our culture. The unknown author of Hebrews undoubtedly saw athletes enter a stadium 'surrounded' by spectators and proceed to the starting line after taking off 'leg weights' used in the pre-game warm-ups. Eyes were set on the finish line, not on the spectators or other runners. Persevering athletes measured the pace of the race and knew when to release the maximum effort.

John Heilpern wrote this story for the *Wall Street Journal*: "In a blissfully funny, vintage Monty Python sketch, there is a soccer (football) game between Germany and Greece in which the players are leading philosophers. The always formidable Germany, captained by Nobby Hegel, boasts the world-class attackers Nietzsche, Heidegger and Wittgenstein, while the wily Greeks, captained by Socrates, field a dream team with Plato in goal, Aristotle on defense and—surprise inclusion—the mathematician Archimedes. Toward the end of the keenly fought game, during which nothing much appears to happen except a lot of 'thinking,' the canny Socrates scores a bitterly disputed match winner."

In the game of life we are limited to time, speed, and the dimensions of love, joy, purpose, and direction of life's opportunity to attain fulfillment. Paul, the athlete, said: "You, being grounded in love, may have power to grasp how wide and long and high and deep is the love of Christ, and to know this love that surpasses knowledge."

The great race of life is a gift to each of us. Join the spiritual athletes. On your mark, get set, Go!

Lord God, may I be a disciplined athlete, focused on the goal of Christ-like love. Amen

You will receive power when the Holy Spirit comes on you,
and you will be my witnesses... to the ends of the earth. Acts 1:8

I am not sure I am man enough to be a nun.

Seriously, I think of the "witnesses" to the love of God in Christ; they are really a tough bunch. Many of the martyr stories are about women missionaries and nuns. Frequently these women gave their lives for people in impoverished conditions amidst despicable tyranny. Killing fields were common.

Along with Jesus, Paul, St. Peter, Joan of Arc, I think of Jean Donovan, born in an upper middle-class home in Westport, Connecticut in 1953. Donovan was a Baby Boomer. She graduated from the University of Mary Washington, Case Western Reserve University with an M.B.A., and earned a management position with Arthur Andersen. In her provocative extant writings is this prayer: "I sit here and talk to God and say, 'Why are you doing this to me? Why can't I just be your little suburban housewife?'" She joined the Cleveland Diocesan Mission Project to work with nuns (she was a commissioned lay-worker) in El Salvador. These Sisters provided shelter, food, transportation, medical care, and love to suffering people. A military death squad murdered Jean Donovan as she volunteered to help women and children refugees from the civil war.

When the signs of mortal threat came, she wrote: "The Peace Corps left today and my heart sank low. The danger is extreme and they were right to leave... Several times I have decided to leave... except for the children, bruised victims in this insanity. Who would care for them... in this sea of tears and loneliness?" Jean Donovan died a vicious death, days after this writing.

God of all, in all places, forgive me when I feel sorry about my trivial problems. Thank you for women, men, and children of courage who follow calls to service of love in Christ's name. Amen

*Because of the Lord's great love we are not consumed, for his
compassions never fail. They are new every morning; great is your faithfulness."
Lamentations 3:22-23*

Rush Kelley told us inspiring and informative war stories. It was a privilege to listen to him. I learned about character, courage, humor, and faith among those in the military service. Rush was a veteran of World War I. His life spanned a century. His intelligence stayed with him to the end. Among other things, he told me what he wanted included in his memorial service, which I did.

One story was about a summons to the command tent on the battlefield. Rush fought in a tank brigade. They had just concluded a risky and successful maneuver against the Germans. He thought he was going to be chastised by the field commander for pushing his tank beyond the exact protocols learned in training. In Rush's words, "Instead of being upbraided, I was upgraded. The general upgraded my rank. That was my first meeting of Lt. Col. Dwight Eisenhower."

"I want a passage of Lamentations read at my funeral," Rush said. "You know that little book in the Bible is like war. War is hell. Lamentations is full of sorrow, loss, suffering, and war. It fascinates me that in the middle of all these cries and 'laments' there is that pure statement of 'how great is God's faithfulness.' I felt that in the war. In spite of all the terror, God's love is real. Read that at my funeral service!"

"Yes, sir!"

What do you want for your memorial service? My mom requested "Pomp and Circumstance." She said, "I'm graduating." She did 'graduate' *summa cum laude*. One U.S.A.F officer requested "Reveille" for his memorial: "It's the morning call, the call to rise."

Great is your faithfulness, God and Father of us all. We praise your name and accept your gracious love. Yours is the Power and Glory forever. Amen

I lift up my eyes to the mountains—where does my help come from?
My help comes from the Lord. Psalm 121:1-2

The things we can do for positive transformation of our personal lives are:

One, Be Curious. Albert Einstein in a lyrical reflection said: "The important thing is not to stop questioning. Curiosity has its own reason for existing. One cannot help but be in awe when he contemplates the mysteries of eternity, of life, of the marvelous structure of reality. It is enough if one tries merely to comprehend a little of this mystery every day." What is one thing my curious mind will pursue in the next twenty-four hours?

Two, Be Yourself. (My wife may say, "No, not THAT one!") Hear e.e. cummings in "Magic Marker:" "To be yourself in a world that is doing its best, night and day, to make you everybody else—means the hardest battle which human beings can fight and never stop fighting." Romans 12:3 agrees with the poet; Paul says, have a "sober" estimate of yourself.

Three, Be Spiritually Hungry. Bishop D. T. Niles of India, a great Christian leader, reminded us that Christians have only one duty. We are, in the eyes of the Lord, only beggars, and ultimately, all we can do in our power, is tell other beggars where to find bread. Of course we speak of the Bread of Life, Jesus Christ. On the San Francisco Theological Seminary's Geneva Library patio facing Mt. Tamalpais, in the beautiful hill country north of the Golden Gate Bridge, my seminary teachers corrected the inaccurate original KJV Bible quote from Psalm 21: "I lift up my eyes unto the hills whence cometh my help." Note the correct translation from the Hebrew in our text. The difference is 'The Difference' in faith's journey. Our yearning for God, can only be satisfied by God, not by nature or natural beauty.

Thank you, God, for allowing me to ask questions, find myself, and seek you. Amen

(A man who was lame from birth was healed) in the name of Jesus Christ...He jumped to his feet and began to walk. Then he went with them into the temple courts, walking and jumping, and praising God. Acts 3:2ff

Everyone needs healing, some time. The man in our text had been carried to the temple gate everyday to beg for money. He survived that way. Often our healing begins when we ask for total mental, physical, and spiritual healing. T.S. Eliot: "Between the idea and the reality; between the motion and the act, falls the shadow. Between the desire and the spasm, between the potency and the existence, between the essence and the descent, falls the shadow. This is the way the world ends, not with a bang but a whimper." We do not have to capitulate to the shadow land.

There is a universal duality placed before everyone. It is the ethical imperative. We cannot control circumstances. We are given choices. We can accept or reject five choices that make the difference between living the essence and ascent of life rather than the descent and death of life.

Admit powerlessness. Two discoveries: "I am not God." "There is a God." In fact there is a God who has proved his love for you.

Trust the ultimately trustworthy One—Christ, who reveals to us the grace and truth of God.

Make a decision: "Not my will but your will, God, be done." Love is the core of the spiritual laws of God.

Turn around: at the turning point of life take "the road less traveled, and it makes all the difference." Christ is our companion on this road.

Forgive yourself: then you will be able to forgive others and accept full forgiveness from God.

God, I make the leap of faith trusting your word of truth. My heart leaps for joy in receiving your serene presence. Amen

Those who live in accordance with the Spirit
have their minds set on what the Spirit desires. The mind governed
by the Spirit is life and peace. Romans 8:5-6

In the joyful beat of 70's music, the award-winning Broadway musical, "Godspell," brought the message of the New Testament gospel to millions of people, first in NYC, off Broadway in 1971, then around the world. Based on a book by John-Michael Tebelak, the lyrics include a prayer from the 13th century by Saint Richard of Chichester: *"Dearest Lord Jesus, savior and friend, three things I pray: to see thee more clearly, love thee more dearly, follow thee more nearly."*

The first Christians enacted the spirit of that great prayer. They responded with deep love to his love and became devoted to Christ's mission to be the presence of God's love in the world. And they accepted the Spirit of God that raised Jesus from death to life as the Spirit empowering their own lives. The concrete historical facts of what that humble band did, what they became, and how they overcame evil is astonishing news to any who have curiosity to see. They were maligned, persecuted, and murdered by the authorities of the Roman Empire. The empire collapsed. Their witness continues to this day.

They were the first community in the history of humanity on earth to live beyond "tribe." With Paul they could say: we are "neither Jew or Gentile, slave or free, male or female, all were one in Christ." They did not argue for the power of the Spirit, they received it. That Spirit of love is present in our world today.

God, three things I pray, to see thee more clearly, love thee more dearly, follow thee more nearly. Amen

The Sovereign Lord said to me, "Prophesy to these bones and say to them, 'Dry bones, hear the word of the Lord! I will make breath enter you, and you will come to life. Then you will know that I am the Lord. I will put my Spirit in you and you will live. Then you will know that I the Lord have spoken, and I have done it, declares the Lord.'" Ezekiel 37:4-14

S pirit of the Living God, hear my prayer. Sometimes my soul feels like bleached bones lying under the desert sun. Where is the sign of life? I ask for faith to see the burning bones of lost dreams raised up to new life.

Your Spirit has the power to shape new forms of life filled with purpose. I recognize that the desert experience is necessary for elemental change to come about. You burn away the dross and behaviors that were shackles on my life. Now, these dry bones are ready to walk around, shout aloud, and celebrate transformation through your Spirit.

I am ready for the new vigor of life, the fervor of courage, the intensity of justice in the new being you create. Each day, whether I see it or not, the great engine star of this heliocentric home, is burning and giving energy to all life on the planet, creatures great and small. Whether I see it or not, your Great Spirit is a burning fire that gives me the energy of love, joy, peace, patience, kindness, and self-control. I pray that 'my heart may be an altar and thy Spirit may be the flame.'

Give me wisdom to understand the larger "burnings" of life. As lightning strikes leaping into massive forest fires that burn bramble bushes away to prepare a place for new wild flowers, so the fires of your justice prepare a place in human history for the new humanity in Christ. Amen

(This Day's devotion includes comments from Anderson Lee, my grandson, age 13, on his birthday.) The message of the cross is foolishness to those who are perishing, but to us who are being saved it is the power of God...for since in the wisdom of God the world through its wisdom did not know him. I Corinthians 1:18ff

I decided not to edit my grandson. Anderson got our attention with this aside: "There is no right answer to life; however, there is a left one. True beauty is on the inside, therefore, this is really an ugly person."

Hold on, there is a provocative question coming. Anderson said, "Don't judge a person based on partial information.

If you judge God because of one coincidence in your life, you really need to look around and see everything God gave you. Look deeper into life. For example, if you heard of a "Dad" who had permitted people, even instructed people, to kill his son, then you would think of him as 'messed up.' (Cf. the biblical story of Abraham and Isaac; God the Father and Jesus Christ). We see the story in the Bible and there is an answer. Look deeper. There is an answer for every action in life. Sometimes a little digging is required."

Anderson added this little jingle, which among other things, shows that a young digital generation American youth has global awareness: "Instagram is a sham/ Pretty much Facebook in a can/ Made for very man./ They don't have a plan/ Pour that can into a pan/ And BOOM!—"Pinterest,"/ Just have eggs for breakfer-est/ You could be the best man/ If you have a game plan/ For Iran and Japan/ Or the Republic of Sudan./Now don't join the Klu Klux Klan/ Cuz you won't be a ladies' man./ I'm out (like a fan!).

Eternal God, thank you for the freedom to develop a game plan for each day, This day, and all the days of our lives. We follow your leadership through Jesus Christ. Amen

(Jesus said to them)"It is not for you to know the times or dates the Father has set by his own authority. But you will receive power when the Holy Spirit comes on you; and you will be my witnesses..." Acts 1:7-8

The effrontery of some people— they play the role of self-appointed prophets of "end times" and "apocalypses." I strongly endorse one of the last utterances of the Risen Christ on earth: "It is not for you to know the times." Let God be God. The end of history is in good hands.

Along this line of thought I return to the memory of being stuck on a railroad siding in East Berlin, August 13, 1961. Taking a break from studies at the University of Edinburgh, my late wife and I decided on a university sponsored train trip through the Soviet Union. There were only four Americans among the fifty travelers and we were assigned to the same rail car once we crossed into a Communist country. First warning sign: our car was detached to a siding in East Berlin as the rest of the train and student travelers went east to Poland. Second warning: soon heavily armed police came through our car checking passports for the third time. That's when we noticed unusual activity outside the train. A high wire fence was being constructed right through the train yard and as far into the city as we could see. Later we were permitted to rejoin our original train group in Poland. After the month long tour in "no-news Soviet Union," returning to London we read what had happened. The Berlin Wall. I never thought I would live long enough to see it come down without WWIII. President Reagan in the 1980's said, "Mr. Gorbachev, tear down this wall."

The wall came down in November 1989. "You do not know the times...the Father has the authority." It is our gracious calling as Christians to be a "witness."

I am not in charge of history.

Thank you, God, I am not in charge of history. Help me, Lord, to be a faithful witness to your authority, love, and blessing in Christ. Amen

*Let the message of Christ dwell among you richly...through psalms,
hymns and songs from the Spirit, singing to God with gratitude in your hearts.
Colossians 3:15-17*

The arts and sciences potentially serve God's will. Boris Pasternak in *Doctor Zhivago* wrote: "Art has two constants, two unending concerns: it always meditates on death and thus always creates life. All great genuine art resembles and continues the Revelation of St. John."

The painter Vasily Kandinsky attended a concert where he encountered the music of Arnold Schoenberg. The composer was "freed from traditional rules of consonance and dissonance...(the tones) seemed to seek their own independent destinies." Following the concert Kandinsky created the grand "Impression III (Concert)." He said, "Concerning the Spiritual in Art, color is the keyboard, the eye is the hammer, the soul is the piano with its many strings." (*WSJ*, 9.23.09)

The theme of both Schoenberg in music and Kandinsky in painting is "liberated from convention." It seems to me that an artist who remains true to his calling and the theme of liberation, and who was forcefully opposed by both communist Russia, and Nazi Germany, deserves attention. As a Christian who believes "for freedom Christ has set us free," I am also a proponent of the artists and scientists who risk life and reputation in opposition to tyrannies.

In 2009 Columbia University's Miller Theatre presented the "Blue Rider." Critics acclaimed it as a breathtaking program of music, image, and movement. Schoenberg and Kandinsky, the composer and the painter, posthumously outlasted the Soviets and the Nazis.

Sing, play, paint, think, and write "to God with gratitude in your hearts."

God, you created the hymn of the universe. Your glorious creation of sound, sight, movement, and melody is everywhere in the cosmos. Thank you for the ancient psalmists and the contemporary artists who seek to express ultimate truths through your gifts. We pray in the name of Jesus who sang as he walked his last night to Gethsemane. Amen

*Therefore, if anyone is in Christ, the new creation
has come: The old has gone, the new is here! II Corinthians 5:17*

If you are a follower of Christ, meditate for a moment on the Greek verb Paul chose in this empowering declaration that deserves the 'screamer' (explanation point) given by the NIV editors (original Greek texts had no punctuations): the verb "has gone" is *parerchomai*. It means 'averted' as in 'averting a disaster.' It means 'perished' as in the 'past is dead.' I can think of a dozen things in my life for which I am grateful they were 'goners,' dead, averted. Thanks to grace and forgiveness.

Immediately now to the future, Christians are challenged not to wait for the future but to be co-creators with God and make the future—the future of churches, the future of professions, the future of society, "the future of the future."

This faith is not for the guys who are all hat and no cattle, the type of future-makers we see in the peculations of a Bernard Madoff. This is more the kind of person Theodor Geisel, "Dr. Seuss," defined: "Be who you are and say what you feel, because those who mind, don't matter, and those who matter, don't mind." True, if you are modeling behavior 'in Christ,' as Paul commends.

We take seriously our new beginnings of life in Christ. T. S. Eliot was rebuffed by more than one agnostic member of the *literati*, for his faith in Christ, but that faith informed the poetry for which he received the Nobel Prize in Literature. Listen to the muse: "What we call the beginning is often the end. And to make an end is to make a beginning." My wife Lolly and I affirmed this thought in our marriage vows. The commitment of love on the first day of marriage creates the future. The ending has already been cast.

Lord God, liberation in Christ is thrilling; with freedom you have given opportunity for creativity, innovative society, and personal responsibility. Thank you, God. Amen.

*We are God's handiwork, created in Christ Jesus
to do good works, which God prepared in advance for us to do.
Ephesians 2:10*

There is a delightful point, counterpoint in the melody of God's creation of humankind. On the one hand, we are 'saved by grace' and that is not of our own doing. This is the first movement of the symphony of life. We are a "work in progress" at best. All of us are on a journey "arriving"…none have "arrived." New Testament teaches a philosophy: *Semper piccata, semper soteri*, i.e., "always sinner, always saved," in defining Christians; salvation is a gift, and we are not complete.

On the other hand, we are charged with the 'ability' to 'respond'—'responsibility' for good works. This view of our calling adds splendid color to the symphony. Albert Einstein said, "If we knew what we were doing, it wouldn't be called 'research.'" Kierkegaard approached good works with a sense of adventure and existential choice: "To dare to risk losing one's footing momentarily; or, not to dare is to lose oneself."

Christian humility is required in the face of doing good works in an incomplete world crossed with multiple waves of chaos. Some Christians act with ideological certainty concerning solutions to society's problems. These persons predict a future like the economist who predicted nine of the last two recessions. Yogi Berra has some advise: "Predictions are hard to make, especially about the future."

Because we belong to that band of believers saved by grace, through faith in Christ, we know Christ calls us "to do good works." We will find our peace and identity in taking the risk of that calling. Taking the risk to do what is right produces the greatest joy in life.

God, we are fulfilled with purpose and filled with joy, accepting our calling in Christ. Amen

The Lord delights in those
who put their hope in his unfailing love.
Psalm 147:11

The Trail of Tears memoirs sadden the joyous heart. In 1839 Cherokee Native Americans were removed from concentration camps in Georgia and neighboring states and forcibly marched to Oklahoma Territory. The U.S. Army handled this relocation in a repressive manner, e.g., pregnant women were allowed two hours for childbirth and rest, and if they could not rejoin the march, they were abandoned. This dismaying chapter in a sometimes glorious history remarkably illustrates the unrelenting human spirit of hope. Among the seeds and plants the Indians brought with their meager belongings were bulbs for daffodils.

Now, in the second decade of the 21st century one can witness the descendants of those first flowers brought from Georgia to Tahlequah, Oklahoma. Witnesses to hope, one of three virtues that last forever. The poets sing:

"Hope is the thing with feathers that perches in the soul—and sings the tunes without the words—and never stops at all." (Emily Dickinson)

"I wandered lonely as a cloud / That floats on high o'er vales and hills, / When all at once I saw a crowd, / A host, of golden daffodils;/ Beside the lake, beneath the trees, / Fluttering and dancing in the breeze." (Wordsworth)

Whence cometh the indefatigable quality of the human spirit? Take hope; it is not from a human source; hope comes from the 'unfailing love' of God.

The Apostle Paul's writing in I Corinthians 13, "The Love Chapter," is known by billions of people around the world this day. Why? We feel assured about 'three things' that outlast everything, including "the black vein of destiny"(Hugo) in the body of our common humanity: Faith, HOPE, and Love remain forever.

Our Father of unfailing love and hope, the surge of resilient joy comes from the gift of hope you place in our hearts, minds, and souls. Amen

The true light, that enlightens everyone, was coming into the world...What has come into being in him was life, and the life was the light of all people. The light shines in the darkness, and the darkness did not overcome it." John 1:1ff

The journey on the high seas of life requires fundamental and trust-worthy instruments of direction.

Herman Melville's classic *Moby Dick* has a scene where Captain Ahab is sailing the Piquod in a perfect storm at sea: no horizon with heaving waves much greater than the vessel, no light from a black sky. The yaw, pitch, and roll of the ship gives no place or object that one can judge simple fundamental balance, what is 'up' and what is 'down.' Except for one thing, the masthead lamp hangs free, swinging from a single pinion. As the ship is violently tossed about, the light hangs steady. It answers to a force beyond the storm: gravity, a fundamental constant. Melville's cryptic line: "Except for a light that reveals the false lying levels about him," peg-legged Ahab would surely have perished at sea. One constant based in reality beyond the storm saves the sailor.

Having passed through the Drake Passage known as the roughest sea in the world on a voyage from Antarctica, we could add our own imagination to Ahab's presence of mind. His sea was more violent than our 55-foot waves and average 77 mph wind. And, we did not depend on a masthead light. We had the steady fundamental instruments of G.P.S., gyroscopes, and computer driven stabilizers.

When we navigate a storm in our lives, we must have a dependable resource beyond our vulnerable selves. It is "the true light, that enlightens everyone."

Christ, you are the light of the world. We thank you for your stable guidance of our lives. Amen

You who pass judgment on someone else for whatever point you judge another, you are condemning yourself, because you who pass judgment do the same things. Romans 2:1

I'd rather have love than life, if that be the choice. There's no desire for Delphi's cool truth, no cavern frothed in ice for me. I rather favor nature's fire on the prairie brush, surrounding all senses with smoky dust, watching wind and flame make stones that glow, hearing crackling heat snapping rocks in two. Christ-like love is the flame of truth burning the past, and the soul is not consumed. Fiery forgiveness clears the personal terrain. In smoldering good-byes to the old, leaving land clean for new wild flowers to grow.

Can you imagine a life without judgment? God gives that to you in Christ. A council of men judged 'an adulterous woman' to death, but the man Jesus (John 8) did not condemn her. The fiery love of forgiveness he gave freed her to walk on a new path to a new destiny.

Speaking to inmates in Sing Sing Prison, Warren Buffet said, "Every saint has a past; every sinner has a future." Sholem Asch, Polish-American novelist noted: "Not the power to remember, but its very opposite, the power to forget, is a necessary condition for our existence." Forgiveness is required.

Are you among the cultured cynics of God's fierce grace to forgive, saying forgiveness is not real? Try a dose of Mark Twain: "It ain't what you don't know that gets you into trouble. It's what you do know for sure that just ain't so."

God of New Life, I saw a burned forest and after the next year's rains, new wild flowers and samplings yearning to be great trees covered everything. It reminded me of your forgiveness in my life. Amen

*Choose for yourselves this day whom
you will serve... as for me and my household, we will serve the Lord.
Judges 24:15*

My dad was sort of a *lingua-phile*—lover of words—so when he announced that our Saturday morning outing would take us to see a "Wing Walker," I thought he was talking about some kind of exotic bird. We arrived at the nearby airbase in Spokane. Yes, we saw and met a "Wing Walker," a seriously acrobatic guy who did tricks on the upper wing of a bi-wing plane as they flew past the grandstand at 100 feet above ground. Dad and I "discussed" (on 7-year-old terms) the brief comments the Wing Walker made after the show, something to this effect, "Your life depends on what you let go of, and what you hang on to."

Decades later that metaphor made complete sense applied to the risky flight of faith in Christ. In the privileged private chapel of your mind, think of things you have 'let go of,' and other things you 'hang on to,' because of your faith.

Years ago Madalyn Murray O'Hair's name was a 'household word' every American knew. She was the 'name' attached to the Supreme Court decision to remove prayer from the U.S. public classrooms. Her name is probably buried in the minds of a few linguaphiles today. Her son, William, became the prototype of a rootless, directionless, malcontent addict by the age of thirty. In an AA Twelve Step program he testified that he was led by the Spirit to simply 'read the Bible.' Conversion followed, and he said, "The Book my mother removed from schools was the place I found God."

William O'Hair became a Wing Walker in faith. He decided what to let go of, and what to hang on to.

God, I pray for strength to make faithful not fatal choices on what I let go of, and what I hang on to, in my airborne journey of life. Amen

> *Follow God's example, therefore, as dearly loved*
> *children and walk in the way of love, just as Christ loved us and gave*
> *himself up for us. Ephesians 5:1*

One person's life may impact for good millions of others through his or her loving and generous purpose for existence.

Donald Worthington Reynolds was such a person. Born in 1906, hawked newspapers at the train station in Oklahoma City as a kid; worked his way through university working in a meat packing plant; started his first business with $1,000 saved and borrowed; purchased and sold his first (Massachusetts) newspaper *The Quincy Evening News*; served in military intelligence in WWII and was in charge of *YANK* read by service personnel around the world; founded the very successful Donrey Media Group; died in 1993. Continuing into the second decade of the 21st century, Reynolds' name and resources are the foundation of hundreds of organizations benefitting the common good of millions of children, women, and men. His love and God-gifted intelligence formed the bedrock of his life.

Three persons who changed for good the history of people of the whole world are three people who never wrote a word that we have, but we quote them somewhere every minute of every day: Socrates, Buddha, Jesus. Here are the themes of their 'oeuvre,' 'the sum of a lifetime work.'

Socrates: "The only true wisdom is knowing you know nothing; wisdom begins in wonder."

Buddha: "We are shaped by our thoughts and become what we think."

Jesus: "Love God with all your heart, soul and mind; and your neighbor as yourself; love your enemies."

Do I have a theme of my life, will there be an *oeuvre* worthy of the opportunities I have been given?

Eternal God, thank you for the gift of the vision-quest I pursue this day. Help me to "follow God's example" in the Spirit and love of Christ. Amen

We who teach will be judged more strictly...Take ships, although they are so large and are driven by strong winds, they are steered by a very small rudder wherever the pilot wants to go. Likewise, the tongue is a small part of the body...it sets the whole course of one's life. James 3:1ff

Ken Burns is one of the greatest storytellers of our generation. His medium is film. He says the storyteller is "an emotional archaeologist." One of his documentary films, "The Civil War," was the most viewed documentary in PBS history: 39 million viewers during the series. Next came his stories from WWII where 16 million Americans served in uniform and 400,000 died. Among his stories is the heroism of Joseph Medicine Crow, grandson of a scout for Gen. George Custer. He achieved a Plains Indian 'War Chief' status in WWII: touched a living enemy soldier whom he did not kill; disarmed an enemy; led a successful war party; and stole an enemy's horse. Yes, in WWII a platoon of German combatants rode horses. At night Crow got behind enemy lines, freed the horses, riding one back to the U.S. side. Brendan Miniter of the *WSJ* (9.19.07) quoted Burns concerning the "huge pang of regret" he had for not getting his own dad's stories of the war before he died.

Our lives are shaped by stories. Each person's life is a story; it has prologue, theme, plot, characters (protagonist, antagonists), climax, and sometimes a conclusion.

For the Christian, we know the Alpha and Omega, the beginning and end of the greatest story ever told, the story of God's love poured out in Jesus Christ. Know your story, know God's story, and tell the stories. "It sets the whole course of one's life."

God, thank you, for telling the story of your motive in creation through the gospel. Help us to tell our stories. Amen

Clothe yourselves with compassion, kindness, humility,
gentleness and patience. And over all these virtues put on love, which binds
them all together in perfect unity. Colossians 3:12-14

Does the text from Paul's letter to the Colossian church sound a bit benign? Soft moral qualities expressed in harsh political realities require men and women of steely courage. *Parade* magazine's David Relin tells the story of a Tibetan, Ngawang Sangdrol, age 72, who came to America for religious freedom: "Before I was born, the Chinese destroyed much of Tibetan culture. When I was 13, I joined some people demonstrating for freedom of religion. All we did was chant 'Long Live the Dalai Lama' and 'Free Tibet.'

"The police tied a rope around my neck, lashed me to a tree and beat me... guards kicked in my head and beat me until I fell unconscious...five (women in the group) were killed by our torturers." Ngawang spent 11 years in prison. She escaped from Tibet and was given asylum in the U.S. (*Parade* 7.2.06)

Why does the second most powerful nation in the world fear religious expression and freedom? Political autocracies cannot survive people who possess the 'Bill of Rights' mentality: freedom of speech and faith. The Dalai Lama is a humble man. It is unimaginable that any powerful person would fear humility. I thought of the fear engendered by the powerful people around a humble carpenter's son from Nazareth. When people pay attention to a person imbued with "compassion, kindness, gentleness, and above all love," they respond with a loyalty that is greater than the bluster and guns of the materially powerful. In Christ, the "meek shall inherit" the earth. If you and I don't believe that, the power brokers of demagoguery do. So, "clothe yourselves" with these Christ-like virtues. You may think you look as harmless as a sheep, but mean guys with power will see you fierce as a wolf.

Thank you, God, for the leadership of Christ and the inspiring virtues bound together in his love. Amen

> *Dear friends, continue to work out your salvation with fear*
> *and trembling, for it is God who works in you to will and to act in order*
> *to fulfill his good purpose. Philippians 2:12*

In the dialogue of love between God and oneself there are two perspectives of this relationship, one from the human side, another from God's.

The human perspective: "It takes so much to be a full human being...few have the courage to pay the price. One has to abandon altogether the search for security and reach out to the risk of living with both arms...One has to accept pain as a condition of existence. One has to court doubt and darkness as the cost of existence." (Morris L. West, *The Shoes of the Fisherman*) This what the Apostle Paul means by working out our faith on the human side of our relationship to God with "fear and trembling."

God's perspective: The '*mysterium tremendum et fascinans*'—the mystery that both awes and fascinates us—comes to us. God initiates, originates the gift of this dialogue of love. This is God's work in the dialogue. It is not magic, it is not "pie in the sky by and by." It is real presence, incarnate presence, and costly presence of God's love demonstrated in the life, teaching, death, and resurrection of Christ.

Jess Walter (*Beautiful Ruins*, 2012) quotes Milan Kunden: "There would seem to be nothing more obvious, more tangible and palpable than the present moment. And yet it eludes us completely. All the sadness of life lies in that fact."

All the gladness of life lies in another fact: 'The Word became flesh' and 'dwelt among us full of grace and truth,' and here, in the dialogue between persons and Christ, the present moment comes alive with lasting love.

Loving Father, we humbly acknowledge our incompleteness; we boldly accept the stupendous energy and joyful gift of the Spirit. In Christ. Amen

In your hearts revere Christ as Lord. Always be prepared to give an answer to everyone who asks you to give the reason for the hope that you have. But do this with gentleness and respect. I Peter 3:15

Sometimes it feels like the church is locked in the silos of sanctity and cannot seriously listen to the hearts, minds, and souls of people outside its membership rolls. Take the Science/Faith dialogue for example. To use the words of Ricky Ricardo ("I Love Lucy"): The church people "got some 'splainin' to do." I think both Jesus and Paul would directly the engage the discussion.

I enjoyed ad hoc lectures at Oxford, often introduced as: "One of the greatest minds in the world, speaking today on a topic of universal significance." Some were the greatest...for example, A.C. Coulson, Professor of Applied Mathematics. He began with a quote from Galileo, "Doubt is a sign of humility," good for both a scientist, and a Christian. Augustine on 'knowledge and belief' said, "Faith precedes reason, but this is reasonable." Coulson went on in his 'splainin': doubt (good questions), humility, freedom of thought, and faith are essential in the journey of good science and true discipleship.

Historians Herbert Butterfield, Fredrick von Weizacker, Reijer Hooykass, and Gunter Howe are a few of the "great minds" who demonstrated how freedom of thought, essential to science, is based on all "freedoms" especially freedom of religion. The Age of Science began in "freedom of thought" nations. The late Max Planck (Nobel Prize in connection with Quantum Physics Theory) ended his autobiography with these words: "Religion and science are fighting a joint battle against dogmatisms, superstition, and the rallying cry for both: 'On to God!'"

God of all reality, thank you for hearts to love you, minds to search out your ways, and wills to follow Christ. Amen

(Response to Peter's first sermon about Christ) When the people
heard this, they were cut to the heart and said to Peter and other Apostles,
"Brothers, what shall we do?"
Acts 2:37.

According to scripture, the first person to help Jesus carry the cross to Golgotha was an African named Simon. Pressed into service by a Roman soldier, Simon was forced to carry Jesus' cross up the streets of Jerusalem. Mark tells the story. Something happened on the way to Golgotha; the influence of the broken figure of Jesus must have "laid its tendrils round his heart." (William Barclay) We know from Paul's writing to Christians in Rome that Simon's son, Rufus, and his wife, became Christians and close companions of Paul. The Apostle tells us that converts from the African town of Cyrene were among the first to hear, believe, and preach the gospel of the risen Christ to the non-Jewish world. Was it Simon, the Cyrene, who bore the physical cross of Jesus, who also carried the gospel of Christ to the African continent?

Perhaps you have seen the documentary film, "Running The Sahara." Three runners of extraordinary ability and endurance raced from Senegal to Egypt across the Sahara Desert. These super athletes ran the equivalent of two marathons a day, fifty plus miles, for 100 days. No days off! They succeeded.

Paul described faith as a great race, and used the metaphor of athletes who are disciplined and focused. I think the young Christians in Cyrene were also disciplined, focused, and successful in accomplishing an extraordinary feat, shall we say, 'Running the Race of Faith from Jerusalem to Cyrene, from the continent of Asia to the continent of Africa.'

Am I spiritually disciplined and focused for the great race of faith in my life?

The text asks the question evocatively: "What shall we do?"

Eternal Father, you have surrounded us with witnesses to endurance in life and faith. Help me to respond to the invitation to apply my faith in Christ to this race of life. Amen

Jesus said, "For the bread of God is the bread that comes down from heaven and gives life to the world." "Sir," they said, "always give us this bread." Then Jesus declared, "I am the bread of life." John 6:33ff

When we celebrate Holy Communion we become one with Christ again. There is not a single person of faith who has not in some way said, "I have a first priority; it is putting God first in my life." In Communion we get to become one with that first priority again. "Again," because there is not a single person of faith who has in some way failed to keep the first priority. Many worship traditions place "Confession" early in the liturgy. There is a good reason for that. Remember the Country music song, "I'll Say 'Never Again' Again"?

Every day starts with a sunrise, a sign of hope. Every day we are refreshed when we commit ourselves to the first priority of trusting God to be God in this day. Annie Dillard in *Teaching a Stone to Talk* writes: "I think it would be well, and proper, and obedient, and pure, to grasp your one necessity and not let it go, to dangle from it, limp wherever it takes you. Then even death, where you're going no matter how you live, cannot you part."

When we partake of the Lord's Supper, or in a daily prayer, we are reminded that we are intrinsically one with Christ who is the Bread of Life given to the world. "Bread" from the Old English *hlaford* is also the root for the word "Lord" in the English language. "Lord" in the Bible is a word for God; and in the New Testament, "Lord" is also a title for Jesus.

Lord Jesus, refresh our bodies, minds and souls, this day, with the Bread of Life, your very presence in our existence. Thank you. Amen

As Jesus was walking beside the Sea of Galilee, he saw two brothers, Simon called Peter and his brother Andrew. They were casting a net into the lake, for they were fishermen. "Come, follow me," Jesus said, "and I will send you out to fish for people."
Matthew 4:18-19

Danish theologian Soren Kierkegaard was a sharp critic of the established church in an era of popular European liberalism prior to the devastation of Europe through two world wars. He cried out, "I have to be against the church in order to be for Christ." He believed the church had become a slave of culture instead of a humble servant of Christ to people in need. Hear one of his battle cries: "The medium for being a Christian has been shifted from existence and the ethical to the intellectual, the metaphysical, the imaginary; a more or less theatrical relationship has been introduced between thinking Christianity and being Christian—and thus being a Christian has been abolished."

Christian faith in the first generation can be an experience; being a Christian because one's parents were, is a heritance; following a culture of religion in the third generation is a nuisance. Every generation must begin with conversion in Christian faith. Paul speaks of knowing Christ through a direct confrontation between the Holy Spirit and the human spirit imbued with self-determination. If we 'test positive' on any of these markers for faith, we may consider again the word of the Apostle Paul: 1. I believe in principles, like tithing, but don't want a pastor or priest to preach about it. 2. I believe we should offer an honorarium to a missionary speaker, if she declines, invite her back. 3. I listen to the meaning of the sermon and scripture with great interest, unless I am thinking of something else. 4. I believe in confession, especially when confronted with the evidence.

Christ did not say, "Follow the church, or follow the best principles." Christ said, "Follow me."

Thank you, God, for the examples of people who are a new creation through Christ. Amen.

Finally, brothers and sisters, whatever is true, whatever is noble, whatever is right, whatever is pure, whatever is lovely, whatever is admirable—if anything is excellent or praiseworthy—think about these things. Philippians 4:8ff

Paul invites us to "think about these things" among which includes nobility. Recently I asked a college audience to define nobility, and it was immediately apparent that the word is not current coinage. Therefore I explained the word via this story, told by my good friend, Ted Findeiss. Ted flew a B-17 in the 385th Bomber Group of the U.S. 8th Army Air Force in World War II.

In 1943, German fighter ace Captain Franz Stigler could have added one more plane shot down to his long list of 'kills.' He came across a crippled B-17 piloted by Captain Charlie Brown. (Yes, this is a true story.) That day 500 B-17's made a bombing raid on an airplane factory in Bremen. Brown's plane was hit by anti-aircraft fire. The nose of the plane was blown off, one engine knocked-out, the surviving members of the crew had blacked out from the force of a diving maneuver from five miles altitude to near ground level.

Captain Brown came to consciousness in time to level out the plane at tree-top height. Then he encountered Captain Stigler in a Messerschmidt fighter plane named "Eva." Stigler could see the dead and wounded through the gaping holes of the B-17. He looked straight into the eyes of Brown and signaled the U.S. Captain to follow. He escorted the B-17, which had no working instruments for guidance, back across the North Sea to England where the Americans landed.

Stigler never reported the incident. He would have been court marshaled. Years later through complicated inter-Air Force relations, Captains Stigler and Brown met at the 50th Reunion of the 385th Bomber Group in Spokane. My friend Ted Findeiss was there. Ted's story made me think about nobility.

Thank you, God, for universal experiences of conscience and virtue, in Christ. Amen

To all who did receive him, to those who believed in his name,
he gave the right to become children of God...born of God. John 1: 12

God of the gifts of life, I confess my hesitancy and inconsistency about one of the most intriguing actions of life. I want to be proactive, co-creative, and an initiator of thought and work; however, you are asking me to be passive, humble, quiet, and open-minded. You have said that Christ, grace, Spirit, and love are to be received. I find it easier to give love than receive love. Master teachers of life have taught me that to be fully human, I must give and receive love.

When I am in the posture of receiving gifts from your hand through other people, am I afraid of exposing my vulnerability? Do I fear that I shall lose control? Am I afraid of accepting the fact that I am accepted? Your grace can only be known and experienced when I let go, and receive what you give.

When I consider your truth revealed through women and men of complete virtue and courage, I see that sometimes they were repelled, rebuffed, and refused by people they loved. Does humble love threaten the self-aggrandized human ego?

Lord, I cannot live very long from the resources of my self-made storehouse of treasure. It is never enough. *I never have enough of the things that are unnecessary.*

When I hunger for your truth, I learn a new axiom: You are love. I must receive love, receive Christ, and receive the Spirit. It is in the recognition of my emptiness that I am ready to receive and be filled. *It is not my doing. It is your giving that fills the empty vessel of my life.*

This day, I choose to receive you, God of love, Lord of grace, in Christ. Amen

I resolved to know nothing while I was with you except Jesus Christ and him crucified. I came to you in weakness with fear and trembling...so that your faith might not rest on human wisdom, but on God's power. I Corinthians 2:2-5

The simple truth is, you and I hold the golden key that may unlock untold joy for ourselves and others. That key is the knowledge of God's love and our ability to share it. Charles Schulz illustrates the paradigm of love: "Why," Lucy asks Charlie Brown, "do you think we are put on earth?" Charlie answers, "To make others happy!" "Well," Lucy says, "I don't think I'm making anyone very happy...and nobody's making me very happy, either." In the last panel of the comic strip we see Lucy screaming, "Somebody is not doing their job!"

In *Serious Talk,* noted scientist and Christian thinker John Polkinghorne wrote: "At the heart of Christian belief is the stupendous claim of Christ's resurrection. The miracle of the resurrection also makes sense as the sign of a deeper insight into the nature of God than is afforded by every day religious experience, and as the anticipation of a destiny awaiting all humanity beyond death. I do not believe this because I was told by some great authority, but because I have derived the ideas of faith in the resurrection from the evidence."

The truth of the Word of God is in the evidence of Christ's life, death and resurrection, and the evidence of Christ-like love given freely by followers of Christ. All of us know a Lucy or two to whom we can give a little love.

Spirit of the Living God, fall afresh on me. Melt me, mold me, fill me, use me. Make my life a living vessel of your love. Thank you for the lavish gift of grace and peace that passes understanding, through Christ. Amen

*Pray in the Spirit on all occasions with all kinds
of prayers and requests. With this in mind, be alert and always
keep on praying for all the Lord's people. Ephesians 6:18*

Admiral John Kirkpatrick added real soul to the membership of our church. His philanthropy, intelligence, and faith complemented a gracious manner accented with wit and wisdom. An evening dinner and table repartee in the Kirkpatrick home created lasting memories. The good Admiral's wife, Eleanor, was the kind of friend every pastor should have. After she thanked me, at a table of twelve, for the regular DVD's of Westminster sermons, remarking among other things "their superior tonal quality," she added: "I'm an insomniac, and the only way I can get to sleep in the early morning hours is listening to your wonderful sermons. Thank you so much!"

John was among a rare few officers in the U.S. military service who attended both the U.S. Military Academy at West Point, and the U.S. Naval Academy. The Admiral served with distinction in the U.S. Navy in World War II. One day he handed me 'The Cadet Prayer,' and said, "I would like this used at my memorial service some day." His hand written note on the side of the pray reads: "Mike, I was introduced to this great prayer in the Cadet Chapel at West Point in June of 1925. It still holds water." (!) The Cadet Prayer:

"O God, our Father, Thou Searcher of all human hearts, help us to draw near to Thee in sincerity and truth. May our faith be filled with gladness and may our worship of Thee be natural.

Strengthen and increase our admiration for honest dealing and clean thinking, and suffer not our hatred of hypocrisy and pretense ever to diminish. Make us choose the harder right instead of the easier wrong, and never to be content with a half-truth when the whole can be won…Soften our hearts to those who sorrow and suffer. Amen."

Whoever drinks the water I give them will never thirst.
Indeed, the water I give them will become a spring of water welling
up to eternal life. John 4:14

Country myth has it that a beloved pastor in a small farm town was known to enjoy his wife's homemade wine. One day the sheriff stopped the parson, "Reverend, you're driving crazy. Are you drinking and driving?" The parson shook his head. The sheriff said, "Let me see what's in that jug next to you." The sheriff whiffed, "That's strong wine!" The pastor said, "Let me smell it… Well, Praise the Lord, he's done it again." I have never seen a miracle like changing 'water to wine,' as in John chapter 2, but I have seen a miracle of water saving thousands of lives.

In a rural region of India, a missionary with a petroleum engineering degree thought of a way to bring water to the crops that fed thousands of people. This region had monsoon rains for two weeks, then triple digit weather and drought for fifty weeks. The missionary arranged for free wheat to be given to the people from the U.S. "Food for Peace" program. Thousands of people 'earned' the food by constructing with hand tools a twelve-foot high earthen dam across the floor of the lowest end of a great wide valley. The engineer had drilled test holes and found that 15 to 20 feet below the clay soil there was a stratum of gravel stones. In the bone-dry summer he organized crews to drill hundreds of dry "water wells" down to the gravel. The monsoons came the next spring, the dam created a lake, the *reverse wells* served like drains in a sink

and filled the gravel cavities with *clear fresh water*. During the next growing season the water was pumped out as needed, the crops grew, the famine ended, the people flourished.

Eternal Lord, each of us needs to fill the inner well of our spiritual lives with your Living Water from which we draw in times of spiritual drought. Amen

*The kingdom of heaven is like treasure hidden in a field.
When a man found it, he hid it again, and then in his joy went and sold
all he had and bought that field. Matthew 13:44*

Henry David Thoreau said: "I went to the woods because I wished to live deliberately, to front only the essential facts of life, and see if I could not learn what it had to teach, and not, when I came to die, discover that I had not lived." All of us would give ascent to Thoreau's dictum: 'I want to live deliberately.' We can.

Jesus spoke a common language, Palestinian Aramaic. The 1st century Aramaic Talmud contains popular stories known to the audience Jesus taught. Jesus used many of these stories. All of Jesus' listeners would identify the 'Pearl of Great Price' story the moment he said, "The kingdom of heaven is like a pearl...." In the Talmudic version of the story, the protagonist is a righteous man devoted to good works who earned the right to come upon the pearl of great price. It was payment for his good deeds. According to that story, he used the pearl to ransom his life from robbers who were willing to kill him for the pearl.

Jesus changed the story. In his revision, the man simply comes upon the pearl of great price because he is lucky. He did not earn it. But wisely he knows its value and changes everything in his life—sells all that he has—to possess the inestimable value of his good fortune in life.

Jesus' story describes the grace of God. It is a gift that changes the values of everything in our lives. We make those changes because of our newly found passion and gratitude. We shall live deliberately with God's grace.

Eternal Christ, thank you for your word taught in the power of the Spirit. Amen

Blessed are those who mourn, for they will be comforted
...Blessed are the pure in heart, for they will see God. Matthew 5:4,8

Jesus began The Sermon on the Mount with a series of "beatitudes," each beginning with the word "Blessed." We frequently use this English word, "blessed," solely on the basis of the overwhelming influence of the King James Bible (1611) on the literary world. The Greek word used by Matthew is *makarios*. Scholars have translated this word as: "happy," "fortunate," "hopeful," "joyful." Robert Gundry's translation of *makarios* (Erdman's *Commentary on Matthew*, 1982) reads "congratulations." I like that.

Witnessing from the podium thousands of faces over many years of various 'Graduation Ceremonies' there are two things I learned. 1. Speeches are not the reason for graduation ceremonies. 2. Those who are graduating are indeed "Happy, Blessed, Fortunate, Joyful, Hopeful." Therefore, Gundry's translation seems apropos, *"Congratulations!"*

Our Lord taught, *"Congratulations* to those who are pure in heart, for they will see God." "He who loves with purity," said Thomas a' Kempis, "considers not the gift of the lover, but the love of the giver."

Only with the empathy of the heart may we apprehend the hard road some people have traveled. Suffering is never desirable, but it often comes with circumstances beyond our control, and certainly beyond anything we have caused or deserved. And yet, Jesus says, *"Congratulations!* You who mourn, you will be comforted." Jesus said, *"Congratulations!* You who are insulted and persecuted because of me; you shall have a great reward in heaven."

As we read the "congratulations" in Jesus' Sermon on the Mount, may we learn again the way of serenity in our hearts in spite of tumultuous events that encompass us. The inward grace of God overcomes all outward conditions.

"Congratulations! You have graduated *'summa cum gratia (grace)'."*

Thank you, living Christ, for your teaching, presence, and grace in my life today. Amen

You make known to me the path of life; you will fill me
with joy in your presence, with eternal pleasures at your right hand.
Keep me safe, my God. Psalm 16:1,11

Isn't 'happiness' an 'inalienable right'? After all, it is written into a foundational document of our nation; 'Life, Liberty and the Pursuit of Happiness' are 'inalienable' rights. A distraught friend said to me, "Don't I have a right to be happy? That is all I ask of my marriage and my job. Is that too much?" She had just described a life of broken promises, financial stress, and the disease of addiction in her home. She had more than a fair share of turmoil and her efforts to make things better backfired. Divorce, bankruptcy court, and rehab changed her circumstances. Still, she was not happy. "Yes, indeed you have a right to be happy." But how?

Christ approached the question about 'happiness' by recasting the question: "Would you like to gain happiness, not by pursuing happiness as a goal of life, but as a by-product of a goal far greater than happiness?" "Yes, I would...I think I would. "In both Psalm 16 and the teaching of Christ, the primary question is, "How do I find God as the central purpose in my life?" Happiness is a by-product of a profound faith in God as the center of our life. Happiness is the by-product of accepting God's acceptance of us. When we trust Christ with all our heart, happiness is a gift of faith. Happiness comes from the euphoria of receiving, and giving forgiveness. Happiness is not the goal of life but the derivative of our unity with the will of God. I paraphrase a 17th century catechism: *Life's purpose is to know God and enjoy him forever.*

Our Father, thank you for your love that pursues us. Help us discover our irrepressible happiness in knowing you, accepting your love, and sharing the joy of life with others. Amen

If you hold to my teaching, you are really my disciples.
Then you will know the truth, and the truth will set you free. John 8:31

God, you are the 'Eternal Now' whom I meet in your creation. Your continuing creation is filled with mystery and the discoverable. You are the One before and after all things. You are the creator of quasars, gluons, and quarks. You are the designer of neurons, neutrons, and the awe-filled numinous. You are the innovator of light, leptons and the mystery of love.

You give me the joy and zeal to use the tools of faith and reason, of hope and science. Give me humility to see that everything in this world has changed, except your grace. I too, must grow, must change, in thought and action. Yesterday shall never return; tomorrow is only a projected vision. Today I live in the motion and miracle of the river of life. It moves through quiet inlets, in narrow rapids, and over waterfalls. You are the same 'yesterday, today, and forever.'

I seek guidance for this path from birth through death to you.

Give me a mind and heart to appreciate the connectedness of all life, to enlarge the circle of understanding other people, to deepen the experience of wisdom, to discover more and more of my self, and to be loyal to the direction of the inner compass of your will.

Thank you for this moment of life, in Christ. Amen

Johann Wolfgang von Goethe wrote: "We must not hope to be mowers, and to gather the ripe gold ears, unless we have first been sowers and watered the furrows with tears. It is not just as we take it, this mystical world of ours, life's field will yield as we make it a harvest of thorns or flowers."

(Paul writing autobiographically) God set me apart...called me by his grace...I did not go up to Jerusalem to see those who were apostles before...I went to Arabia...then after three years went to Jerusalem...then after fourteen years...I met privately with (the apostles of Christ). Galatians 1:15;2:2

Paul had a sudden turning point in his life when he changed from persecuting Christians to following Christ with Christians. His life was not an immediate jump into leadership: "three years" in Arabia, a euphemism for a long desert retreat and training in discipleship; "fourteen years" internship service before being accepted as a peer among leaders of the young church.

Sometimes slow is fast. Perhaps we should all slow down. Of course we live in a universe of speed. Our little planet is moving at 1,037 mph at the equator; earth orbits the sun once a year, at 92,956,957 miles from the sun that means we, on earth, are moving in space at 66,595 mph; our solar system speeds around the center of the Milky Way Galaxy at 497,000 mph.

Slow down now, spiritually speaking.

Benjamin Wagner an executive with MTV described a serendipitous weekend with Mr. Fred Rogers of TV fame. Wagner said the slow quiet pace of Mr. Roger's personal life was the authentic copy of his television *persona*. Wagner said: "I complained about the jump cut sound bites of the MTV world, and I told him, I have a PBS mind." Rogers responded with this sage thought, *"I feel so strongly that deep and simple is far more essential than shallow and complex. Spread the message."*

God grabbed hold of Paul in a furious moment of a thunder and lightning storm. But the disciple was slowly, patiently prepared for the ultimate purpose of his life.

God of the universe, as summer approaches, let me find time and places for stillness where I may hear your voice. Amen

Jesus said, "Who do people say the Son of Man is?" They replied, "Some say John the Baptist; others say Elijah; and still others, Jeremiah..." "But what about you?" he asked. "Who do you say I am?" Simon Peter answered, "You are the Messiah, the Son of the Living God."... Then Jesus said to his disciples, "Whoever wants to be my disciple must deny themselves and take up their cross and follow me...whoever loses their life for me will find it." Matthew 16:13-16; 24-26

Consider this day "Matthew's Christ." The writer of the first Gospel describes a Messiah/Christ that was unique in his time in history. Matthew's Christ is existential. He is a Messiah of action. Love is not just an attribute of Christ; it is the condition and essence of the Messiah's way of life. Matthew's Christ is provocative, he asks the hard questions of everyone: "What do you gain if you the possess the whole world but lose your soul?" Matthew's Christ is universal, he is Christ for everyone...who would accept his invitation to follow him: Jews, Roman military leaders, social outcasts, foreigners to Israel—that is, "Gentiles"— the Greek word for "all nations" of people, rich, poor, women, children, and men. Matthew directs his Gospel to a primarily Jewish audience and then highlights the story with "inclusions" of all the diverse tribes, clans, cultures, and nations of the world.

Matthew's background list of "names," the genealogy, that make up the lineage of the Holy Family includes good guys, bad guys, and questionable characters. In fact he makes it clear that Jesus is the Messiah planted firmly in the milieu of common humanity. God in real flesh, incarnate, invades the sordid, splendid human history of the world. This incarnate Messiah is the hope of the world, all the world. All persons.

Christ, this day, I accept your invitation, "Follow me" as an imperative not an alternative to set aside. Amen

A man with leprosy came to (Jesus) and begged him on his knees. "If you are willing, you can make me clean." Jesus was indignant. He reached out his hand and touched the man. "I am willing," he said. "Be clean!" Immediately the leprosy left him. Mark 1: 40ff.

Mark's Gospel is the gospel of love and truth in action. He tells us about meeting the One in whom we meet the Living God. It is a great mystery. The actions of Jesus are not a mystery. Everyone saw the action. Mark, in his unsophisticated manner, avoids the obfuscation of erudition. He is a plain, clean, clear window through which we see Jesus at work, the action of love and truth. Mark writes with a youthful enthusiasm. In chapter 3, for example, Mark has 34 phrases, all incomplete sentences in the original Greek, tied together with "ands." Thirty-four "ands" with just one verb. Mark is excited to tell us what people saw in the actions of Jesus.

Mark's story is about what people saw the penniless preacher from Nazareth do. What they saw was the revelation of perfect love. On the one hand, this Jesus reveals to humanity all that God is. On the other hand, this Jesus reveals the essence of the ultimate meaning of our humanity: What is God like? What does it mean to be fully human?

Mark's society was organized so that the power structure always stayed with an elite group, protected by the taboos of social relationships. Judaism denied it had a caste system, but it did. The lowest caste were called "lepers," more than a biomedical term, it included the disenfranchised. Lepers were tormented, bullied, and forced 'outside the walls' of the protected city. A leper asked Jesus to heal him. Jesus, Mark writes, was "indignant." Not at the leper, at the taboo. We see God's love revealed in the action of this moment.

God, thank you for sending us your Word in Jesus. Our human need and destiny are revealed in Jesus. We meet you, the Lord of Life, in Jesus Christ. Humbly, we thank you. Amen

(Following the crucifixion the disciples were gathered together and)....Jesus himself stood among them and said, "Peace be with you." They were startled and frightened. He said, "Why are you troubled, and why do doubts rise in your minds?" When he had said this, he showed them his hands and feet. They still did not believe it because of joy and amazement. Luke 24:36-42

Through the writer Luke, we are given a Gospel of Inalienable Astonishment. The essence of life that makes it really worth living is a good surprise. Every good story must have a surprise. Every good life has a surprise.

Consider the disciples. No one had better evidence for belief. No one had more experience in the presence of Jesus. No one had more providential opportunities to know the essence and truth of God's love. And yet, they "still did not believe." But Luke adds a phrase that fits the theme of his Gospel of Inalienable Astonishment. "Because of joy and amazement" they did not comprehend what transpired before their very eyes.

Back in an era when we used to get our news from newspapers and magazines, *Life* magazine sent a team of reporters to "get a story" on one of the best known theologians in the world, Paul Tillich. He escaped Germany to find a safe place in America in the time of World War II. While doing his life story a reporter asked him, "Could you simply say in a word what is the crux of your philosophy and theology?" Tillich said, "Yes, I can say it in one word. The root of all my thought is this: *astonishment.*"

As we scan the brief twenty-four chapters of the Gospel of Luke, we witness from the birth of Jesus, through his year of teaching, through the horrid time of crucifixion, and in the resurrection, one consistent reaction that ultimately leads to splendid belief. It is astonishment, the inalienable right of astonishment.

Thank you, God, for the stupendous surprise of joy in the gospel of Christ. Amen

"The word became flesh, and made his dwelling among us.
We have seen his glory, the glory of the one and only Son, who came
from the Father, full of grace and truth. John 1:14

We have all played, or observed the "Ain't It Awful Game." Contestants seem to vie with one another about the 'worst thing going on.' With Alice of Wonderland, we may sing: "It's gonna be the worst day, it's gotta be the worst day of my life...my life has gotten so complicated, so underwhelming and overrated..." Elie Wiesel, a survivor of a Nazi concentration camp, said this about the worst sin: "The opposite of love is not hatred, it is indifference. The opposite of life is not death. It is indifference. The opposite of faith is not heresy. It is indifference. The indifferent person is dead before he or she dies."

Consider the nature of God. God is not indifferent. The incarnation of God in Christ reveals the true nature of God: love, life, faith, and the art of glory and beauty are manifest in Christ's real presence in human history.

The Gospel of John enunciates three grand categories of thought for meditation. One, the grace of Christ is sovereign. It is everywhere in the world, never confined by the human societies' barriers of tribe, race, or birthright. The Greek word that describes this grace is *poikilos*. That translates to "manifold," "many colored," as in the whole spectrum of light, a rainbow of colors that surround us and runs through our history. Two, the *logos,* the "Word" of God, is in the being of Jesus. The Living Christ is the Living Word. Three, each believer is a "gospel" to the people surrounding our lives. We are living stories of the presence of Christ in the world.

We stand in awe, Eternal God, when we behold the mystery of your presence in us, in the person of Jesus Christ. Thank you for revealing your story, the Gospel, in the story of each of our lives. Amen

Therefore I tell you, do not worry about your life, what you will eat or drink; or about your body, what you will wear. Is not life more than food, and the body more than clothes?...Can any one of you by worrying add a single hour to your life?Matthew 6:25ff

God, you are the 'same yesterday, today and forever.' I change every day. Aging is your gift of life to me. The ages of life have many blessings, though some are realized in retrospect.

In life's first age of innocent dependence, you gave me a familial heritage that reflected your love. I thank you every day for this blessing.

The age of learning, as I see it now in the mirror of memory, was a miracle. We are living beings created in your image and gifted with billions of brain cells eager for a new experience to store enduring remembrance. Thank you for the choices of adventures placed before me.

Thank you for the age of rebellion when you permitted me to learn, unlearn, and relearn the way of life. Thank you for the teacher called "failure." The crucibles of life were essential to the metamorphosis of a truer self. Here I learned the strength of surrender and transformation in the cauldron of creative chaos.

Gratitude overwhelms me when I consider the amazing age of productivity. When I accept the co-creator work you call me to do, I am privileged to witness your work.

With all the gifts of the ages, I ask for one more—the gift of the age of wisdom. May I have wisdom to discern your will in the manifold complexities of the human story. Thank you that my journey of life is not from birth to death, but birth through death to you. You are the means and end of all the ages of life. Amen

When the fullness of time had come, God sent his Son.
Galatians 4:4

Thanks to Alexander the Great, Greek was the most common language of the empire in which Christianity originated, therefore, the New Testament was written in Greek. The Greek word for "time" used in our text, is *kairos*. Unlike *chronos*, which is measured time as "the time" on your smart phone, *kairos* means a special time, a chosen time, a timing of things like a "turning point" in history. Paul instructs, "at just the right chosen time," God made the incarnation happen. Christ entered the history of the world.

A good friend of mine, Dr. Fred Silva, is a notable pathologist who also is an acclaimed lecturer on the subject of Science and Faith. Fred reminded me that "God made 'time' so that everything wouldn't happen at once."

Dr. Thomas Lewis, one of the greatest science writers in the past century, was asked by his publisher to write a book on the "seven greatest wonders in science." He did, and said he saved the best for last, *The Wonder of the Human Child*. From father and mother two cells join and begin to divide. Each soma cell divides until 10 hundred trillion soma cells later, there is a human being. Each of these trillions of cells has a strand of DNA through which one can trace the origins of our biological history back to the beginning of time. This same coding will be carried forward to the end of all time.

As Dr. Lewis Thomas says, the timing of this complex universe of activities inside each cell with incalculable interactions of nucleotides and enzymes is "ordained from the beginning." Thomas is speaking about "biology" not "theology." Right timing is written into the code of life. From the perspective of the New Testament, the right timing, the *kairos*, for everything is from God.

God, I am humbled by the beautiful complexity of all the creation about us, from a single cell, to the vastness of the universe. Thank you for ordaining the time of Jesus Christ. Amen

What good is it, brothers and sisters, if someone claims to have faith but has no deeds? Can such faith save them?...Faith by itself, if it is not accompanied by action, is dead. James 2:14ff

Martin Luther called James "an epistle of straw." Fortunately, the strong-minded reformer was not the measure of what books should be in the Bible. This writing by James, thought by many to be the brother of Jesus, is for me almost too clear. I cannot read James prayerfully without asking myself, "This idea of faith and action is true; am I doing this? What must I do now to have integrity in my belief?"

The late Chuck Colson was a lightning rod around the questions of faith and action pronounced by James, argued for and against by Christians of all political and religious party affiliations—liberals, conservatives, evangelicals. Colson was in prison for Watergate (President Nixon) affairs. This experience led to his conversion to believe Christ, commit his life to Christ, and more importantly, for today's thought, to follow Christ. Colson founded a ministry to inmates that changed for the common good tens of thousands of human lives. Eighty percent of inmates incarcerated in the U.S. return to prison for future felonies—recidivism. Those who graduate from Colson's Prison Fellowship, the "largest compassionate outreach to prisoners and their families in the world" (Michael Gerson, *Washington Post*, 4.24.12) have more than reversed this figure. Ninety percent of those do NOT return to prison. Colson's fellowship

that takes seriously the writing of James, and the instruction of Jesus ("I was in prison and you visited me," Matthew 25) serves men and women in 100 nations of the world.

"Show me your faith without deeds... even the demons believe...and I will show you my faith by my deeds." (James 2:18)

Eternal Christ, you have given us a faith that transforms our lives. Help me to have actions that reflect my convictions. Thank you. Amen

I kneel before the Father, from whom every family in heaven and on earth derives its name. I pray that out of his glorious riches he may strengthen you with power through his Spirit in your inner being, so that Christ may dwell in your hearts through faith. Ephesians 3:14-17

This scripture is a picture of the Sanctification of Nearness. With the presence of Christ, the mundane becomes the super mundane. Saint Therese of Lisieux, known as "The Little Flower," taught how to make common tasks into the beautiful place of the presence of God by silently repeating the scripture, "Whatever you do in word or deed, do everything in the name of the Lord Jesus." (Colossians 3:17)

Every home may have a time to practice the sanctification of the nearness of God. Years ago I remember our family having a brief "devo" (devotional time) together. All participated. Nicole, youngest and four years old, said her memorable prayer: "Thank you, God, for gravity. Amen." Where does a young mind get that thought? The sanctification of nearness is real when you consciously remember to thank God for the physics of the universe.

Church members can sanctify the nearness of God in the simple way they meet other people in the context of the routine affairs of a congregation. I shall never forget the first time Dan Joslin visited our congregation. His signature dress code always included a sports jacket so loud you wanted to cover your ears. With a handshake and smile he addressed members after a sermon and said, "You don't believe all that Jesus stuff, do you?" But the members continued to listen to Dan, love Dan, and include Dan. Eventually he joined the church. He asked me for the microphone when I was introducing the new members at a televised worship service, and said, "I want to thank all of you for giving me a home for faith. I love Jesus, and I love you."

Thank you, God, for the sanctification of your nearness in our lives. Amen

Has a nation ever changed its gods? (Yet they are not gods at all.) But my people have exchanged their glorious God for worthless idols. Be appalled at this, you heavens, and shudder with great horror. My people have committed two sins: they have forsaken me, the spring of living water, and have dug their own cisterns, broken cisterns that cannot hold water. Jeremiah 2:11-13

"The World is Not Enough" is a phrase Ian Fleming, creator of "James Bond," borrowed from the heraldic motto on the coat of arms of the (real) "Bond of Dorset" family. This motto is over 400 years old. Jeremiah described his people trying to create "a world that is enough" ending up with broken cisterns that hold no water. Hard as we try, all the stuff of the world is not enough to fill the emptiness of the human soul, the thirst of the human spirit. Ultimately, living a life sold out to the world is like drinking dust from a cup dipped into an empty well. We go through the motions of living; we come away thirsty. We are parched to the depth of our souls.

Reinhold Niebuhr, one of the most sophisticated theologians in America history, told this simple story of faith. "As a child I spent a day with my grandmother. Toward evening a severe storm began. How would I get home? My father came. He put his big blue coat over my head—grabbed my hand—and off we went. I couldn't see anything. We splashed through puddles and mud, rain and thunder claps all around. I would have been a fool if I had complained...protected by my father's coat...led by his strong hand. Father knew the way...when the coat was parted, we were home."

This world is not enough. With the leadership of God we are led through the world to our ultimate home. Take hold of the Strong Hand of One who sees the way.

Lord, even when I am lost, I fear not. Holding your hand, I trust you know the way. Amen

Woman, why are you crying? Who is it you are looking for?
John 20:15

Not unlike Mary Magdalene, one of the first persons to encounter the empty tomb of Jesus Christ, we may be very near that ferocious moment of God's wonder and not experience it, nor believe it. Mary had all the right training, right teaching, and right stuff to be a disciple of Christ. Like Mary, our preconditioned patterns of thought may preclude our seeing the wonder of an event taking place before our eyes.

My aunt Esther who attended Washington State University described the experience of enjoying a fellow student destined for a remarkable life. If you watched intently you may have glimpsed the possibilities in the making of your classmate, Egbert Roscoe, from Polecat, North Car-

olina. He was raised by a farmer dad who went broke, therefore went "West" looking for new opportunities, and a mom so paranoid about Satan that she would not answer the telephone with "Hello" because "that word contains the name of Satan's home." Egbert was a leader on the debate team that included Aunt Esther. He was one of the first to graduate with a degree in "Radio Broadcasting" and W.S.U was one of the first universities in the world to offer that degree. History, destiny and the providence of God melded, creating the rest of the story. Egbert became a famous broadcaster covering World War II from the frontlines, and the most famous television broadcaster of his generation. Yes, he changed his name from Egbert Roscoe to Edward R. Murrow.

On an infinitely larger scale, Mary Magdalene could have been a colleague of Jesus and never have known the risen Christ. That can happen to persons today, steeped in religion, but foreigners to the Spirit of God and the gift of belief. Mary listened, opened her eyes, and accepted the graceful gift of God's power in the Risen Lord.

Open my mind and heart, O Lord, that I may see your presence in the resurrection of Jesus Christ. Amen

Cast your cares on the Lord and he will
sustain you; he will never let the righteous be shaken. Psalm 55:22
Cast your anxiety on him because he cares for you. I Peter 5:7

The validity of faith is deeply existential. When we put our faith to work in the midst of serious predicaments, crisis events, loss of life and love, then, we may truly believe for the first time what we have experienced for the first time, "the Lord will sustain you," "he cares for you." There are many arguments against faith in the bland confrontations or dialogues on "belief" and "disbelief" that take place in the seminar rooms, the dining rooms, and the bar rooms. I have noticed that all of these lack context. In the context of financial failure, divorce, death, depression, and addiction, faith has a sharp edge. To use a biblical image, sharper than a two edged sword—it cuts both ways. We do not superficially test our faith in the polite and protected environments of church meetings, retreats, and Christian conferences. Life itself will bring real times of testing that we neither anticipate nor control. The faith we learn from Jesus Christ prepares us for the inevitable and unpredictable vortexes in the deep seas of our voyage of life.

1. We are what we believe. If we have built our house on the sands of fear, we shall always have proof that our belief in negativities is valid. 2. When I am angry, I almost always am angry about something outside of myself. When I find a solution to anger, I find that I am a part, or a large part, of the cause. 3. Choice is a powerful tool of the mind and soul. I may choose to see harsh events from another perspective, the mind of Christ (to use a phrase of the Apostle Paul). 4. I decide, "This Day," not to judge, anyone at anytime for anything.

God, help me to put the teaching of the Bible into the practice of my life, today. Amen

After Jesus was born in Bethlehem in Judea, during the time of King Herod, Magi from the east came to Jerusalem and asked, "Where is the one who has been born King of the Jews? We have come to worship him...having been warned in a dream not to go back to Herod, they returned to their country by another route. Matthew 2:2,12

Trying to control the fortuitous circumstances of life is like trying to sink a pig in a pond. It wears you out and it annoys the pig. Get accustomed to reality. We are not in control. Control is not the point of living. In the story of the Magi, the Wise Men from the East (modern day Iraq and Iran), Matthew has a subtheme, a nuance, to the grand narrative of the Gospel about God's love in Jesus Christ. The Magi came, met, and worshipped the gift of God in Jesus. They listened to the inner compass of God,

"warned in a dream," and they "returned by another route."

When we sincerely come to that meeting place where we encounter the truth of Christ, and when we listen with the heart to the will of God, we shall always "return by another route" to our daily lives. We may come to God on the roads of seeking approval from other people, especially important persons. We come to simply "feel better." Then, if we encounter the stunning presence of Christ and his grace, we leave by a different road. It shall be "the road less traveled," another route, without needing to perform, without pretense and patronage of societal mores. "Returning by another route" in life we discover for the first time a new spiritual topography that includes love, joy, and peace. (We shall meet the Magi again during *The Twelve Days of Christmas* in *This Day*.)

Help me to image the surprise of the Magi upon seeing Jesus for the first time, seeing the Living Lord of faith in the life of a person. Amen

With what shall I come before the Lord? He has shown you, O mortal, what is good. And what does the Lord require of you? To act justly and to love mercy and to walk humbly with your God. Micah 6:6ff

Albert Einstein was one of the most interesting persons in modern history. His influence was enormous. Einstein is quoted frequently for his scientific sagacity, and infrequently for his views on faith. Once he wrote, "I want to know how God created this world. I am not interested in this or that phenomenon, in the spectrum of this or that element. I want to know His thoughts; the rest are details."

Many years ago I visited a Buddhist Temple in Hawaii. The guide pointed out a saying at the entrance: "You have been given the key that opens the gates of heaven. The same key opens the gates of hell." There is a paradoxical duality common to both faith and science. In each domain the "gifts" of the respective disciplines may be used for good or evil. Einstein noted that about the power of nuclear physics; the Prophet Micah noted that duality about the gift of faith which can be inverted to do evil: "You leaders who despise justice and distort all that is right, who judge for a bribe, and priests teach for a price." (Micah 3:9f) True faith always has a moral imperative. Jesus used the words of the prophets to annunciate the gospel.

In his later years, Einstein wrote a "Letter to the 75th Anniversary of the Ethical Culture Society" in New York. He said: "I believe, indeed, that overemphasis on purely intellectual attitude...has led directly to the impairment of ethical values...The cultivation of this most important spring of moral action is religion, without this there is no salvation for humanity."

May I hear the truth of your justice, mercy and love, O God, and commit my life to your perfect will. Amen

You did not choose me, but I chose you and appointed you. John 15:16
Everyone who believes in him receives forgiveness of sins
through his name. Acts 10:43

The discussions about free will or predestination will probably not end this side of heaven. A professor of mine speculated that on the "Pearly Gates" of heaven there would be on the earthly side a sign that read, "Whoever will, shall come." And, on the heavenly side looking back at the entrance, another sign, "You did not choose me, I chose you."

Consider Christ's choice of disciples. Five fishermen, one tax collector, four zealots, and undocumented resumes for several. No one could ever charge Jesus with training an elite guard planning to take over an empire. But this humble collection of disciples with a few hundred women and men set out on a course that soon overcame the mightiest empire in history. Pogroms, imprisonments, exiles did not deter the movement of faith. Arrest a man named Paul, bring him to Rome for trial and execution, and soon the palace guard of the Romans, leading centurions, met Paul, heard his story, became Christians and they took the gospel to the far reaches of the empire in their deployments.

We have mentioned previously that the word for "witness" in Greek is the same word we translate "martyr." The motley band of disciples was indeed both witnesses and martyrs for Christ. Their influence continues twenty centuries later.

Consider the price they paid to say, "I believe Jesus is the Christ, the Son of God." Peter, crucified in Rome; Andrew crucified; James, beheaded by Herod; John, exiled to Patmos; James ("the younger") crucified in Egypt; Thaddeus, martyred in Persia (today's Iran); Philip, died in Hierapolis (today's Turkey); Bartholomew, flayed to death; Matthew, martyred in Ethiopia; Thomas, martyred in India; Simon the Zealot, crucified.

God, I am humbled in remembering the costly gift of faith in which faithful men and women through the ages made the ultimate sacrifice that I may live in faith and freedom. Amen

God will meet all your needs according to the riches
of his glory in Christ Jesus. Philippians 4:19

Elie Wiese tells this story. (Please forgive my paraphrase): "There once was a Rabbi named Eisik of Cracow. Starving with his poor family he had a dream. A voice in the dream told him to go to Prague and under the great bridge near the royal castle, he would find a hidden treasure. The dream was repeated three times, and so he decided to go.

"Eisik found the bridge. The bridge was guarded by soldiers. So he could not dig for the treasure. As he loitered in the vicinity, one of the soldiers asked him what he had lost. He told the soldier about the dream. The soldier burst into laughter. 'Really. You poor fool. You have worn out your shoes and yourself, coming all this way. I too once had such a dream, and it told me my treasure was hidden in Cracow, in the house of some old Rabbi named Eisik. The dream even said the treasure would be found in a dusty corner behind a stove. But being a reasonable man and not trusting dreams, I of course did not go.' The Rabbi thanked the soldier, returned to Cracow, dug behind the stove, found the treasure that saved his family."

This parable strikes home. Any of us can come to that impoverished time in life when we feel diminished and helpless by the obstacles before us. We go at great lengths to solve our problems. The greatest treasure is near at hand. But we must search and find, ask and receive. Then, this day, "God will meet your needs."

Thank you, Christ, for being our trusted Friend and Companion in the vicissitudes of life. Thank you for meeting our needs in all circumstances. Amen

In Christ all the fullness of the Deity lives in bodily form, and in Christ you have been brought to fullness...When you were dead in your sins...God made you alive with Christ. He forgave us all our sins. Colossians 2:9ff

The Twelve Step Program of Alcoholics Anonymous creates a modus operandi for discovery of truth and reformation of life. The Twelve Steps are practiced by millions of people worldwide. I offer here a simple Christian theological paraphrase of the Twelve Steps. I believe they are consistent with New Testament thought.

1. We admit to God and ourselves that we are powerless to save ourselves. 2. We accept God in Christ who alone is a power greater than our addictions, and who can restore sanity in our lives. 3. We decide to turn the control of our lives over to God. 4. We begin a fearless inventory of our moral strengths and weaknesses. 5. We admit to Christ, and to at least one other person, the true nature of our wrongs. 6. We willingly receive God's help to transform our lives. 7. We humbly ask God to remove the obstacles in our character. 8. We make a list of persons we have harmed, and with whom we desire reconciliation. 9. We take affirmative steps to create relationships in the love and truth we learn from the teaching and life of Christ. 10. We repeatedly assess our new life, making changes where necessary, being willing to admit wrong, and being responsible for commitments in love to others. 11. Daily we seek God's will through prayer, and the strength from God to follow his perfect will. 12. As we experience the transformation of life in spiritual awakening, we follow Christ in service to the true needs of others.

God of all life, renew within me a new mind, a courageous heart, and a good conscience. Amen

*Very truly I tell you, whoever believes in me will do the works
I have been doing, and they will do even greater things than these. John 14:12*

The followers of Christ will do greater things than the work and ministry of Jesus? Yes. As pessimism cloaks many American and European Christians about the status of the church today, the reality is this: from 2002 to 2012, the world experienced the greatest growth in Christian faith than any of the two hundred decades since the ministry of Jesus on earth. Unless you have seen what is happening in Africa, South America, China, and parts of Asia, you may have missed this headliner.

One example how this growth actually works: in the early 20th century Belgium controlled the Congo as a colony, administered from Europe. Missionaries from numerous countries served there. An eccentric Christian spokesperson, Simon Kimbangu, was considered by the Belgium overlords to be a threat to colonial power. He was imprisoned in 1921 and died in prison in 1951. During his prison years, he was visited by his sons, who became strong leaders of an indigenous and independent church. The Kimbangist Church in Zaire and the Republic of the Congo now has over five million followers. (By comparison, the Presbyterian Church in the U.S.A. lost members, from over five million to less than three million). The Kimbangist Church belongs to the World Council of Churches, cooperates with the Roman Catholic Church, and the Salvation Army in Africa.

Christ's last words to his followers concerned The Good News that would traverse all the nations of the world. "Go, and make disciples in all nations." It is happening now. You can see it if your mission perspective is not dwarfed by local constraints. You can see it, if your God is not too small.

Thank you, Christ, for letting us see the exhilarating times of faith in your global family. Amen

(Concerning the resurrection) When Jesus rose early on the first day of the week, he appeared first to Mary Magdalene...When they heard that Jesus was alive and that she had seen him, they did not believe it. Mark 16: 9-11

God of infinite wisdom, miracles surround me and I miss most of what happens. Even when it is as obvious as the ground upon which I walk, the person with whom I talk, the sky whose light I use, miracles often elude me. Sensitize me, Lord. Make me aware of your power of raising me from death to life. You raised Christ to life again from the

'agony of death, because it was impossible for death to keep its hold on Him.'

I have been at times, like the first disciples who heard about the resurrection and the story "seemed to them like nonsense." When death had consumed my love and locked me behind the doors of fear and loss, such stories of raising the dead seemed like an illusion wrapped in fantasy. Then, you broke through those doors where I was shackled in death's throes. You turned days of sunsets into dawns. Death was transformed to life again. Resurrection is here and now.

There are many things in my life that must die, in order that I may truly live: unmitigated self-centeredness, obsession with outward appearance, fears about fate controlling the future, and the heavy burden of the residuals from the pursuit of immediate gratification.

Your Spirit, that raised Christ from death, is now raising me to new life. The past is forgiven. I am released. The future is insured by your providential love and grace.

Your gift of this persistent springtime within my human condition is a cosmic event that changes for good all of life and history. Glory unto you, our God, unto Christ our Savior, unto the Spirit our Guide. Amen

(Paul, writing from prison in Rome) I thank God every time I remember you. I always pray with joy because of your partnership in the gospel... The peace of God, which transcends all understanding will guard your hearts and minds in Christ Jesus. Philippians 1:3; 4:7

"The mass of men (women and children) live in quiet desperation," according to Thoreau, writing from the beautiful secluded enclave of Walden's Pond. I am not sure Thoreau found the key to unlock the prison doors of desperation. Paul had that key. While he could not literally unlock the doors of a prison in Rome, nor prevent his unjust and hateful beheading ordered by the Emperor, Paul did have the key to the mystery of indefatigable serenity and joy. Philippians, written from prison, is called The Epistle of Joy.

The great Saint Augustine searched for that key to life. Like many, regardless of outward appearances and in spite of the collection of "things" surrounding their physical existence, Augustine felt *mad, had, and sad*. He wanted to feel honestly *glad*. What's the secret? He said, "I kept looking for that 'without my life' (meaning the external environment). What are the new things I could discover that would create a better sense of life? All of a sudden, I discovered it was not 'without,' but 'within' that the answer could be found."

Paul found the key: we live by faith in Christ who is the completely empowered emissary of God's grace, forgiveness, and giver of joy and peace. All circumstances, good and bad, are external forces that have no power over the inward strength of Christ; therefore, I can face everything in life "through him who gives me strength." (Philippians 4:13)

Today, Lord, you remind me to not seek joy in external stimulations of materialism and additive habits. Thank you for the inward present of your Spirit, the source of love, joy, peace, and steadfastness. Amen

*May the Lord give you the desire of
your heart and make all your plans succeed. Psalm 20:4*

Victor Hugo said, "Greater than the marching of armies is an idea whose time has come." John Dewey wrote, "Every great advancement has issued from a new audacity of imagination."

Here's an example: a guy born in 1944 finds himself in a Yale economics class in 1962, offering, per assignment, a "big idea" to the professor who said, "That's stupid. If that could be done, it would have already been done." Undaunted, this college student went into the U.S. Marines and earned the Silver Star, Bronze Star, and two Purple Hearts from the 200 combat missions he flew. He was emboldened about his "big idea" from things he learned about logistics in the military. In 1973, he, Fred Smith, founded FedEx and proved that the "stupid" idea worked. One could organize a system in which overnight deliveries could be made from anywhere to anywhere in the U.S.A.

Among the last words of Christ to his rather motley band of followers was this really audacious idea: take the Good News to the ends of the earth. Jack Dorsey co-founded Twitter, he said, "to enable a short burst of inconsequential information." Twitter has put 22 Arab nations on the alert. Twitter is one means of communication for millions of Christians in over 200 nations of the world.

Remember the "Big Idea" of the Gospel of Christ: The Kingdom of God is within you; There is no human mediator between you and God; God who is in Christ encounters us directly with forgiveness and love; The Holy Spirit of God empowers us with love, joy, and peace. This Big Idea comes from the audacity of God's imagination.

Thank you, God, for giving us the freedom of audacious imagination. Amen

Think of yourself with sober judgment, in accordance with the faith God has distributed to each of you...We have different gifts, according to the grace given to each of us. Romans 12:3ff

Does Paul really mean that we may change our emotional state by the way we think? Emphatically yes. We can choose to be 'niggling nabobs of negativity,' or positive passionate persons of principle. Paul focused on the image of Christ, not in the mirror of memorized regrets. From his prison cell Paul spoke of the joy of faith and that he "learned to be content" in all circumstances. Paul had come to that turning point in his life when he was confronted with the Living Christ. Projecting what Paul could have heard from God's encounter: "Paul, you are accepted by me, you are forgiven. Your past life of destructive hatred, your self-centered control of others, your fear of the success of my liberated people—all of this is forgiven. If you accept forgiveness, practice love, and walk by faith, all the past is changed. You shall be transformed to the new humanity in Christ. But first, you have to let go of the past, let go of your ego, and let go of judging others."

Guillaume Apollonaire wrote: "Come to the edge./ No, we will fall./ Come to the edge. / No, we will fall./ They came to the edge./ He pushed them and they flew."

The leap of faith may seem abrupt, absurd, not common sense. It is all of these. And it is our opportunity to fly on the wings of God's strong presence in every night and day of our lives.

Lord, this day let me be freed from the trivial dribble of ideological babblings that I previously let pass for belief. I have stood on the edge of the cliffs of human intelligence and logic too long. While I may fear the abyss below, nudge me. Let me find that faith is not a descent but the ascent to the realm of your buoyant joyful presence. Amen

There is now no condemnation for those who are in Christ Jesus, because through Christ Jesus the law of the Spirit who gives life has set you free from the law of sin and death. Romans 8:1-2

Vince Lombardi said, "Winning is a habit, unfortunately so is losing." Part of the reason for this, is 'momentum,' a term used frequently in sports. Winners have a momentum, an inner force, an inertia that keeps them moving toward the goal of winning even when unforeseen and uncontrollable circumstances intervene, such as injury to a key player.

Once upon a time I chartered a forty-five foot boat for a family vacation. I read a book, passed a nautical test, and was given a piece of paper that said I knew how to be the pilot of the boat. My family was the crew, four children ages 4 through 12, and my wife, second mate and chef. We disembarked from Seattle and headed our boat "Victory" out through Deception Pass toward the American San Juan Islands. Eagerness was the strong suit of Captain Brave, supplemented by ignorance. I had read about those waters, but never experienced them. The incoming tide was moving at 14 knots, with a strong wind. To head west through the pass we confronted the wind and tides with an old boat whose top speed was 10 knots. The boat did not have enough momentum to carry it safely through the pass, a pass lined with shaggy cliffs on one side, rocky shore on the other, literally, our Scylla and Charybdis. The power against us was greater than the power with us. We made it to a safe harbor because the forces of nature determined our direction and destination, in spite of the captain.

The momentum in our lives comes from positive and negative forces greater than our selves. Choose the momentum of the Spirit of Christ over the momentum of self-will.

Our Father in Heaven, please enable us with the power and momentum of your Spirit. Amen

Be transformed by the renewing of your mind.
Romans 12:2

The beginning of the work of Christ in our lives is only a beginning. "Renewing of your mind," is always a 'work in progress.' Sometimes ministers forget that, and act as though the ministry is only three things: "They're hatched, matched, and dispatched." (Baptismal ceremonies, marriage ceremonies, and memorial services.)

Napoleon is credited with saying: "Alexander the Great and I conquered the world by the force of our armies, with power, and our empires have vanished. Jesus of Nazareth conquered the world with love and his kingdom will never end."

Consider the math in this plan of God, conquering the world through love in Christ. It has to do with the influence of one person on two persons, those two on four persons, in a continuous procession throughout history. Ray Kurzweil in *The Age of Spiritual Machines* tells an old story that illustrates this exponential math.

Once there was an Emperor of China who loved the game of chess and wanted to reward the inventor: "What could I give you as a reward?" The inventor said, "A grain of rice on the chess board. One grain on the first square, two on the second, four on the third, and double the amount on each square for the remainder of the board."

The Emperor agreed until he discovered that the last square would have 18 million trillion grains of rice. At ten grains of rice per one square inch of soil, this would require rice fields covering twice the surface of the earth. In one version of the story, the Emperor killed the inventor of chess.

The math of how the gift of God's grace in Christ transforms the lives of tens of millions of people works on this exponential scale. Tell your story to another person.

God, thank you for the infinite scale of the love you reveal in Christ Jesus. Amen

Blessed are the meek, for they will inherit the earth.
Matthew 5:5

One example of this axiomatic truth from Jesus' "Sermon on the Mount" is the story of Ruby Bridges.

Ruby was born in 1954. At the age of six, her parents agreed that she would be the one, and only one, person to integrate a "Whites Only" public elementary school. National media attention was focused on this event. Ruby had to walk a gauntlet of hostile people lining the sidewalk to the front door of William Frantz Elementary School in New Orleans. The white citizens present were angry and hateful. The whole world, via television, heard and saw the rage, death threats, and curses.

In a providence of coincidence happening, a young U.S. Air Force officer stationed in Biloxi took acute interest in this event—Dr. Robert Cole. Cole was an M.D., Ph.D. who specialized in children's health. Knowing the setup of this monumental event, he wanted to know how a little girl could cope with such a horrendous undertaking. He introduced himself to the family and they accepted his daily counseling. A conversation with Ruby, after one of the many days of confrontation, went like this: "Are you OK?" "Yeah." "Feel good?" "Yeah." "Any headaches?" "Nope." "Eating right?" "Yeah." One day he witnessed what he thought was Ruby talking to the people in the gauntlet shouting at her. "What were you saying?" "I wasn't talking to them. My pastor and mother taught me that Jesus had to do some hard things, like facing angry people who shouted at him and wanted to kill him, and Jesus prayed for the crowd, so, every day I pray for this crowd, too."

Cole became one of the most famous and popular professors in the history of Harvard. Standing room only crowds attended his lectures.

Ruby became a spiritual example of Christ's sermon for all to see.

Thank you, God, for the witnesses to your truth revealed in Jesus Christ. Amen

There is no fear in love. But perfect love drives out fear,
because fear has to do with punishment. The one who fears is not made
perfect in love. I John 4:18

"I don't believe in God, but I miss him," reads Julian Barnes' opening sentence in *Nothing to be Frightened Of.* Barnes describes himself as an atheist turned agnostic. He wants to know why anyone fears the afterlife that he doesn't believe in. Can one be frightened of 'Nothing?' Barnes admits to Thanatophobia. (*Thanatos* is the Greek word for "death.") "Pitched from sleep into darkness, panic and vicious awareness that this is a rented world (in which I am) awake, alone, utterly alone...shouting 'oh no OH NO.'" His dreams include being shot by a firing squad for an act he never committed. He envisions himself locked in an overturned sunken ferry. Barnes says, "I had no faith to lose." His only experience with church, he lives in the U.K., is visiting them for architectural interests "to get a sense of what Englishness once was."

I have no idea where the "rest of the story" leads for Julian Barnes. I do know that some of the fiercest agnostics in history have amazing turning points in their lives, people like H. G. Wells. He wanted to write a history of the world. The more he studied the detail of the life and influence of Jesus and his teaching, the more he became convinced that Jesus is the Christ to be trusted and believed. As a believer he said, "The penniless preacher of Nazareth has irresistibly become the center of history."

It is only when one witnesses the love and mercy of God in concrete human action that we can finally say, "Once I was blind, but now I see."

Lord God, with a disciple of Jesus I pray, 'Yes, I believe, help my unbelief.' You graciously allow me to experience doubt as the opposite side of the coin of faith. Amen

The Spirit searches all things, even the deep things of God
...We have the mind of Christ. I Corinthians 2:10ff

"Every one of us gladly turns away from his or her problems," C. G. Jung wrote. "If possible, they must not be mentioned, or, better still, their existence is denied...The artful denial of a problem will not produce conviction; on the contrary, a wider and higher consciousness is required to give us the certainty and clarity we need."

The memorial service for a decorated veteran of the U.S. Air Force, husband for thirty years, father of three children, was concluding. The presentation of the flag to the family, twenty-one gun salute, and the Taps. I have a hard time holding back tears whenever I hear the Taps played on such a somber occasion. The background of the Rocky Mountains gave this moment in the outdoor service an additional sense of lasting reverent presence. I concluded with the committal prayer to the Risen Christ, and before saying, "Amen," the twenty-five-year-old daughter of the deceased jumped out of her front row chair, ran forward, threw her wide open arms across the top of the casket and cried out: "Daddy, I never told you I love you!"

The back story: this young girl joined a protest movement and commune in university days. She told her dad she hated him, for everything, especially his military career, and never wanted to see him or talk to him again. She kept her word. In the following years she was in "artful denial" of the problem. Now it was too late for the conversation her deepest level of consciousness desired. In the following months the crucial and painful steps forward were taken: acknowledgment of denial; clarity to oneself about the deepest regrets; confronting Christ's forgiveness and accepting forgiveness; and receiving restoration for oneself, family, and friends.

God, you teach us that it is never too late to accept your forgiveness. Amen

Do you not know that in a race all the runners run, but only one gets the prize? Run in such a way as to get the prize...We do it to get a crown that will last forever. I Corinthians 9:24-2

This day let us consider the dual demands of 'running' and 'resting.' The human spirit and the Spirit of Christ teach us that both are natural and true.

Running: I like to watch Usain Bolt, the fastest human in history. His personality and running style are captivating. Bolt's top speed is 30 mph. He averaged 23.5 mph over 100 meters when he set that record; at 200 meters record he ran 19.9 mph. Bolt is 30th on the list of the fastest sentient creatures on record; white tail deer, warthogs, grizzly bears, and house cats are faster. An Arabian horse has run 60 miles averaging 16 mph. That may be the fastest creature at distance running; the current record in the marathon for a human is 2:03:59. (My first marathon was 3:55:45; the winner had attended the awards ceremony, had finished the press conference, and had left the stadium when I plodded in.)

Part of our life is "running." God has "marked out for us" the race with a focus on Jesus. Jesus' race, according to Matthew, lasted twelve months from his first teaching through the gruesome crucifixion.

Life in Christ, and life as a living creature in God's grand creation also requires "resting." Jesus withdrew to "a solitary place" numerous times according to the Gospels. "Resting" is built into the created order, according to Genesis 2:1: "God rested from all his work."

Let us run with perseverance. Let us rest in solitude.

This day, Lord, I thank you for life, for a race 'marked out for me.' And, I thank you for rest, retreat, and renewal of life and spirit. In Christ. Amen

As you come to him, the Living Stone, rejected by humans...you,
like living stones, are being built into a spiritual house. I Peter 2:4-5

Solitude builds strength for the community. There is a natural togetherness in Christian experience. Some kind of communal experience is essential for biological and spiritual life. Isolation is not natural. Solitude is required.

Listen to Thomas Merton's poetry: "Be still/ Listen to the stones of the wall./ Be silent, they try/ To speak your Name./ Listen/ to the living walls./ Who are you? / Who/ Are you?/ Whose Silence are you?"

My research studies created an investigative trail from New College Oxford to Salisbury Cathedral, home to an archive dating back to 1258 A.D. I would take breaks from the research to enter the great nave of this magnificent cathedral to rest, listen to the great organ and Mozart's music. The stones in that structure fascinated one's contemplative instinct: 70,000 tons of Chilmark stone, Jurassic age fossils in the stone, same quarry from which Stonehenge was built, 'what were the intrinsic differences between Druids of Stonehenge and the monks at Salisbury,' who were the craftsmen who worked 38 years to build the cathedral, what could the stones say about the people drawn to this worship center over the last 800 years, why is the best of only four original copies of the Magna Carta kept here for eight centuries?

I now contemplate the Living Stone of Christ and 'living stones,' ourselves, being built into the spiritual temple of God. This "spiritual house" will never be destroyed, even the "gates of Hades shall not prevail against it." (Matthew 16:18)

Solitude in the house of God builds strength in the community of Christ.

Eternal Christ, today I pray for your church. May each of us as 'living stones' in the 'spiritual house' reflect the true story of your mercy and grace. Amen

He must become greater; I must become less.
John 3:30

God of all time, matter and energy: Lord of the universe and Creator of microcosms; let me commune with you about the size of my place in the reality of life.

When I doubt what you can or shall do, I am saying that 'my God is too small.' Often I have envisioned myself too large with my frenzied activities and my desires for accumulation of material things. You are the Great God who is the light of the world. You commission us to reflect your light to others. Can anyone see your light through the opaqueness of my life?

I am the one who needs to downsize. I need to de-emphasize desires, postpone gratifications, discipline appetites, and make space and time for enlarging the realm of love and holy presence in my life.

I meditate upon Christ. He had no trust fund, no endowment, no institutional position of power, nor a popular front organization. He chose to downsize his divine prerogatives and took on the form of a servant of humanity. In his humility, there is infinite power. In his apparent weakness, there is overwhelming strength. In his death, there is resurrection to eternal life.

In downsizing desires, acquisitions, and self-focused attention, may I let your love increase, the love that is boundless in this brief history of time. Help me, Lord, to enlarge the spiritual habitat of your will and diminish my own. I pray with John the Baptist, "Christ must become greater; I must become less." Amen

Christian simplicity is the very perfection of the interior life—God, His will, and pleasure as its sole object. Jean Nicolas Grou, *The Hidden Life of the Soul*

Beneath the crude shell of materialism there lies in most persons an innate longing for the spiritual and the eternal. John LaFarge, *An American Dream*

The law of the Lord is perfect, refreshing the soul. The statutes of the Lord are trustworthy, making wise the simple. Psalm 19:7

In Dostoevsky's *The Brothers Karamazov* recall the courtroom scene after Dmitri has been sentenced to imprisonment in Siberia. Exhausted, he fell asleep on a hard bench. When he awakened he found someone had placed a pillow under his head. He had no idea who the angel of the night might be. He had thought he was alone in a merciless universe of tyranny. The pillow was a sign that in the bleak winter of repression there is still someone with a heart of compassion. Dmitri commits to keeping God's name alive in the godless gulag of suffering.

We heard a U.S. Air Force officer describe his seven years in prison in Hanoi with unspeakable harsh conditions, where survival seemed nearly hopeless. One morning he stirred awake in his 'tiger cage' and found a Christian cross beautifully woven from straw. Only North Vietnamese guards had access to his prison. He knew he was not alone in his faith. A secret follower of Christ intermittently brought morsels of food, symbols of faith, as a ministry to a prisoner.

We are reminded not to put off another day the opportunity to bring the moment of affirmation, the morsels of the Bread of Life, the symbols of spiritual presence to someone who is locked in a prison of despair. We all suffer a bit from procrastination, as Groucho Marx wrote to his friend Leo Rosten: "Dear Leo, I haven't gotten around to writing you a letter because I've been so busy lately not writing letters to anyone that I didn't have time to write you."

Today I commit myself to take the gift of love 'that replenishes the soul' to someone isolated in loneliness.

Lord, among his last words, Jesus said to visit the prisoner and that visitation was received by himself. I pray for wisdom and will to follow this mandate of love. Amen

For whoever wants to save their life will lose it, but whoever loses their life for me and for the gospel will save it. What good is it for someone to gain the whole world, yet forfeit their soul? Mark 8:35-36

She was the most forgetful person I have ever known—my mother. I do not mean cognitive deficiencies. She could forget her ego nearly in every situation. In my mom, I could see the truth of Jesus' teaching—forgetting one self and finding one's true identity. Tolstoy said to "forget yourself in the dream of daily life." This ability is a gift of grace. We live in a culture of infinite self-consciousness: "How do I look? Is this the right car to attract attention? How does our second and third vacation home compare to the ones I see in *Architectural Digest*? Who else do we know who goes to that church? Does that university have the right elite image that will help my kid's career?" The list goes on *ad infinitum, ad nauseum.*

The writer of Proverbs described a woman of noble character. This could be my mother. "She is worth far more than rubies. Her husband has full confidence in her and lacks nothing of value. She brings him good, not harm. She works with eager hands. She gets up while it is still night; she provides food for her family, her lamp does not go out at night. She is clothed with strength and dignity; she can laugh at the days to come." (Proverbs 31:10ff)

Albert Schweitzer said "service" is the greatest word in the dictionary, and only service can make us fully human. (With his four doctorates in medicine, theology, music, and history, I imagine he knew a ton of words.)

Who is the most forgetful person you know?

God, thank you for the loving service of others in my life…parents, friends, and mentors. Amen

On one occasion an expert in the law stood up to test Jesus. "Teacher," he asked, "what must I do to inherit eternal life?" (Jesus told the story of the 'Good' Samaritan) Jesus told him, "Go and do likewise." Luke 10:25ff

Jesus' ministry in word and deed was inclusive of people outside of the narrow definition of orthodoxy and culturally established rules of religion. In this familiar story of the Samaritan the good guy is the outsider, the baddies are two 'insiders' of religion. The teaching applies to us.

An unusual opportunity arose following a Board of Trustees meeting at San Francisco Theological Seminary. I cancelled my flight to meet the person of this opportune time, His Holiness, the Fourteenth Dalai Lama. After discussions and a small luncheon and a short speech by the Dalai Lama, I drew these estimations of our Tibetan visitor to America: humble, contentedly happy, and grateful for life with all the dimensions of love, hate, repression, and notoriety that he endured. As Jesus taught, I needed to hear, learn, and understand someone from outside the orthodox confines of my own experience.

From notes on the Dalai Lama's comments: "I am thankful to be awake this day. I will not waste the present time. I will expand my heart to other people. I will have kind thoughts about others and want my energies applied to benefit others."

(This day's prayer is by Kirstin Lee, my daughter, on her birthday.)

Hi God, thank you for the gift of Gratitude. It is such a glorious force that takes us away from ourselves and helps us to focus on: the fabulous sunrise, the kind UPS delivery man*, delicious food, a healthy child, a joyous run on the beach, the growth realized from suffering, the beauty of being human, and the grace of amazing love that you give to surround us. We are grateful to be grateful. I love you, God! Amen

(* Kirstin informed us that her UPS deliver man and friend died in a tragic accident a few weeks after she wrote this prayer. He was loved by his family, customers, and God.)

(The devotional today is in honor of my 17-year-old step-granddaughter, Taite Sandefer.) Blessed are the pure in heart, for they will see God. Matthew 5:8

The word for "pure" in Matthew's original Greek text is *katharos*. In Greek it was used to mean "unadulterated," "unmixed with alloy." We have noted before that the Greek word for "blessed" may best be translated "happy." Let's paraphrase the text: "You shall have true happiness when, with unmixed motives, you seek God. Then, you shall see God." Kierkegaard said, "Purity of heart is to will one thing and one thing only."

In this season of the year the whole world will hear about the American Declaration of Independence, which we celebrate tomorrow. In Jefferson's first draft, pre-committee editing, he said our "rights" are the "pursuit of life, liberty and property." Jefferson was probably thinking with his old English legal mind that only "property owners" would be voters if and when we formed a new republic. The wisdom of the committee prevailed. The "pursuit of happiness" is nearly the universal and dominant instinct of our 21st century culture. A recent poll shows "seeking happiness" as the first goal of Americans.

Happiness is elusive. Forget the "pursuit of happiness." That is like chasing a black panther in a dark jungle at midnight and you are blindfolded. The panther not only wins, she is laughing at us. Most of our "pursuits" are laughable; it's the stuff of Tina Fey and Larry David's comedic shows. So, if you have Shadow Fatigue

(chasing the shadows of elusive happiness) perhaps the time is now for the prescription offered by Jesus Christ: "Happiness comes from the purity of heart." What you receive, what you "see" is God.

True happiness is a by-product, a reward, and a gift of a faithful life.

Lord, I keep looking for happiness in myself. I am an empty vessel. Fill me with your Spirit, the fresh water of love for you and others wherein I may find peace and joy. Amen

You will receive power when the Holy Spirit comes on you;
and you will be my witnesses in Jerusalem, and in all Judea and Samaria,
and to the ends of the earth. Acts 1:8

These words recorded by Luke, writer of Acts, are among the last words of Christ on earth. On these words the whole world pivoted on its political and social axis. Power is given to the people.

A true reading of the New Testament, we were taught by Reinhold Niebuhr, shall inevitably lead to democracy. The first Christians practiced democracy for all: rich, poor, women, men, all tribes and nations were invited to Christ's communion.

The greatest single fact of change in the 21st century, a century of change, is the democratization of the world. Fifty years ago one third of the world experienced democracy. Today nascent or fully developed democracy grows in more than two thirds of the world. Everywhere the hue and cry is 'power to the people.' A cowboy philosopher from Oklahoma had it right, "Democracy is a terrible form of government and it's the best there is." (*Thanks, Will Rogers.*)

Three intrinsic principles of life and action in the New Testament message lead to democracy. One: God created all humankind in his image. That's the equal footing principle. Two: God reveals the perfect image of what it means to be human in Jesus, "the center of history." Three: God gives the insight of his truth to "everyone" (John 1:9). Take note, not black, white, people of color, or people of a chosen cultural affinity. In this context, The Declaration of Independence, 1776, is abundantly clear.

"We hold these truths to be self-evident, that all (persons) are created equal, that they are endowed by their Creator with certain unalienable rights...Governments... deriving their just powers from the consent of the governed."

Thank you, God, for the privilege of liberty to practice faithfulness, to love one another. Thank you for the sacrifice of service to others, celebrated this Fourth of July. Amen

As a deer pants for streams of water, so my soul pants for you, my God. My soul thirsts for God, for the living God. My tears have been my food day and night, while people say to me all day long, "Where is your God?" Psalm 42:1-3

Brave people in every generation have stood in the breach between tyranny and liberty, between death and life. People of faith are tested to the core of their belief. Dietrich Bonhoeffer, pastor and theologian, found himself at the precipice of death awaiting execution in a Nazi prison in Flossenburg. He prayed: "O God, early in the morning I cry to you. I cannot do this alone. In me there is darkness, but in you there is light. Lord, whatever this day may bring, may your name be praised." Bonhoeffer died the next day, Monday, April 9th 1945, death by hanging. His witness to Christ remains forever.

Lech Walesa was another staunch witness to faith and liberty. He became one of the most prominent leaders of the Velvet Revolution that brought down the Berlin Wall, the Iron Curtain, and the Soviet Union. On August 14, 1980 he stood on a tractor and spoke to a crowd of shipyard workers in Gdansk, Poland. Perhaps his speech is the most influential speech of the 20th century, marking the beginning of a revolution without a war. We heard him speak a few years after he was President of liberated and democratic Poland. In the Q & A he was asked how he managed to defy the police and military force of the repressive Communist regime, and he said, laughingly: "I didn't do anything smart or great, or profound. I simply told the truth. The truth promoted me—promoted me first to one jail then another. Courage is like being pregnant. Either you are, or you're not."

God, I pray for the courage required of my convictions. Prevent me from depending on others to tell the truth. Thank you for the witness of Jesus' courage. Amen

The Lord bless you and keep you; the Lord make his face
shine on you and be gracious to you; the Lord turn his face toward you
and give you peace. Numbers 6:24-26

Creator of all life, I thank you for the gift of faith to believe in life after birth. There were times when I lived as if I did not believe in the life that was gifted to me. Talents and treasures, loyalties and loves, were wasted, neglected, and abused. If I believe in life after birth, I live with aspiration. Aspiring to gain not substance, not money, not advantageous opportunity: I desire you in my life.

Thank you for giving me a trusting relationship in you. You are the object and subject of my deepest joys and transcending serenity.

God, I desire for you to be in my consciousness that I may meditate. Be in my conscience that my behavior shall honor you. Be in my heart that I may love you. Lord, be in my emotions that I may rejoice in you. Be in my countenance as I look up to the beatific vision of Christ.

Loving God, with all the gifts from you, I am bold to ask for one more—the gift of gratitude. You are the Bread of Life. When I come to you, I am never hungry. You alone can fill the emptiness of my soul with gracious presence. Undeserved grace is the indefatigable source of my existence.

Thank you, my Creator, Redeemer, and Comforter. Amen

Mercy, peace, and love be yours in abundance. (Jude verse 2)

To him who is able to keep from stumbling and to present you before his glorious presence without fault and with great joy—to the only God our Savior be glory, majesty, power, and authority, through Jesus Christ our Lord, before all ages, now and forevermore. Amen (Jude verse 24)

Your word is a lamp for my feet, a light on my path.
Psalm 119:105

Many years ago, near the height of the Cold War, my wife and I took two contraband books into the Soviet Union. One was a paperback copy of the Bible. The other was Boris Pasternak's *Dr. Zhivago*. The books were coveted by various Russians we met. Eventually we gave the books to two University of Moscow students. The students had heard about the books, even quoted passages from both, but had never seen a copy of either.

From *Dr. Zhivago* there is a lyrical passage that connects the cosmic Christ of the New Testament to the universal condition of the world: "Into this tasteless heap of golden marble he came. Lightness and an aura. Emphatically human. Deliberately provincial, Galilean. And since he came, gods and nations ceased to be, and full humanity came into being."

How things changed. The Berlin Wall is down, the Soviet Union is gone. For a time the new Russia invited guests from the U.S.A. to bring Bibles to hand out to high school students. These public schools inculcated Bible study into the curriculum. Tens of thousands of Bibles in the Russian language were distributed. My sister from Menlo Park, California was one of those couriers. Cultures change. That openness has ended and yet the mission of Christ in today's Russia continues.

I am a firm believer that the "Word that is a lamp for my feet, a light on my path," can never be suppressed by regimes of any kind. In the most inhospitable environments the Word of God cannot be extinguished, in the long run. China is a good example. Some worry that the Bible's "Light" may be overshadowed by cultures so open that everything is taken for granted. Could indolence, indifference, and ignorance to the Bible happen in America?

What do you think?

God, please keep me from careless inattention to the gift of your Word. Amen

I press on to take hold of that for which Christ Jesus took hold of me... One thing I do: Forgetting what is behind, I press on toward the goal to win the prize for which God has called me heavenward in Christ Jesus. Philippians 3:12-14

In the movie "City Slickers" Jack Palance, representing 'country wisdom' addresses Billy Crystal and the 'city slickers.' Gesturing with one index finger waved in Crystal's face, Palance says, "THAT is the secret of life: ONE THING." Great idea, what is the "one thing?" The movie never explains.

All of us want to find the meaning of life that is more than 'monotony tinged with hysteria.' Will and Ariel Durant had finished their monumental, *History of the World.* Will Durant said, the "one thing" that all humans seek is "liberty as a product of order." Robert Frost, "You have freedom when you're easy in your harness."

We continue to question: "What kind of liberty, what kind of order, and whose harness?"

We get a little closer to the answer with Voltaire's seminal work, *Candide.* At the end of the narrative, after much experimentation, the hero has learned what the "one thing" is: "*Il faut cultivar notre jardin.*"—"cultivate your garden." Of course it is a metaphor, we must cultivate the gifts given to us. For a believer, these gifts are from God. Read again Paul's "one thing" he must do from our text.

Bonhoeffer nailed the answer to our "search for meaning, for the one thing that makes all the difference in life." He said, "Discipline is the doorway to freedom." He begins with faith in Christ and being a "disciple" is being "disciplined." It comes to this: to whom, to what, will I give my ultimate loyalty in order to be liberated and possess my destiny?

God, this day I choose the grace of Christ as the "one thing" guiding my destiny. Amen

Put on the full armor of God...the belt of truth... the body armor of righteousness... feet fitted with readiness...the shield of faith...the helmet of salvation...the sword of the Spirit which is the word of God. Ephesians 6:10ff

This was an embarrassing moment. Having been selected in high school to the All State Football team (Washington State) we were getting ready for an exhibition game in the University of Washington football stadium. Hype, pretense, and personality performance games were taking place in the locker room at our first meeting. We were handed our equipment, instructed to put it on, come to the field for photo ops. Dressing next to a huge tackle, a total stranger, I began to put on the pads as usual. There was one set of pads I had never seen. I stepped into the harness, thinking they were some kind of hip pads that I had never worn (as receivers we sometimes wore a small pad inserted into our pants). I looked like a fool and felt like one. My locker mate quietly said: "Those are rib pads, you have them upside down." He must have thought, "Wow. Who is this bumpkin? Can't dress himself."

I have made myself a fool on an infinitely larger scale. I have not worn, or used the whole armor of God given by the Lord who 'supplies all our needs.' Name all the pieces of equipment Paul describes. At one time or another I have not correctly 'put on the pads' for the contest of life. Tennessee Williams in "The Rose Tattoo" says, "Fear and evasion are the two little beasts that run in that revolving cage, constantly in our nervous life." Was it not fear or evasion that caused me at times not to put on the helmet of salvation, not to pick up the sword of the Spirit, or, not to grab hold of the shield of faith?

Stop fretting about life. "Put on the whole armor of God."

Thank you, God, for equipping us to face all circumstances of life. Amen

I will be their God, and they will be my people. Jeremiah 31:33

My daughter Nicole witnessed this scene at a market. An elderly lady, a customer or two ahead of her in the checkout, needed a taxi to return home. The lady asked the checkout assistant, "Would you please phone a taxi for me? Here's the number." The word "assistant" in this case had no relationship to the word "assistance," and the dear lady was given the brush off. The dejected lady slowly walked to the door. Nicole intercepted the lady in need, gave her a ride home, became good friends, and kept in regular contact. In time Nicole and her two daughters said goodbye to their best "older" friend at the lady's memorial service.

We shall call this woman Mrs. Z. Nicole introduced us, I saw her writings, she demurred—"I am not a writer, I am not worthy." She wanted the ministry of anonymity. She is a writer and she is worthy. (Mrs. Z's poem is our prayer this day. Her pronoun "YOU" is "God").

"Take the beauty of a sunset, mix it well with summer skies,
Take the something you see shining in a child's sweet touching eyes.
Take the strength from the mountains, take the grandeur from the sea,
Take the promise of tomorrow and the life that is to be.
Take the winds that blow gently and caressing, then merciless in mighty storms,
Take the mist that early in the morning falls upon the moor and marshland farms.
Take the songs of choirs on Sunday as they sing of God's good grace,
Take the ageless wisdom painted on a saintly old man's face.
Take all these things and magnify ten thousand: if this you carefully do,
You shall in multiplying, not told my faith in YOU."

For freedom, Christ has set you free. Stand firm,
then, and do not let yourselves be burdened again by the yoke
of slavery. Galatians 5:1

W.H. Murray was a member of the Scottish team whose expeditions were the first to conquer several Himalayan Mountains. His comment is worthy of those considering an expedition putting the Christian faith into action: "Until one is committed there is a hesitancy, the chance to draw back which creates ineffectiveness. In all acts of initiative there is one elementary truth, the ignorance of which kills countless ideas and splendid plans; that the moment one definitely commits oneself, then Providence moves too."

Goethe said: "Whatever you can do, or dream you can, begin it. Boldness has genius, power, and magic in it."

Duque Hernandez story (*Newsweek*, 1.12.98) is an example of Murray's axiom.

Duque worked for eight dollars a month as a physical therapist in a Havana psychiatric clinic. The commitment to escape Cuba was made, plans laid, and the journey began. The last song he sang at a dance in Havana was *"Ay Dios Amparame."* ("Oh God Protect Me."). Duque and several others escaping Cuba launched a twenty-foot boat made from scrap wood. They had four oars, a compass concocted from household magnets, provisions of spam, water, and bread. The leaky boat sank, the escapees swam to Anguilla, a deserted split of land belonging to the Bahamas. For four days they ate seaweed and raw conch. A U.S. Coast Guard helicopter rescued them, took them to Freeport. Duque said, "Finally all we had was faith; the only thing we are looking for is freedom." El Duque is a four times World Series Baseball Champion today. Welcome to freedom.

The freedom road in the race of life always begins at the starting blocks of commitment.

Lord, I commit myself this day to you, to do your perfect will. Amen

Accept one another, then, just as Christ accepted you,
in order to bring praise to God. Romans 15:7

After one hears positive reports in several countries spanning three continents concerning the work of a specific mission organization, it is time to take notice. That was my experience with World Neighbors. This grass roots mission's strategy is in the "hand up" not the "hand out" genre of charity. Going into some of the most isolated and impoverished rural communities in the world, World Neighbors puts a philosophy into action. I saw the points of this strategy on the wall of a village community center in the mountains of Honduras. I believe the most sophisticated business start-up, church, or charitable organization could learn from these organizational steps. I think it applies to individuals going through life's changes. The title of the program is the Spanish word, *Filosophia* and the steps are translations from a poster in Honduras. Whatever you teach, do it yourself first. Respect the cultures of other persons. Start small. Plan a small budget; plan to keep the costs low. *Con Mucha Motivacion.* Instill the project with much motivation. Responsibility: each person must be responsible for the work done. Satisfaction: celebrate the successes with gratitude.

Consider the beginning of the Christian faith. Churches began in homes. People of all tribes and cultures were respected. The small gatherings were under severe persecution in some times and places and yet through sharing they survived and thrived. The *con mucha motivacion* of the church was the Spirit of Christ. The church considered itself the "body" of Christ in which each person was a 'member' of a complex body; responsibility applied to everyone. No one would doubt the church's satisfaction. They sang songs, spiritual songs, hymns of praise and joy.

If you are an agent of change, try this simple formula.

Lord God, thank you for the living witness from agents of change and reconciliation in the whole world. Amen

Carry each other's burdens and in this way you
will fulfill the law of Christ. Do not be deceived: God cannot be mocked.
A man reaps what he sows. Galatians 6:2,7

First I want to thank my good friend Bob Fitzpatrick for the notes he took from a Loc Le presentation we both heard. Fitz is a retired F.B.I. agent and his copious notes and professional attention were far superior to mine.

Loc Le lived in Da Nang Province, Vietnam. He had attended school in France, spoke French, and received an engineering degree from the University of Saigon. He owned a factory and a trucking company with 350 trucks. In 1975 he and eighteen members of his extended family were forced to flee Vietnam. For a time the family was among the 'boat people' aboard a merchant ship packed with 2,700 refugees. Via Guam the group finally got to Camp Pendleton. Loc Le possessed only the clothes on his back, no shoes, even lost his eyeglasses in the ordeal at sea. It was nearly impossible to relocate his family because they wanted to remain together, all eighteen. Finally Our Lord's Catholic Church in OKC sponsored them. Loc Le had never heard of Oklahoma.

In his first job in OKC Loc received $2.10 an hour. He saved enough money to make a down payment on a failed dirty little restaurant named Jimmy's Egg. (You can guess where this story is going.)

Loc Le kept the "Jimmy's Egg" name...now 16 restaurants, four in Florida, and many patrons call Loc "Jimmy."

This story has all the components of a New Testament history saga: faith in God, fellowship in Christ, and follow the guidance of the Spirit. What one sows one reaps.

We add to this the factor of 'good luck,' i.e., 'providence.'

God, thank you for your hand in the story of people around the world. Christ, thank you for your grace. Spirit of God, thank you giving people love, joy, and peace. Amen

Come, let us sing for joy to the Lord; let us shout aloud to the
Rock of our salvation. Let us come before him with thanksgiving
and extol him with music and song. Psalm 95:1-2

Our rented flat in Edinburgh was near the university and several libraries. Looking out at the Edinburgh Castle the quiet tomb like qualities of the 18th century building, named Ramsay Garden after the famous Scottish poet, this flat seemed like the ideal place to glue oneself to the writing desk and compose a doctoral dissertation. Until one day I discovered that a musician practicing for the Edinburgh International Music and Arts Festival had moved in next door. This guy practiced by the hour, by day, by night. Maybe on the third morning, I failed to tame the savage spirits of irritation when the musician, a cellist, began playing the scales—for two straight hours. So I went to introduce myself and talk about this problem. I was also plain curious; he really played beautiful music. Why would any one this good be playing scales for two hours?

Two minutes later I learned this: my neighbor was Mstislav Rostropovich from the U.S.S.R. Some say the "greatest cellist of the second half of the 20th century." "Why the scales?" I asked. He said, "I have to prepare for a concert. It is essential for me to practice the fundamental notes. Each note must be as nearly perfect as I can play it."

I thanked him for the meeting, said, "I love listening to your practices," and learned a lesson again. *We must never forget the fundamentals of the game.* I heard that from coaches on the playing field, from professors in the seminars. There are some fundamentals of our faith that must be practiced intently to produce the grand symphony of belief: dedication to Christ, forgiveness, acceptance of others, openness to the leading of God.

Thank you, Christ, for your followers who do the basics of faithfulness. Amen

God was pleased through the foolishness of what was preached to save those who believe...Just as a body, though one, has many parts, but all its many parts form one body, so it is with Christ...Now you are the body of Christ. I Corinthians 1:21; 12:12ff

What would the ideal community of faith look like? Once I was in a "think tank" (a somewhat self-aggrandized name) at a research center whose job assignment was to "think of the ideal community for the future needs of a state." One scientist had been a member of the Apollo Space Program management team. He had lots of ideas about the ideal "space community." These are notes from what I heard. The scientist credited Buckminster Fuller, *et al*, for these ideas. It was important stuff to consider in the context of the "eminent demise of the earth's population through apocalyptic events," some of those think tank scientists reasoned. The ideal community's social criteria:

A common script to which each is absolutely committed. Commitment to work as an ensemble, not unanimity but harmonically. Uniformity for the common good, and diversity for individuals to co-exist. Group practices conducted daily to concentrate psychic energy on the transcendental. Expect conflict between the "engineer" and the "poet." Community expiation must be provided to protect morale.

I think I read about these six points years before attending the so-called "think tank" meeting. These six points are two thousand years old! See Paul's "Letter to the Church at Corinth," written in *circa* 55 A.D.

By the way, I like Bucky Fuller's motto: "Dare to be naive." I like Paul's too: "The foolishness of God is wiser than men."

Whose naive fool are you? You get to choose your leader, and choose your community.

Thank you, God, for making us a part of the Body of Christ serving the world with his grace. Amen

(This day's devotion is by Jeff Sandefer, my son-in-law, on his birthday.) A good name is rather to be chosen than great riches, and loving favour rather than silver and gold. Proverbs 22:1

My great-grandfather was president of a small religious college for over thirty years. He is buried on the campus, and engraved on his headstone are the first words of Proverbs 22:1: "A good name is rather to be chosen than great riches."

I never met my great-grandfather. He died before I was born. But as a small child I often visited that campus, and the words on his headstone have had a powerful impact on my life.

The scripture spoke clearly one point: money and riches would not lead to happiness, satisfaction, or fulfillment. But still I struggle with the epitaph. What does it mean to have a "good name?"

Certainly a "good name" had little to do with fame. Still, the phrase suggests that one should be known for something. For moral conduct? Perhaps, but the Pharisees thought of themselves as having a spotless moral record, that included sending Jesus to His death. To act in a kind way? Yet, sometimes, speaking the truth is necessary, even if it doesn't seem kind.

I'm still praying for inspiration and direction as to how I should lead my life, so as to "choose a good name." As I've grown older, the last part of Proverbs 22:1, the part left off my great-grandfather's headstone, has called to me more and more. Perhaps the most precious "silver and gold" in life comes from being in relationship with God, from which a "good name" will naturally follow.

For certain, we all long to hear that blessing so beautifully written in Matthew, a blessing that tells us that we have found favor with our Lord: "Well done, my good and faithful servant."

Thank you, God, for the rich heritage of our faith passed to us by men and women who received your loving favor. We thank you for their disciplined faithfulness. In Christ. Amen

Dear friends, let us love one another, for love comes from God. Everyone who loves has been born of God and knows God. I John 4:7

Do you ever get a little negativity in your daily dose of reality? Some times we solve a problem by withdrawing from it. Simply turn off the TV or smart phone streaming station F.E.A.R. News. A healthy way to recover the attitude of gratitude is to see love in action.

Nearly always, truth is a relationship. I cannot conceive of an idea, or definition of "truth" for a person that does not in-volve a relationship. I read a study by a research scientist on this subject; she had both M.D. and Ph.D. degrees. She stud-ied the biographic data of scientists who voiced agnosticism about the validity of faith. The list included some famous and some lesser-known scientists. An inter-esting correlation ran through the cases in the study. Largely, this group of men and women did not have good relationships with parents and other adult mentors in the homes they experienced as children and youths.

Arguably we can surmise that our un-derstanding of any "truths" regarding our lives and personhoods are learned and be-lieved because of some relationship with one or more other persons. This means we cannot discuss the validity of a "truth" that involves our minds and emotions in a purely objective dimension. To know the "truth" about love in my life is sub-jective, and always involves a relationship with someone. These relationships may be negative and destructive, or positive and affirmative, forming how I know the "truth" about love.

Is this not why the "Incarnation of God's Love" in Christ is crucial? We know God's love in the relationship of faith in Jesus and the relationships of those who believe Christ.

We thank you for meeting us, O God, in human flesh and history, in Jesus Christ. Amen

Once, on being asked by the Pharisees when the kingdom of God would come, Jesus replied, "The coming of the kingdom of God is not something that can be observed, nor will people say, 'Here it is,' or 'There it is,' because the kingdom of God is in your midst." Luke 17:20-21

This revolutionary theme makes faith in Christ unlike all institutional religions. The presence God is 'in your midst.' God's rule is not confined to the place of priestly presentations of culturally accepted mores of an organization representing God. The radical (the Latin basis of this word is "root") truth of faith in Christ sets the believer free from the human structures and positions of power that attempt to control followers without setting them free, forgiven, and loved. New Testament theology is grounded in this primary premise of Jesus' teaching—"the kingdom of God is in you." It is closer to you than the priests, pastors, and properties of the church. It is nearer to you than the words, wisdom, and communications of the church, synagogue or temple. God's true altar is in your heart and his Spirit is the flame.

This new message of Jesus is not popular to persons who confine the conveyance of the Word to a special class of people selected by an institutional order empowered by habit and tradition.

This new message of Jesus, 'the kingdom of God is in your midst,' sets the faithful disciple free, on the one hand, but on the other hand, like "liberty," that gift comes with "responsibility." The Latin antecedent of "responsibility" is *re-spondere*, which means "answer, or, to answer." I deeply appreciate the gift Jesus announces in this teaching. I accept the gift. Now, the hard question: "Am I able to 'answer to God' for the way I use this gift?"

Lord, help me be a responsible citizen in your new kingdom of love and grace. Amen

Then their eyes were opened and they recognized him. They asked each other, "Were not our hearts burning within us while he talked with us on the road and opened the Scriptures to us?" Luke 24:31-32

There are times we are overcome with love to the extent that is hard to find words to describe the feeling. Such is the case of two, unnamed persons by the writer Luke, who met the risen Christ on the road to Emmaus. W.H. Auden took scintillating excursions into the descriptions of love; however, in one definition of real love, Auden simply said: "Among those whom I like, I can find no common denominator, but among those whom I love, I can; all of them make me laugh." I am sure there was laughter in the hearts of those who knew and loved Jesus. It is there today, in the hearts of those who know and love Jesus.

The witnesses to this joyous reality of love are everywhere. For example, *GQ* magazine's cover photo and feature story (September 2013) on RG3, Robert Griffin III, quarterback for the Washington Redskins, cannot dismiss or minimize the pure joy, love, and laughter around RG3. His life is grounded by faith in Christ and love of family. The fact that RG3 is a great athlete influences others to question, and perhaps find, the same source of joy.

Once I heard the world famous writer and psychiatrist Erick Fromm lecture on the topic of his best selling book, *The Art of Loving.* Not a few in the large university audience at Cal Berkeley would be in the category of "the cultured despisers" of faith. Fromm emphatically said: "Love is the only sane satisfactory answer to the problem of human existence."

I heard no one say, "I don't understand what he's saying." True love needs no collaborative witnesses. Real love is a truth that stands on its own record. God has shown his love to us in Christ.

Lord God, I humbly thank you for the joy and love experienced through faith in you. Amen

The cords of death entangled me; the torrents of destruction overwhelmed me. In my distress I called to the Lord: I cried to my God for help...I love you, Lord, my strength. The Lord is my rock, my fortress and my deliverer, in whom I take refuge. Psalm 18:1ff

Elizabeth Barrett Browning, in "Proof and Disproof," gives voice to the distressed heart of one pressed by the 'torrents of destruction that overwhelm' the soul. "Dost thou love me, my Beloved? / Only thou canst answer yes! / And, thou gone, the proof's disapproved, / And the cry rings answerless—/ Dost thou love me, my Beloved?"

In Greek mythology, the story of *Tantalus* pictures the condition of human yearning in the midst of continuous distress. Tantalus was condemned for his crimes to stand forever in water up to his neck. Trees laden with luscious fruit hung over his head. When he was hungry and tried to reach the fruit, the bows moved the fruit out of his reach. When he was thirsty, and bent down to drink, the water receded. All efforts were futile. This continued forever. It is from this story that we have the word "tantalizing" in our vocabulary.

In the crucible of an unbearable distress, we have one choice left, the leap of faith. Put the old proverb into action: "Whatever you can do, or dream you can, begin it. Boldness has genius, power, and magic in it." Paul said, "Work out your own salvation with fear and trembling, for God is at work in you." The Psalmist felt the hopelessness of the 'cords of death that entangled him,' and that is when he "cried out to God," in a grand leap of faith, and found he was not alone. God is there, in the abyss of despair. God is our Rock and Salvation.

By your intervening grace, O God, save me from the abyss of despair. You are my Rock and Salvation. Amen

(Today's devotion is by Betty Catching, my mother-in-law, on her birthday.)

For this reason I kneel before the Father, from whom every family in heaven and on earth derives its name. I pray that out of the glorious riches he may strengthen you with power through his Spirit in your inner being, so that Christ may dwell in your hearts through faith. And I pray that you, being rooted and established in love, may have power, together with all the Lord's holy people, to grasp how wide and long and high and deep is the love of Christ. Ephesians 3:14-19

Lord, I come to you—just as I am—seeking solace, seeking affirmation, seeking acceptance, forgiveness—seeking you, your presence, your voice. Where shall I find you? Your voice comes to me, "Rejoice, rejoice, rejoice! I will never leave you nor forsake you; it's a promise. I'm with you always."

The Lord is my strength and my salvation. The Lord is perfect in all ways. He is in control. He guides me, orders my life force, puts people and places and things before me in perfect timing—never too early, never too late. He has the plan. He works the plan. His plan works! Praise God, all is well. He will take my burdens, my concerns, and work them out to his plan.

Help me, God, to follow your course laid out for me. Help me to see others as you see them, to see situations as you see them. Help me to listen to your voice, obey your commands, accept wherever and whatever situation I find myself in, knowing you will turn whatever evil—or my own stubbornness and arrogance—into good.

My prayer, Lord, is that everyone could feel your glorious presence—may I doubly request this exuberance for my specially loved ones whom I've prayed for these past years. You know them so well. My prayer is that they will know you intimately as well. Amen

Who among the gods is like you, Lord? Who is like you—majestic in holiness, awesome in glory, working wonders? (Moses' song of deliverance after God led Israel out of Egypt) Exodus 15:11

Eternal God, Creator and Redeemer of life, I humbly thank you for the mystery of this momentous moment. I am praying. I cannot explain this experience to anyone who has not experienced prayer, nor can I explain love to anyone who has never loved.

Is it that we are indeed 'created in your image?' That the ineffably sublime existence of your loving and holy presence becomes a part of my deepest consciousness, if I stand still in awe and wonder?

Give us this day our daily wonderment.

Miracles are with me each day as the earth is bathed in sunlight. If I come into the open from behind the walls of self-concentration, perhaps then I may see. Let me not look down like Narcissus who gazed into his own image until drowning in fascination with himself. I must look up to the highest power and glory, to you, Almighty God, to you, loving Christ, to you, comforting Holy Spirit.

I searched for you in human constructions of thought. I searched for you as the reasonable word that completes a logical syllogism. I did not find you at the conclusion of a mathematical principle. I found you in the equation of love.

You were pursuing me; you found me. Soon I found "the heart has reasons that reason knows nothing of."*

You are the living Spirit that fills my empty heart. May I pause before the simple astonishments of life in reverence for the blessings of air, food, water, wine, and the nourishing companionship of others.

Every thing good comes from you, including this communion of prayer. Amen (Pascal)

*Unless a kernel of wheat falls to the ground and dies,
it remains only a seed. But if it dies, it produces many seeds
...For this reason I came to this hour. John 12:24ff*

Mount Saint Helens stood in a noble line of the Cascade Mountains of my home state. Mountains seem to be monumental reminders of grandeur that you can always count on—changeless, constant, solid, visible markers of true direction. We need those "feelings" engendered by mountains. Unlike the timeless mountains, our era is marked by aimless mobility, and restless ambiguity of mores.

Nevertheless, even mountains experience massive upheaval and change.

In 1980, Mt. St. Helens erupted in a volcano. The beautiful symmetrical snow capped apex blew up into the sky. Four thousand degree molten lava mowed down forests, filled emerald colored lakes, and scraped to the bare bones of black rock her millennia old soils. Some said, "Life will never come again to Mt. St. Helens."

Three years later. A forest ranger found a clump of wild flowers growing tenaciously on an escarpment. He looked again. The flowerbed was in the perfect form of an elk, lying on its side. Investigating the scene he discovered that plants had sprouted from the organic material where an elk had been struck down and buried in the volcanic ash from the fiery mountain: *A Patch of Flowers on a Mountain of Death.*

When we follow the gospel with the teachings of Jesus, his horrendous death, the glorious resurrection, and the Spirit that creates a church of disciples, we are following the steps of God's creative renewal in human history. Like the mountain, everything is changed, everything seems to be destroyed, and yet, everything is new and transformed, and one thing is constant: God and his grace.

God, thank you for the hope given in your creative grace that transforms despair, destruction, and death in my life. Amen

Forget the former things; do not dwell on the past.
See, I am doing a new thing! Now it springs up; do you not perceive it?
Isaiah 43:18-19

Lord, you are the creator of the earthy aromas of life. Imaginatively, you have given us the pungent memories of events, places, and living beings. Thank you for the memory of scent: the scent of a baby's skin, soft as a rose petal; the scent of newly plowed soil; the scent of a horse's neck touched by the rider's face as he whispers 'thanks for a great ride'; the scent of the desert at midnight when the cactus is in bloom; the scent of the kitchen at the ranch house filling the country air with an invitation 'hot cinnamon rolls are ready'; the scent of the ocean borne on the Pacific breeze.

Thank you, God, for the urban memories; each city has its collective scent of individual aromatic signature. Each of these places are home to millions of people you love, each is fragrantly distinctive: Bangkok, Beirut, Cape Town, Hong Kong, Paris—sweet, musky, spicy, piquant.

Memories of the preferred perfumes and colognes of beloved ones remind us there is lovely beauty and the holiness of life. Memories of the sensuous aromas of springtime—the crocuses, anemone, sanguinaria, ghost flowers, hyacinth, and daffodils pushing through the last springtime snow—these are symbols of resurrection.

The whole earth itself is a great temple filled with the swirling incense of tens of thousands of scents. Lord, the memory of 'imagined' scent deepens our love and attraction to the truth—the fragrance of the costly perfume a woman poured on the feet of Jesus as she wiped his feet with her hair; the fragrance of the perfumes brought to the birth of Jesus in Bethlehem; the perfume poured out on his body at the tomb in the garden after Golgotha. We remember, and we thank you, God, for all the dimensions of love enlarged by *the scent of life.* Amen

These people who have been turning the world upside down have come here also. Acts 17:6

Jesus entered the narrative of history at an inauspicious time and created a dramatic turning point. Rome had 'conquered the world,' a euphemism for the greater Mediterranean countries on three continents. Palestine was the least prominent province. Galilee was its 'outback.' Widespread poverty created the seedbed of revolt. The Roman army instilled political and economic order. The leaders of the Temple in Jerusalem tried to supplement political order with social and religious order.

Into this heap of rigid political and religious orthodoxy Jesus came. He spent time with 'sinners' and 'tax-collectors' making him unpopular with the orthodox religious leaders. He allowed an 'unclean woman' into his fellowship at a banquet observed by the public. He endorsed the faithfulness of a non-Jewish Roman centurion saying he had not seen faith so great in all of Israel. Jesus broke the Jewish rules of Sabbath-keeping. He touched and communicated with lepers, the 'untouchables.' Jesus gave healing and spiritual counsel to a Samaritan woman. Jews hated Samaritans, and of course, Jesus was a Jew. Having zealots as some of his disciples made Jesus suspect to Rome.

Jesus raised fears of both religious and political rulers for two reasons: he associated with all of the 'wrong' people, and worse than that, he was popular with the general public, therefore, dangerous.

The 'penniless preacher from Nazareth' was put to death. After the resurrection of Christ and with the Spirit's leadership of his followers, this band of Christians became known throughout the mighty Roman Empire as "people who turn the world upside down."

What do you think the power of this movement is? I will accept the simple answer of Paul, who had been among those tyrannical religious bigots against Jesus. The power is the grace of God in Christ Jesus.

This power is alive here and now.

God, I am overwhelmed by the humble strength of your grace to accept, forgive, and renew the spirit within me. Thank you. Amen

*Love the Lord your God with all your heart and with all your soul
and with all your strength. These commandments that I give you today
are to be on your hearts. Deuteronomy 6:4*

St. John of the Cross, in the 16th century, wrote an evocative comment: "In the evening of life we shall be judged by love alone." I say 'evocative' because it raises for me a really strong question: I believe the statement is true, will it be true for my life? Imagine an opportunity to ask God one question, and imagine God's answer to your one ques-tion. I would ask the question raised by philosophy throughout the ages: "What's this thing called life all about?" I imagine God's answer would be, "It's a love story."

Paul gave the rationale of his letter: "I want you to grasp, to know the love of Christ than surpasses knowledge." How do we know the unknowable?

First: we must see a new reality. Astronauts who return from space journeys tell us stories of what it is like to see planet earth from space, this world, this place we call 'home;' fragile intertwined networks of oceans, continents seemly suspended, floating in light and darkness, a spherical temple of beauty that is one spinning gem in a space full of billions and billions of larger stars and planets, a single entity interconnected. "God so loved the (whole earth) he sent his son" to reveal that love to us. We cannot see that much love. We can see Jesus through the record of scriptures. He shows us the 'unsearchable' heart of God.

Second: we know the unknowable when we truly love, and have been truly loved. 'Love has reasons that reason doesn't know.' The truth of love is in a relationship.

This day, Lord, I am overwhelmed by your love, and I am delighted by faith that I may love you. Amen

> *I will praise your name for your unfailing love and your*
> *faithfulness...When I called, you answered me; you greatly*
> *emboldened me. Psalm 138:2-3*

Gratitude dispels negativity. I wish I could only remember the conferences I had with people in crisis that had successful outcomes. This is one. A husband and wife wanted to visit about their "marriage problems." That is not technically correct; it should read, "A husband came with his wife who wanted to talk about their marriage problems." Both wife and husband had verbal lists of grievances. One item she listed, "He never, ever thanked me for anything I have done or who I am." "Is that true?" "Suppose so." "Do you like your three kids? They seem like good kids." "Well, yes." "Let's start there: please, looking into your wife's eyes, say the name of each child in a sentence, 'Thank you for your part in the birth of _____.' Repeat this for each of the three kids." After he did this for the first born child, the couple began to cry, first apart, then arm in arm. The guy never got through the 'naming' of all three children. Without dealing with 'all the issues' of the marriage, the couple began to talk about the things for which they were grateful, specific items, about their life together. They're still together.

Some wrongly see the "Old Testament" and "New Testament" as dispensations of different gods. The "old" God is a lord of "laws." The "new" God is a lord of "love." "God is Love" can be said of all the ages and forever. The Hebrew Scriptures use a beautiful word describing God. The word is 'mercy,' in Hebrew *khehsed.* It means 'steadfast, loving kindness, mercy.' Psalm 138:8: "Your *khehsed* endures forever."

Gratitude dispels negativity. Gratitude saves marriages.

This day let us be grateful for God's loving kindness, the *khehsed* and *agape* of the Lord.

Forgive me, Lord, for my days and nights of ingratitude. This moment I begin a new day with a grateful heart. Amen

Your Father has been pleased to give you the kingdom
...For where your treasure is, there your heart will be also. Luke 12:32ff

Commitment is the source of contentment. The most debatable point of this axiom is "commitment to what, to whom." Over the years I have seen the general truth of this declaration in persons who have this in common: each has a sense of contentment because each has made commitments to God in work, wisdom, and wealth.

Not everyone has abundance in all three gifts, but all of us have the potential to make commitments to God in two of the three categories. Some followers of Christ make commitments of wealth and wisdom, some work and wealth, some work and wisdom. Christ is served by each one.

Laurence Olivier was one of the greatest actors of all time, however, he said: "I do not want to be known as a great actor, I want to be known as a workman. I think God is a workman who works at his creations. God has made this beautiful creation and recreates it, reworks it, and remolds it. He is a workman." Over and over again when we see greatness displayed in a performance, we are witnessing a "workman" at work. Great performances do not just flow miraculously in the spontaneous moment of our observation. Warren Buffet works at his field of expertise, investment wisdom. Serena Williams works at her tennis profession with hundreds of hours of disciplined practice year after year. Leontyne Price practiced 10,000 hours before she became an opera singer. The late Millard Fuller, the founder of Habitat for Humanity, worked years to develop wealth, and then worked hard, using Christian wisdom, to give away his wealth.

Lord God, I have some portion of three gifts: work, wisdom, and wealth. May I be committed, generous, and experience contentment in your kingdom. Amen

Where the Spirit of the Lord is, there is freedom.
II Corinthians 3:17

The gospel sets us free. Freedom is quintessential to the New Testament message. Give an enslaved person, or an enslaved people, the New Testament and the potential of revolution is at hand. The lyrics of this freedom song come from William Cowper: "Ye fearful saints fresh courage take; the clouds ye so much dread are big with mercy, and shall break in mercy upon your head."

This is a frequently quoted medieval fable. A stonecutter was working a great quarry cutting stones for a cathedral. He saw a rich merchant walk by. He wished he were that man. His wish was granted. He met a king, and wished to be that man, and he became a king. He saw the mighty sun in the sky, and wished to be the sun and so it was. A cloud divided the sun from the earth, he wished to be a cloud, and so it was. The cloud struck against a mighty mountain of rock, he wished he were the rock, and so it was. He saw a stonecutter fashioning stones for a cathedral…"

In Christ we are set free from the past through his forgiving grace. In Christ we are free to become the true person of our calling and vocation from God. 'Freedom sets me free, to be me.' Audaciously claim the gift God has given you. Don't compare yourself to someone else, as John Lydgate said (circa. 1440): "Comparisons are odious."

Lord Christ, I hear your words that you 'came to us to give us life and have it more abundantly.' Thank you for calling me to be free to serve you, love others, and discover my true identity. You graciously let me repent of old destructive forces in my life. You freed me from the shackles of regrets. You empower me with your Spirit. May your Great Name be Praised. Amen

*Now there was a Pharisee, a man named
Nicodemus who was a member of the Jewish ruling council.
He came to Jesus at night. John 3:1ff*

Good things happen at night. It is true that "darkness, midnight, and shadows" often are metaphors that connote "fear, despair, and regret." God "who never sleeps or slumbers" is Lord of both day and night. God called us "out of darkness into his marvelous light." The power of the cross was at work in the blackest night of time. Nicodemus heard the gospel from Jesus at night. Good things happen at nighttime.

I see Mr. Wise Old Owl, who lives near our home, go to work at night. His passion to feed his family is a nocturnal mission. Many beautiful flowers bloom only at night. Their white, pink, yellow, orange, and purple blossoms concoct a splendid palette of colors, if you have night vision. The nocturnal sphinx moth pollenates flowers at night. In the cool midnight breeze the evening primrose shows off its gorgeous yellow blossoms. The same primrose is famous for its medicinal powers. Night bloom water lilies are deep crimson red or pink with night-time blossoms measuring ten inches in diameter. Moon flowers blossom only in moonlight. And the night gladiolus (from the Latin word meaning "sword") shows off creamy yellow petals that attract butterflies and bees. The Creator demonstrated special interests for women who love expensive perfumes, and men who pretend not to be influenced by them. The Casa Blanca lily, more fragrant at night, is used in exotic perfumes.

Fear is a condition of the brain. The nighttime of God's world is not to be feared. God meets us in our "nights of fear" and calls us into his marvelous light.

You, O Christ, are the light of the world that we first see in our own night times of fear. Amen

> *Each of you should give what you have decided in your*
> *heart to give, not reluctantly or under compulsion, for God loves*
> *a cheerful giver. II Corinthians 9:7*

Consider these stages of giving: 1. 'Give a little' and grouse about the recipient organization. 2. 'Give a little more ' and feel ambiguous about it. 3. 'Give more until it hurts,' and quit giving. 4. 'Give even more until it feels good' and enjoy your giving cheerfully. Some people are all hat and no cattle when it comes to giving. Others are real. Here are examples of giving as an expression of faith and personal calling. I chose persons of capital means because too often they have been 'dissed' as a group.

Grace Groner: Grace worked as a secretary at Abbott Laboratories for 43 years. In 1935 she bought three shares of Abbott stock at $60 per share. Her investment grew. She lived modestly and when she died, she willed to her alma mater, Lake Forest College, the largest gift in its history—$7 million.

Karl Rabeder of Austria earned millions of dollars, spent millions on homes, vacation sites, luxuries. He didn't like it, said his lifestyle was "soulless." He sold all the "stuff." He plans to spend all his wealth through a micro charity he created to serve poor people in Central and South America.

Chuck Feeney made a fortune from co-creating Duty Free Shoppers Group in airports from Hong Kong to Honolulu. His enormous donations are given through Atlantic Philanthropies for the aging, children in need, reconciliation, and human rights. Chuck doesn't own a home or a car.

Grace, Karl, and Chuck experienced the joy of giving. God, the giver of all we possess, knows the joy of giving: "For joy set before (Christ) he endured the cross."

God, the giver of grace and liberty through Christ, we dedicate our giving to you. Amen

Each of you should look not only to your own interests,
but also to the interest of others. Your attitude should be the same
as that of Christ Jesus. Philippians 2:4ff NRSV

Lord of life, I live in a world where justice is in jeopardy. I pray for a world where people experience balance, the balance of power and justice. You have shown me, O Lord, that I could not be free without justice. I pray that the powerless shall not be dispossessed, and the powerful may be just.

You revealed the balancing of power and moral right in Jesus, who never compromised justice for popularity or privilege. Christ, your justice is hard, not because it is without love, but precisely because it is love. You teach me, O God, that all the true justice I experience has come from sacrificial living of others. Christ, you suffered and died that I may live. You have created in me a heart that is restless in the presence of injustice. You have shown us what is right. In your will, Lord, justice is compassion in action. Evil hates justice, but never succeeds against your love.

Christ, you reveal the final victory of love over evil in the cross. Your agape love creates reconciliation where the forces of culture demand retaliation. You vindicate the sacrificial lives of those who served others with the supreme goodness of justice. Your grace is astonishing.

Lord, I use the words of your servant* to confess: "Life *without you is* but a walking shadow, a poor player, that struts and frets his hour upon the stage, and then is heard no more; it is a tale told by an idiot, full of sound and fury, signifying nothing." You have overcome the fury of nothingness with the substance of redeeming grace.

Let me share power with those who are powerless, and love with those who live without justice. In the name of the Father, Son, and Holy Spirit. Amen
*William Shakespeare

*You have searched me, Lord, and you know me...Before a word
is on my tongue you, Lord, know it completely...Search me, God,
and know my heart. Psalm 139:1ff*

This day our devotion is on the subject: "God's Discovery of You." According to the Bible, God creates, initiates, redeems, and sustains the relationship of love with persons. The Psalmist does not write, "I searched for you;" rather, "You, Lord, searched for me."

Let's do a retrospective on our faith: "How did my faith begin?" "Who started the relationship?" I believe most would say, "God did. God used intermediaries." God is not a passive role player watching the human drama from the wings of the stage.

French biologist Jacques Monod, who calls himself an agnostic, makes this assessment: "The ancient covenant is in pieces; man at last knows that he is alone in the unfeeling immensity of the universe, out of which he has emerged only by chance. Neither his destiny nor his duty have been written down."*(Chance and Necessity)*

Monod is old energy. Hosea said the same thing more than 2,700 years earlier.

"There is no truth or mercy or knowledge of God in the land. By lying, killing, committing adultery...my people are destroyed for the lack of knowledge of God." (Hosea 4:1ff)

The evidence of history shows the conditions described by Hosea and Monod are not static. God intervenes in history. God invades in history, the human story. God takes the initiative to reveal his loving kindness and presence of a man, Jesus, who is the true Christ.

There is always a race between belief and unbelief, between faith and catastrophe. Fear not. God shall never forsake his creation. Christ shall never withdraw his grace. His grace is sovereign.

Lord, you came to us in Jesus Christ as the Word made flesh, to love the world, not to condemn the world. We accept; we believe; we follow your love in Christ. Amen

When the fullness of time had come, God sent his Son...God has sent the Spirit of his Son into our hearts, crying, "Abba! Father!" So you are no longer a slave but a child, and if a child then also an heir, through God. Galatians 4:4 NRSV

"Fullness of time" is, translated in Greek, *kairos. Chronos*, on the other hand, is "measured time" such as the "time of day" you see on your smart phone. *Kairos* is "a special time, as in good-timing." A great quarterback has a perfect read on a wide receiver who breaks into the open, away from an equally fast cornerback, to catch a football that is "there" *just at the exact instant* to be caught for a winning touchdown. In the post game interview we hear the words to the quarterback, "you had perfect timing" on that throw. That's *kairos*, not *chronos*.

What was the perfect timing for the birth of Christianity? God chose it. *Pax Romana*, the Roman Empire's 'peace' insured by its broadly cast military; education in two common languages—Greek and Latin; Roman roads and Roman protection of water routes that enhanced trade, travel, and international commerce; cultural exchange and the existence of a monotheistic ethical religion in a multinational setting—Judaism. These are a few of the ingredients that made the first decades of the 1st century the "fullness of time." This *kairos* was chosen by God to invade the world by incarnating his presence in the personhood of one human being. The Chosen One is the penniless Teacher of Nazareth. There was not a better *kairos* before, or since, for this historic turning point to take place. Christ became the center that makes sense of the human narrative.

This "timely" presence of God provides a needed center to my tiny personal 'universe,' without which I am spinning out of control in an undefined geometry of meaninglessness.

Thank you, Eternal Father, Lord of all life, for intersecting our humanity in the time and place of Jesus of Nazareth. In Jesus Christ we meet you and receive the Spirit in fullness of grace and truth. Amen

Therefore this is what the Sovereign Lord says
...I will create new heavens and a new earth...I will rejoice over Jerusalem
and take delight in my people. Isaiah 65:13,19

The writer of our text is not reticent to describe the emotions of the Lord God. I hope you can feel a bit of inner joy as you meditate on the "delight" of God. When I was at the University of Edinburgh, one of my favorite mind-wanderings was to think about the life and times of the many great persons who graduated from that Scottish university. As I walked by the offices of the College of Humanities, I was reminded that Eric Liddell, who enrolled in 1920, lived at 56 George Square. It was easy to 'see' him running to class.

The Academy Award-winning movie, "Chariots of Fire," introduced Liddell to the world. He held the world's record in the 400 meters set at the 1924 Olympics in Paris. For reasons of his Presbyterian faith, he would not run in the 100 meters race because the first heats were held on Sunday. Liddell was known for his speed, his modesty, ordination to ministry as a missionary, and holding to his convictions in all circumstances. He died in a Japanese interment camp in China in 1945. He was one of a few selected to leave the camp in January of 1945, but he gave his 'pass' to a pregnant woman. He died of malnutrition and related illnesses a month later. The war ended in August of 1945.

Eric Liddell said, "I believe God made me for a purpose, but he also made me fast. And when I run *I feel His pleasure.*"

It is my prayer that you delight in the Lord, for he delights in you. And when you do the purpose in life for which God calls you, may you *"feel His pleasure."*

Thank you, God, for the integrity and joy revealed in witnesses to your presence in life. Amen

Wide is the gate and broad is the road that leads to destruction, and many enter through it. But small is the gate and narrow the road that leads to life, and only a few find it. Matthew 7:13-14

Luke Skywalker speaking to Yoda, his Jedi Knights instructor: "I'll try to do it." Yoda: "For Jedi Knights there is no 'Try.' There is only 'Do,' just do it."

When we face what seems to be an impossible task, such as working and praying for a major change in the moral direction of life, for a person, or a society, perhaps we will consider Yoda, and Jesus. 'Take the road less travelled' by entering the 'narrow gate' that 'only a few find.'

I believe major league sports have done more to overcome the injustices of racism in American society than all the churches' efforts combined. Eleven a.m. on Sunday is the most segregated hour of the American week. Of course sports and church cannot be separated, because it is the moral instinct of Christians who are members of churches who, in part, have been instrumental in changes for good. Take, for example, Branch Rickey, a Methodist Church member.

Before he became President of the Brooklyn Dodgers Baseball team, he was coach at Ohio Wesleyan University. One night, before a game with Notre Dame, the team was checking into a South Bend hotel. One black player, Charles Thomas, was on the team. The clerk looked at Thomas and said, "No." Rickey said, "He will sleep in my room." That night Branch Rickey saw Thomas crying, looking at his hands... "If only I could make them white." Rickey said, "Come on, Tommy, snap out of it, buck up. We'll lick this one day." Rickey, Yoda-like, taking the narrow road of Jesus, was a huge force for good in the next decades of change in the U.S.A. Think Jackie Robinson, Brooklyn Dodgers!

Lord, give me courage to enter the narrow gates of doing the hard 'right' thing and not follow culture's crowd through the wide gates of popular self-aggrandizement. Amen

I know that there is nothing better for people, than to be happy and to do good while they live, that each of them may eat and drink and find satisfaction in all their toil—this is the gift of God. Ecclesiastes 3:12-13

Jeremy Bentham is almost famous for two legacies. A philosopher and social reformer at University College London, he wrote the official British counterpoint to the Declaration of Independence, in 1776. His writing went nowhere, and it seems he was strongly influenced by the Americans. Bentham was against slavery, for free speech, for the separation of church and state. Some of his students were famous, like John Stuart Mill. Bentham was almost famous for his "Auto-icon." As per instructions of his will, Bentham's 'head' and 'body' were posthumously mummified, according to an ancient New Zealand rite, and put on display at the university.

As recently as 2013, at the 150th Anniversary of Bentham's death, the College Council brought "Bentham" (head only) to its board meeting. The official minutes of the meeting read: "Present but not voting."

Bentham is almost famous for inventing the Law of Diminishing Marginal Utility used by economists to this day. Some things are "marginal"—one does not have to have them, but some of those things have a useful purpose, that is, "utilitarian."

The law is at work all the time, in our lives, our marketplace and our purses and wallets. *We can become 'marginal commodities' in our consumer-oriented culture and lose our identity.* When given the status of god, materialism becomes a demon. The Law of Diminishing Marginal Utility takes control. The materialistic demon can destroy our soul.

I choose this day to be alive, "present and voting," for satisfaction that comes from work ordained by the Lord.

This day, Christ, I choose to follow you and discover the disciplines of the abundant life you have given us. Amen

Therefore, I urge you, brothers and sisters, in view of God's
mercy, to offer your bodies as a living sacrifice, holy and pleasing to
God—this is your true and proper worship. Romans 12:1

You never know in advance whom the Spirit of God calls to be the firebrand and leader of ethical reform that changes laws and behaviors of the whole society, but be ready to be surprised. It may be your sewing teacher.

Donaldina Cameron came to San Francisco in the 1870's to be a sewing teacher. She became the leader of a movement that has saved tens of thousands of lives. The Presbyterian Church started the Occidental Mission Home for Girls in 1874. It became the Cameron House. You have heard the phrase, "I've been Shanghaied," meaning one who is forced into captivity to do something you abhor doing. This happened to thousands of Chinese in the 19th century. Forced with threat of death onto ships in Shanghai China, sometimes sold by their destitute Chinese parents, they were brought to California to work gold mines, build railroads, become 'domestics'—slaves, and prostitutes. Donaldina Cameron organized a ministry that served the Chinese victims of horrific violence and discrimination. She raised money, offered protection, provided hospitality, created one of the best educational institutions in San Francisco, and worked with powerful political leaders to create just laws.

Great resume for a sewing teacher. She offered herself as a "living sacrifice" and we can be assured that her work was "holy and pleasing to God." As recently as the 1970's the Cameron House served 20,000 refugees a year. These were Chinese citizens who fled Mao Zedong's murderous political changes in China (estimates of deaths range from 30 to 100 million). Today, many of the leaders in the Bay Area are Asians who graduated from the Cameron House.

Disraeli said, "Justice is love in action." This sewing teacher put Christ's love into action.

To the greater glory of you, Eternal God: we are grateful for your servant, Donaldina Cameron, for her faithfulness to Christ. Amen

A person finds joy in giving an apt reply—and how good is a timely word. Proverbs 15:23. When Jesus had finished saying these things, the crowds were amazed at his teaching because he taught as one who had authority, and not as their teachers of the law. Matthew 7:28-29

Who are the three greatest teachers of all time? It could be Jesus, Buddha, and Socrates. Over one half of the 7.108 billion citizens on planet earth follow one of these teachers. (Some say Socrates never existed. I say if he didn't, he should have.)

The "Socratic Method" of teaching has continued for twenty-five centuries. Jesus employed the "*elenchus*" method of Socrates' dialectical style: refutation by 'a negative method of hypothesis elimination.'

A popular 'Socrates story' is paraphrased here. "A student wishing to confound the teacher, Socrates, with a question he could not answer, asked, 'I am holding a bird in my hand, is it dead or alive?' If Socrates said 'dead' the student would let the live bird fly away; if he said 'alive' the student would crush the bird and open his hand. Socrates replied, 'Whatever you will, it shall be.'"

Much of the truth taught by Jesus, the Living Word, comes down to this existential fact. What will you do? Christ's word is nothing if we do not hear, obey, and follow the teaching. Christ's word is everything if we do hear, obey, and follow the Word.

I don't agree with some teachings of William Jennings Bryan. I do like this thought: "Destiny is not a matter of chance, it is a matter of choice; it is not a thing to be waited for, it is a thing to be achieved." Jesus concluded The Sermon on the Mount, saying: "Therefore everyone who hears these words of mine *and puts them into practice* is like a wise man who built his house on the rock."

Thank you, eternal Father in heaven, you have sent us good mentors and teachers, especially I thank you for the teaching of Jesus Christ. Amen

Start children off on the way they should go,
and even when they are old they will not turn from it. Proverbs 22:6

"The Lion King" carries me to the heights of theatrical entertainment. All three of 'us' love this show: the 'child within', the 'seasoned adult,' and my 'alter ego' of unrequited optimism. Timon, the meerkat (Nathan Lane's voice in the movie) is a character based on Shakespeare's Timon of Athens. In Greek, the name means "he who respects." Timon's good friend is Pumbaa, a warthog, and his Kiswahili name means "careless." Timon and Pumbaa find Simba, a young cub in the desert, and save him from dying. They vow to protect Simba and raise him with a simple philosophy: "*Hakuna Matata!*" Kiswahili for "no problem, no worries!"

Simba grows happily under their tutelage. One day, his childhood friend, Nala, finds Simba; Timon and Pumbaa learn the true identity of their young charge. Simba is the *Lion King of the Pride Lands*. The four happy souls with their *Hakuna Matata* view of life go to the Pride Lands where their philosophy is challenged in a war against Scar and the Hyenas. The good guys win, and that's the part that assuages my alter ego.

How does "goodness" fair in this world? It does not always win the battles, but goodness wins the war. Was there ever a presence of "goodness" like we see in the key characters on the New Testament stage? Mary, the mother of Jesus; the converted Paul; Lydia, the 'seller of purple goods;' Thomas, after doubting his way to belief; Peter after becoming a real man; and of course, the lead character, Jesus. They faced good and evil circumstances with peace in their hearts. When the Lord wills it, "*Hakuna Matata!*"

Lord, you know I like a good ending to the story of life. In spite of momentary challenges, may I truly believe that you are the Lord of history and yours is the final victory. Amen

Blessed are those who are persecuted because
of righteousness, for theirs is the kingdom of heaven. Matthew 5:10

On August 10, 258 A.D., deacon Lawrence of Rome was executed by burning. The Roman emperor Valerian decreed all Christian bishops, ministers, and deacons put to death. Stories follow that time of persecution into the 21st century. It is said that Lawrence, a deacon under the leadership of Bishop Sixtus II, took the treasury of the Christians and gave the money to the poor. When asked by the magistrate in charge of the executions to surrender the money, Lawrence referred to the sick, the blind, and the beggars of Rome as the treasure of the church. Lawrence was tortured and burned to death.

One hundred years later, the famous Bishop Ambrose of Milan wrote about Lawrence in manuscripts we may read today. Emperor Constantine had a chapel built in Lawrence's memory. Later, Rome's Church of San Lorenzo (St. Lawrence) was built as a memorial to Lawrence's faithful ministry to Christ.

The whole world watched the televised rescue efforts at the mining accident site in Copiapó, Chile, in 2010. The successful rescue was called "Operacion San Lorenzo," after the martyred deacon St. Lawrence.

On August 10, annual remembrance services around the world recall the witness of Lawrence's "righteous" and courageous life. In subtle and surprising ways, the words of Jesus always come true, "Blessed are those who are persecuted for righteousness."

Lord and God of all, Risen Christ, the true head of the Church, Holy Spirit our comforter, I humbly acknowledge my inability to imagine the suffering paid for my life of faith and freedom today. I prayerfully remember Jesus on the cross. I remember the martyrs of unwavering courage. I remember the warriors in wars of liberation. I shall never forget the price paid for this priceless life. Amen

Keep me free from the trap that is set for me, for you are my refuge. Psalm 31:4
Does a bird swoop down to a trap on the ground when no bait is there? Amos 3:5

The scriptures give us two points of view about the various "entrapments" and conflicts that embroil our lives in despair, dissolution, and depression. The Psalmist pleads for help because *circumstances for which I have no control* have trapped me. To borrow a phrase from W.H. Auden, I live in a world "where ogres act like ogres." The first case is *Innocent Victim Trapped*. On the other hand, we have the prophetic perspective. I am caught in a trap, and as I gain insight into the predicament, I realize the trap was baited: *circumstances in which I have control*. I took the bait. *Preventable Entrapment*.

At the International Edinburgh Arts Festival I attended a "Fringe Festival" presentation featuring a mime. The mime was hilarious and provocative. Quiet Mediterranean music filled the background as the soundless mime acted out entrapment. In a small room, the audience soon learned the mime was caught in a room behind three locked doors. Of course the audience does not "see" the walls or doors that trap the mime. He hilariously bumps, bashes, and bangs against the adversarial constructions that trap him. As the silent narrative comes to the climax, the mime stops all activity, pauses, and walks off the set through the space where the back wall should have existed. It did only in the mind of the audience. We were all surprised. The superb acting of the mime had us believing he was trapped in a four-walled room, but he had never given any evidence that the back wall existed. Isn't this a parable of most of my problems? *Preventable Entrapment!*

Consider whatever entrapment affects your life: Innocent Victim, or Preventable Entrapment. Help comes from the One who is our Rock, our Refuge, our salvation.

Lord, you are the force that protects and rescues me from the entrapments of life. Thank you. Amen

*I praise you because I am fearfully and wonderfully
made: your works are wonderful, I know that full well. Psalm 139:14*

There is room for everyone in the science and faith dialogues. What is at stake is universal. For example, my ancient Scottish family motto is *Nil desperandum auspice Deo.* Is that true? Putting a motto on a coat of arms does not make it so. When I think, pray or meditate, I have come to believe that *Nothing is to be despaired under the guidance of God.*

Experience has taught me to trust good science. This includes among other things, two total knee replacements, open-heart surgery for aortic value replacement and the Maze Procedure for atrial fibrillation—repairing damages incurred from rheumatic fever at age 13. And I trust the good theology of our family motto, "Nothing is to be despaired under the guidance of God" whose presence "I know…full well."

A Nobel Prize winner, physicist Charles Townes puts the science and faith complementarity in clear words. "Science wants to know the *mechanism* of the universe, religion the *meaning*. The two cannot be separated. Many scientists feel there is no place in research for discussion of anything that sounds mystical. But it is unreasonable to think we already know enough about the natural world to be confident about the totality of forces."

Einstein lecturing at Princeton Seminary on May 19, 1939, with Europe already in war (his reason for being in the U.S.A.) told his audience: "It is clear that knowledge of what *is* does not open the door directly to what *should be*. I cannot conceive of a genuine scientist without that profound faith. The situation may be expressed by an image: science without religion is lame, religion without science is blind."

Lord God, I am grateful for great doctors who know good science, and a great and loving family and friends who believe in prayer. Amen

In the past God spoke to our ancestors through the prophets at many times and in various ways, but in these last days he has spoken to us by his Son...the radiance of God's glory and the exact representation of his being, sustaining all things by his powerful word. Hebrews 1:1ff

High in the hills of the Hindu Kush, with the Himalaya Mountains as background, we visited a peaceful Hindu "chapel" named after Ramakrishna. Upon entering, one sees pictures of Hindu religious leaders. Near the front is a picture of Jesus. I asked our Hindu guide about the picture, assuming that this must be an anomaly. He said, "No, in the view of Samsara and the Wheel of Life, we see Jesus as a part of the natural cycle of existence."

Sometimes when listening to a person wrestling with life's purpose, I may ask, "Do you feel like you are caught in a power of fate, a karma, a wheel of fortune over which there is no control?" Samsara is inculcated in Hinduism, Buddhism, and Taoism. It means "continuous flow" or "continuous cycle-existence." The Hindu guide used this term to explain his belief. The cycle-existence, represented by the 'Wheel of Life,' is an immutable motion. It cannot be changed by an outside force. Samsara believes we are moved through "six realms of existence." These are: gods, demigods, humans, animals, ghosts, and hell beings. Souls transmigrate, through reincarnation, through the cycle-existence.

"Parkway Drive" is a popular Australian Metalcore (fusion of punk and extreme metal) band. It is not a coincidence that their "hot" 2012 album's first song is entitled "Samsara." I think many people believe in determinism; every thing that happens is inevitable; "it is what it is, can't change a thing."

Consider an alternative faith described in Hebrews chapter one.

Thank you, God of sovereign love, for choice: I choose to follow Jesus Christ, I choose to enact his love in my relationships. I choose to do your will. Amen

*Now when Jesus saw the crowds, he went up on a mountainside
and sat down. His disciples came to him, and he began to teach them.
Matthew 5:1-2*

A teacher can cut the shackles of despair and create a sunrise of hope in a person's life. All good teachers have three qualities they transmit with ease to their students. A good teacher informs, delights, and inspires. Methods of teaching vary, but methodology is secondary to substance.

I hope you have heard this case history. It is the story of a person's life being saved by good teachers. The documentary film and *The New York Times* best selling memoir of Liz Murray illustrates what good teachers can do in the transformation of a person.

Liz went from homelessness to Harvard. The little girl Liz grew up in the Bronx, NYC. Her parents were hippies who became drug addicts; welfare checks were used to buy drugs; the church's gift of a Thanksgiving turkey was sold to buy a hit; no money for food, Liz recalls eating ice-cubes with her parents to "make us think we were eating;" they did share the contents of a tube of toothpaste, for dinner.

Mom died of AIDS; dad moved to a homeless shelter. Liz became a street person, homeless in the Bronx. Dad died of AIDS.

Liz had an epiphany. Go to high school at night. Got A's; teacher was wonderful; the teacher took Liz and nine others to visit Harvard; she received a *New York Times* scholarship; graduated from Harvard; received Oprah's "Chutzpah Award;" met the President of the U.S.A.

Today Liz is a motivational speaker positively influencing thousands of teenagers worldwide: "Don't use childhood hardships for excuses; drugs and gangs are killers; you have choices."

Jesus had a short time for his mission. He chose the role of "teacher." Matthew describes how the greatest mission of transformation in all of time began: "His disciples came to him, and he taught them."

God, thank you for the inspiration, instruction, and delights from teachers. Amen

*Love never fails...For now we see only a reflection as in a mirror;
then we shall see face to face. Now I know in part; then I shall know fully, even
as I am fully known. I Corinthians 13:8,12*

John Stuart Mill said, "There are many truths of which the full meaning cannot be realized until personal experience has brought it home." Saint Augustine reminds us that humble people may have a grand learning advantage over sophisticated "learned" people. He said, "See how the unlearned start up and take heaven by storm whilst we with all our learning grovel upon the earth."

Let us pray:

God, you came to us as a rabbi, a teacher. The first persons to accept you were learners. I have much to learn. Lord, continue to be my rabbi. I want to be a disciple. In learning, I must be willing to risk failure. In learning, I must be able to see change for good when it occurs in others, especially the beloved closest to me. I may learn from everybody. From the talkative, I learn silence. From the rude, I learn civility. From the heartless, I learn kindness. Help me, O God, to learn that humble wisdom is more important than many facts. I must confess that what I think I know can sometimes prevent me from learning what I don't know. When I face new truth, help me to be willing to unlearn and relearn.There are two vast spheres of being I yearn to learn more about. One is the mystery of you, Father, Son and Holy Spirit. The other is myself. I know very little about myself. I 'see only a reflection as in a mirror.' Continue to teach me about personhood in others and myself. Continue to teach me about the creation you have formed in this intricate web of life. Amen

*The hand of the Lord was on me, and he brought me out by the Spirit
and set me in the middle of a valley; it was full of bones. He asked, "Son of man,
can these bones live?" Ezekiel 37:1ff*

Ezekiel was among a thousand young men taken captive from Israel and marched in chains to Babylon (modern Iraq). His vision and inner conversation with the Lord probably happened as he passed through the desert area where a flock of sheep had died. He could not forget the impression: dry bones parched white by the desert sun. He was beginning to see that as a vision of his own demise—his brain suffering from dehydration, lack of oxygen, and racked in pain, a perfect troika causing hallucinations.

Ezekiel dreamed he could hear the inner voice of God. "You are a captive, helpless man. Are you also hopeless? See the valley of dry bones. Can these bones live? Yes. Watch the *Ruah* breathe life into these bones." It happened. The dry bones of the prophet's desert experience came to life. *Ruah* in Hebrew means "breath" or "Spirit" as in the "Spirit" of God.

Case history: What the Spirit of God can do for a person caught in a death march in a desert time of life. Meet "Audrey" of Seattle. Graduate of the "right Ivy League school" with an M.B.A. Hired by Microsoft. Broke through the glass ceiling. On the day of receiving the most important post she ever imagined holding, she also received news that "the biopsy is positive, the tumor is growing fast." She knew this type of cancer often leads to death.

Audrey, like Ezekiel, endured the desert experience, and slowly, over several years came to experience affirmation in her faith. She lived creatively ten more years, and died at age 55. She called her life a victory for the Spirit of God.

God, meet me in the desert of my journey. Bring the Spirit to breathe life into my dry spiritual bones. Thank you. Amen

God created humankind in his own image, male and female, he created them. God blessed them and said, "Rule over...every living creature."...God saw all that he had made, and it was good. Genesis 1:27

What happened to this beautiful and glorious garden, paradise? Humans lost it. I paraphrase: "We humans let a humble animal symbolized by a lowly snake on the ground dominate our judgment and behavior." Hear this: the key sin of humanity that causes us to lose paradise is *apathy, and its identical twin, inaction.* To be created in the image of God is a stupendous gift, with a commensurate responsibility. We were given power to exercise good or bad judgment. We did bad. "We served the creature," as Paul said (Romans 1:25), a lowly snake.

The metaphors in Genesis transcend their apparent simplicity. The 'possessors' of the earth lose their possession through apathy. Are we not made the fool at times because of the most impotent situation? Adam and Eve are archetypal humans. What are 21st century examples where a lowly 'creature' controls our humanity? Perhaps the snake in the field of our culture seems sophisticated, however, the subtlety of seduction lies not in the seducer's power. Our apathy gives power to the seducer.

Simon Weil wrote, "All sin is an attempt to fill the void within us." Augustine said, "Sin is nothing, and persons become nothing when they sin." The idea of sin is the inversion of the idea of God. "We do not need to conjure up a sense of sin," wrote Henry Emerson Fosdick, "Take one swift glance at the state of the world today. Evil is still the central problem."

Here's the good news. The realization of our full humanity lost through our inaction is regained through the action of grace, the power of God for salvation. When Adam and Eve left the garden they went "East of Eden." God met them there, East of Eden, outside of paradise—where all of us live in this generation.

Lord, have mercy on us, apathetic about the gift of creation. Thank you for redemption. Amen

God is not human, that he should lie, not a human being,
that he should change his mind ... Does he promise and not fulfill?
Numbers 24:19-20

Anxieties and questions arise among devout believers: "Is God in charge, or not?" We are very close to the world. We are very close to the internal problems of our lives: issues with loved ones, families, and friends. We get caught up in the mood of William Yeats' poetry, "The Center Cannot Hold."

"Turning and turning in the widening gyre/ The Falcon cannot hear the falconer; / Things fall apart; the centre cannot hold;/ Mere anarchy is loosed upon the world,/ The blood-dimmed tide is loosed, and / Everywhere the ceremony of innocence is drowned,/ The best lack all conviction, while the / Worst are full of passionate intensity."

The back story in the passage from Numbers relates to the same issues we have: 'where is God in the affairs of this sordid world where injustices prevail?' The messenger, Balaam, in good Hebrew prophetic style, is not reticent to "ask the Lord" for the message, and he delivers it in the first person. Paraphrased: "It appears, God, that things are falling apart, the center we trusted does not hold..." God spoke to Balaam who relays the message, "I, the Lord says, am not like a human being who goes back on his word. What I speak, I do. I have blessed you. There is no misfortune seen in Jacob, no misery observed in Israel. I, the Lord, brought you out of slavery in Egypt. There are no evil omens against you."

We cannot understand history from only the human point of view. God's sovereign love is being brought alive through the actions of millions of disciples. After the history books are written, you may join the prophet (verse 23): *"See what God has done!"*

Lord God, help me to keep my faith. Take not thy Holy Spirit from me. Amen

The Lord be with your spirit. Grace be with you all.
II Timothy 4:22

What is the greatest word in the Bible? Luther said it is "forgiveness." What do you choose? I choose *grace.* Our text today is probably the last words Paul wrote before he was executed in Rome. "Grace be with you all."

In fifth grade Sunday school—my dad taught the class—we were given an acronym to remember and define 'G.R.A.C.E.' "Gifts Received At Christ's Expense."

Christianity is the only religion in the world that says, "You are saved by grace."

Paul writes the "thesis" for the complete New Testament dissertation, saying, "For it is by grace you have been saved, through faith—and this is not from yourselves, it is the gift of God." (Ephesians 2:8)

The grace of God in Christ is the most powerful force in the world because it can change the human heart. It is also a humble power, because it requires consent, from the human side of the gift. Tillich described it: "Christ accepts you, as you are. Now, accept the fact that you accepted." Grace requires consent.

Bonhoeffer commented that our faith is "religionless." He meant that our faith does not depend on the traditions and infrastructures of institutional religious organizations. The gospel does have a libertarian spirit about it that is fascinating. "There is no mediator between God and people, except Christ," Paul told Timothy, a trainee for leadership in the church.

In 1978 Erma Bombeck published a book with this question for its title, *If Life is a Bowl of Cherries What am I Doing in the Pits?* (It's still a five star in *Goodreads* reviews.) A better metaphor of God's grace may be: "Life is a Dish of Fresh Peaches on Homemade Ice Cream." Taste and see, there is delicious love served up by God.

One must accept the glorious gift to behold its goodness.

Eternal God, each day nudge me, when I forget to voice my gratitude, for the gift of grace in Christ Jesus, my Lord and Savior. Amen

The Word became flesh and made his dwelling among us.
We have seen his glory, the glory of the one and only Son, who came from
the Father, full of grace and truth. John 1:14

There is a story about a philosopher who did not believe God. He thought the incarnation of Christ was preposterous. One day, walking on a beach, he saw an anthill that he knew would be destroyed by the zenith tides that come once a year. How could he save the ants? He thought of many ways, most of them using natural structures. It occurred to him, if he really wanted to save them, he would have to somehow communicate with them. The ultimate way to do this would be through an ant who understood the impending destiny of all the ants. 'Becoming an ant' would require the ultimate 'creative' power. Could that be God, the ultimate creative power? But, why would he do this? He thought, only if I really cared, if I loved them. The philosopher answered his own question about the absurdity of the gospel, "God so loved the world that...the Word became flesh."

The greatest "why" question the philosopher had ever considered was answered intuitively...God had the power to manifest his ultimate being in a person. God did this in Jesus of Nazareth. The ideas of God, the words about God, the ancient mystical thoughts of the nature of God, were manifested in one grand, glorious act of grace. God comes to the human stage of existence, as a human being.

"We have seen his glory, glory of the one and only Son, who came from the Father, full of grace and truth."

Thank you, God, for meeting us in the life, teaching, death, and resurrection of Jesus Christ. Amen

233

The nations will see your vindication, you will be called
by a new name. No longer will they call you 'Deserted.' You will be
called Hephzibah. Isaiah 62:4

Hephzibah is a beautiful name, if you speak Hebrew. It means, "my delight is in her." God is giving Israel a new name to show his love for the nation that suffered captivity in Babylon— Israel returning home humbled by experience and rededicated to the Lord. The Lord is happy. The Hebrew writers are expressive in their descriptions of the Lord's emotions. "A wise son brings joy to his father" Solomon writes. (Proverbs 10:1) The same joy is emoted by God for his faithful people.

What had they done to cause God's delight? According to Isaiah, "I, the Lord, love justice; I hate robbery and wrongdoing. In my faithfulness I will reward my people." (Isaiah 61:8) Simply put, Israel started to be obedient to the law, summarized by the Ten Commandments. Read the commandments colloquially translated by the Cross Trails Church in Fairlie, Texas, a small town between Wolfe and Commerce; the style of the translation fits the style of the people— country and Texan:

1. Just One God. 2. Honor yer Ma & Pa. 3. No telling tales or gossipin'. 4. Git yourself to Sunday meeting. 5. Put nothin' before God. 6. No foolin' around with another fella's gal. 7. No killin'. 8. Watch yer mouth. 9. Don't take what ain't yers. 10. Don't be hankerin' for yer buddy's stuff.

God is "delighted" in the people who keep his law, not because he is an insecure Cosmic Dictatorial Policeman. God is happy because you and I are happy when we keep the divine guidelines of life. If we do, we like others, enjoy the community, and think positively about ourselves. God has "delight in her, and him" when we do the hard "right" versus the easy and destructive "wrong."

Thank you, God, for your Word that is a light and guide on the difficult road of life. Amen

All of them were filled with the Holy Spirit and began to speak in other tongues as the Spirit enabled them. A crowd came together in bewilderment, because each one heard their own language being spoken. Utterly amazed, they asked: "Aren't all these who are speaking Galileans?" Acts 2:4,6

The size of your dream determines the size of your experiences. To make a dream become a reality we must first learn to listen to the wind.

My first solo sailing experience was an utter disaster. It is so embarrassing I won't tell anyone about it. Please keep it a secret. After launching a very cheap little sloop, I hoisted the sails, pushed away from the dock, caught a lucky break in the wind driving off the shore. I could feel the cool 57-degree waters of the Puget Sound. Mount Rainier stood up in all its glory, saying, "All is right with the world," or so I thought. What I had not anticipated was the rapid change in the wind, nor did I realize in time its power. I was "flummoxed." For me that was a nautical term. End of story.

Yes, that's the end of my first solo sailing experience. The capsized sloop sank before rescue boats could pull it out. Fortunately a guy in a fishing boat pulled me out. "Biggest sucker I caught today," he must of thought.

The last four words of the Risen Christ recorded by Luke are Jesus' instruction to the disciples to stay in Jerusalem until they would be clothed with "Power from on High." They stayed; Pentecost happened. The power was the Spirit. In New Testament Greek the word for "spirit" and "wind" is *"pneuma."* (Hence, 'pneumonia, pneumatic').

Learn to listen to the wind. Know its direction. Use its power. The Holy Wind/Spirit is the power of God working through our lives.

Father in heaven, I thank you for the gift of life, the strength of the Spirit, and the love of Jesus Christ. Amen

For God so loved the world that he gave his one and only Son, that whoever believes in him shall not perish, but have eternal life. For God did not send his Son into the world to condemn the world, but to save the world through him. John 3:16-17

Sir John Templeton said that Agape (love)— Christ-like love, pure and unlimited love for every human being with no exception— has been "the goal of my life for eighty-six years." Templeton cites Manitonquat, a Native American poet, and keeper of lore of the Wampanoag Nation of Massachusetts. "Medicine Story," (the meaning of his name) said:

"Life is the Sacred Mystery singing to itself, dancing to its drum, telling tales, improvising, playing, and we are all that Spirit, our stories are but one cosmic story that we are love indeed, that perfect love in me seeks the love in you, and if our eyes could ever meet without fear, we would recognize each other and rejoice, for love is life believing in itself."

Rabbi Hillel endured derision from a caustic critic and continued to expound his views of the love and mercy of the Lord. Finally the critic said, "I will convert to the faith if you can recite all the laws of God while standing on one leg." Hillel stood on one leg and said: "Whatever is hateful unto thee, do it not unto thy fellow. This is the whole law." The Hebrew word for the providence of God is *paqad*. This concept is "to attend with care, or kindness." The Bible is a history of God's love and kindness.

Faiths around the world from all nations of people tell the story of God's love. It is only in Christ we know who God is. Only in Christ can we see how perfect love is manifest in a human being.

Lord, examine my heart and mind. I want to meditate on the meaning of Christ's love for all persons. Imperfect as I am, may I in some way reflect Agape love to others. Amen

"Come, you who are blessed by my Father; take your inheritance, the kingdom is prepared for you since the creation of the world. For I was hungry and you gave me something to eat...I was a stranger and you invited me in"...The righteous will answer him, "Lord, when did we see you hungry and feed you? ...When did we see you a stranger and invite you in?" ...The King will reply, "Truly I tell you, whatever you did for one of the least of these brothers and sisters of mine, you did for me."
Matthew 25: 34ff

What, you and I may be asked, is the distinguishing mark of our lives? What should be the distinguishing mark of our church? According to Matthew the parable quoted in our text is among his last words to his followers. Taking this cue from Jesus, I think the distinguishing mark of my life should be "compassion." I trust that "compassion" should be the distinguishing mark of the church.

In my years of ministry I was pastor in two churches: University Place Presbyterian Church, Tacoma, Washington, and Westminster Church in Oklahoma City. I thank God for traits of compassion in both churches. For example, they tolerated me. Both congregations had humble beginnings. University Place first convened for worship services in an old barn, a tomato shed donated by a farmer. Westminster began services in a rented dance hall. Today these two churches continue a myriad of ministries whose hallmark is compassion. T. S. Eliot wrote: "What we call the beginning is often the end, and to make an end is to make a beginning. The end is where we start from."

This may or may not apply to tomato sheds, dance halls, and churches, but if you think about, perhaps it does.

God, I pray that the distinguishing mark of my life honors you, Father, Son and Holy Spirit. Amen

*Therefore, if anyone is in Christ, the new creation
has come: The old has gone, the new is here. II Corinthians 5:17*

Faith is not unlike being on a runaway horse. (Repeating a metaphor from March 14) When a person
takes seriously the love of God as the
supreme value of personal existence,
this force of faith takes you where a will
greater than your own is in charge. Get
ready for an unexpected ride. If I give my
life to Christ, I am no longer in control.
Events and circumstances happen that
I could not have foreseen in my wildest
dreams. This faith does not avoid the dark
side of human affairs. Faith takes us near
the cliffs of frightening insanity. Faith
takes us into the black heart of humanity's cruelty. Faith lets us see "the ghoulies and ghosties and long legged beasties
and things that go bump in the dark." (R.
Burns) Faith means "the new creation has
come." The wild ride, it turns out, has
purpose. It is not led by fear even when
ancillary experiences are fearful.

As mentioned before in *This Day*: the
starting gun for the runaway horse was
thunder and lightning. I knew from the
outset I was not in charge. Bit and bridle
were negated in the mind of the horse. As
a mere rider on a force I had never felt
before, I was excited. Delusions were
gone, primarily the delusion of who's in
control. Directions by another being, obstacles surprisingly avoided, and a delir-
iously happy homecoming at the end, all
this and more, comprised the ride I did
not plan.

You and I are surrounded by heroic
examples of people who have been willing not to dismount this wild runaway
ride of faith.

I invite you to get out of the paddock,
let's go for a ride. *Let Go, Let God.*

God, thank you for taking me to places, to meet people, to have experiences
that I never dreamed of possessing. God,
you made life, bigger than dreams, come
true. Amen

This is how God showed his love among us: He sent his one and only Son into the world that we might live through him. I John 4:9 The one who is in you is greater than the one who is in the world. I John 4:4

"Love all God's creation, both the whole and every grain of sand," Dostoevsky writes in *The Brothers Karamazov.* "Love the leaf, every ray of light. Love the animals, love the plants, love each separate thing. If thou love each thing then thou wilt perceive the mystery of God in all; and when thou perceives this, then thou wilt thenceforward grow every day to a fuller understanding of it."

Dostoevsky and John have a common thesis about the ultimate meaning and concern of life. "God is love. Love is the inner structure of true life." "Perceiving the mystery of God" is a tall order from our Russian friend, but let's try these axioms of love, based on the Letter of John and the thought of Dostoevsky. (I use 'axiom' in its sense from the Greek word *axioma,* meaning "self-evidently worthy.")

Six Axioms of Love:

1. Perfect love casts out fear. 2. We love because God first loved us. 3. The unloving know nothing of God. 4. God dwells in us when we love others. 5. Love will never come to an end. 6. Love cancels innumerable sins.

This day meditate on opening our eyes to see love in every "ray of light, every grain of sand." Let us look at suburbs, towns, and cities with the eyes of the heart, as Jesus did. Remember he looked up at the City of Jerusalem and wept. Oh, what passionate love he felt in his heart for the people. It is self-evident. Love opens the eyes of the heart.

Thank God our Father, Christ our Savior, and Holy Spirit our Guide, for the gift of love. Amen

Where can I go from your Spirit? Where can I flee from your presence? If I go up to the heavens, you are there; if I make my bed in the depths, you are there...Search me, God, and know my heart; test me and know my anxious thoughts. Psalm 139:7-8,23

There is a *majestic instancy* in our meeting God. There is neither time nor place that he cannot search and find us. A New Testament Greek word used for our English word "world" is *cosmos. Cosmos includes all dimensions of creation*: sentient beings (including people of course), places, and things. God so loved the "world" is the Bible's way of saying God loves all that is. Therefore, expect his *majestic instancy* to show up anywhere, at anytime.

Francis Thompson (late 19th century) became an incurable addict. Homeless in London, "homeless' in soul, mind and body. Near death he scribbled out a poem that led to his discovery and recovery through agents of Christ, Londoners who had compassion for him. The thesis of the poem, "The Hound of Heaven," is the reality that there is no place God cannot find you. In the poem, "The Hound" in pursuit is God.

"I fled Him, down the nights,/and down the days;/ I fled Him, down the arches of the years;/ I fled Him, down the labyrinthine ways / Of my mind; and in the mist of tears./ I hid from Him, and under the running laughter."

The 'running laughter' is the joyous Hound of Heaven in pursuit of his mission.

God through Jesus Christ is pursuing you and me. From God's perspective of the sovereign pursuing Christ, there is cosmic laughter. "Where can I flee your presence?" *Nowhere.* Perhaps that is the meaning of scripture that says of Christ, "For the joy set before him he endured the cross and scorned its shame." Christ knows the joy of love in its pursuit of the loved—you and me.

God, we humbly praise your Name for pursuing us, finding us, changing us through the *majestic instancy of love,* in Christ. Amen

Walk while you have the light, before the darkness overtakes you.
John 12:35

Following his brilliant speech on space travel and new discoveries in science, I asked the speaker, Wernher von Braun, "What, for you, is the most remarkable phenomenon in the universe?" He answered quickly, in one word. "Photosynthesis." He was serious, and added, "All of biological life as we know it lives off this miraculous mechanism, directly or indirectly. The power of a cell to transform the energy of the sun into nutrients of life through photosynthesis is a wonder to behold."

There is a spiritual analogy here. Christ, "the light of the world," taught that everyone has a light to carry into the world, a light of love and justice. It is a light that shines in the darkest recesses of human experience. Spiritual photosynthesis? Yes, and it works through individuals, as if 'cell by cell' the whole of life is permeated with love.

Let me give one example. The words "football" and "Oklahoma" define each other in the State of Oklahoma, and the Selmons are the First Family of OU Football. Jessie and Lucius Selmon, Sr. raised nine children, three football stars at OU and in the NFL. (Lucius, Dewey, and Lee Roy) Each of the family is an exemplary Christian. After retiring from the Oakland Raiders, Dewey, his wife and children, came back to Oklahoma to receive the "Family of the Year Award." A reporter asked Dewey's four year-old daughter, "With your dad travelling at football, how does a busy family like yours keep so close together?" She answered, "Well, we hold hands. And we hold on real tight."

The word that defines the pervasive power of "spiritual photosynthesis" is love. We are created so that the light of love in us is transformed "into the nutrients of life."

God, thank you for the light of Christ that shines in our hearts and transforms our relationships with love. Amen

Now to him who is able to establish you in accordance with my gospel—to the only wise God be glory forever through Jesus Christ! Amen. Romans 16:25

There is an *ecstatic* epiphany in faith that one hopes comes in time to live with purpose the life that follows. It is this: One alone is God and I am not. We are not in charge of history; we are ambassadors. The Bible never calls us emperors; it does call us ambassadors of reconciliation by appointment of Jesus Christ. "God, who reconciled us to himself through Christ, gave us the ministry of reconciliation." (II Corinthians 5:18)

Bill Wilson, co-founder of Alcoholics Anonymous once said, "Years ago, I used to commiserate with all people who suffered. Now I commiserate only with those who suffer in ignorance, who do not understand the purpose and the ultimate utility of pain. In God's economy, nothing is wasted. Through failure, we learn a lesson in humility that is probably needed, painful though it is. Our program is no success story in the ordinary sense of the word. It is a story of suffering transmitted under grace into spiritual progress."

One of the first things we surrender in faith through Christ is the role of playing god in our own lives. It does not work. It is destructive. The god-complex certainly destroys relationships with family, with friends, and with the community. When we surrender to Christ's will in faith, it is not a loss of perspective about a good life. We surrender trying to be in control, so that we make good choices about what controls us—not drugs, alcohol, sex, money, power, prestige, and comfort.

After the ecstasy, there's the laundry. There is work to do. We are "saved by grace…in order to do the good work" of life in Christ. (Ephesians 2:8ff)

Our Father, I surrender to you my desire to control others around me. Thank you for forgiveness and freedom to make this choice. Amen

They remembered that God was their
Rock, that God Most High was their Redeemer. Psalm 78:35

Gracious God, I thank you for the gift of remembering.

Let me *remember to remember.*

Remembering the gentle love of my dad as he carried mom in his arms from the car to her bed. Remembering her days of recovery and the fight with cancer, I thank you for recollections. I remember dad's story about her disease, and instructions to all the family about the new shares of work the family would have. I remember his prayers. I remember her joyous presence in the nascent passages of time allotted my life. Thank you.

There are poignant remembrances of your grace from times when my own actions separated me from doing your love and justice. I remember trying to fill the void in my life with substitutes for truth. I remember how you have shown me the way towards love. I remember that Jesus' passion was not without sacrifice and that Christ's priceless love is given to me without cost to me. Christ paid the price of perfect love. Remembering my redemption overwhelms me with gratitude.

Thank you for the memories of a phalanx of your servants united in the common good of the human community. I remember that their wealth, work, and wisdom create a place for the tree of life to grow and yield its harvest. I remember the fruit of that tree has nourished me.

I remember the freedoms experienced in a nation whose history is marked by a few great visionary people and tens of thousands who also had compassion. I *remember to always remember* the sacrifices of those who have made this extraordinary encounter with liberty a part of my life and memory.

Remembering that you gave your Son because you loved the world, let me never doubt that you are the Good Shepherd for all people everywhere.

Most of all, I remember your amazing creation, your tender kindness, your subtle providence, and your loving redemption. Amen

Great is the Lord and most worthy of praise;
his greatness no one can fathom. One generation commends your
works to another; they tell of your mighty acts. Psalm 145: 3-4

What is it like when a wall that divides one's dreams from reality comes down? There is the joy that dreams can come true. There is a monumental emotion—hope, vitality, gratitude, and serenity are combined. Earlier in this month's devotions we mentioned the "Berlin Wall." What was in the minds of people there at the moment that Wall, a phenomenal metaphor of division, came down? Let's hear German witnesses involved in Mauerfall.

Gunter Schabowski was 60 years old at *Mauerfall,* 'the day the Wall came down.' Gunter was a member of the communist regime's Politburo. He said the event was set up in part by an erroneous announcement to East Berliners that restrictions in passing from East to West were being lifted. Twenty years after the event, he is delighted that Mauerfall has brought freedom to millions of people.

Lt. Col. Harald Jaeger describes how 25,000 Germans from the communist East Berlin showed up at the Wall guarded by thirty police. Jaeger was in charge of the crossing at Bornholmerstrasser. He decided to let the crowd pass. "I'm happy that the only thing that flowed was fear-induced sweat and not blood." He ordered the gate opened at 11:20 p.m. A turning point in history happened in the next few hours. The Berlin Wall came down without World War III being ignited.

There are many "political walls" in the world today. We can pray for change in those conditions causing injustice.

There are personal walls near ourselves that we may bring down. Perhaps "fear-induced sweat" will flow. When these walls come down, the monumental emotion combining hope, vitality, creativity, gratitude, and serenity take the place of the impassable wall. Do you have an existential *Mauerfall* in your family for which you thank God? I do too.

God, thank you for breaking down the barrier walls in my heart and mind. Perhaps there are other secret walls that I don't see; please show me. In Christ's Name. Amen

Now get up and go.
Acts 9:6

Saul, a Pharisee, days after the cru-cifixion and resurrection of Jesus, used his religious authority and his polit-ical connections, as a Roman citizen, to become, shall we say, the 'self-appointed Czar of Persecution Procedures against all Christians.' He would stop at nothing, including murder.

As providence would have it, the un-expected happened. Saul was converted to be a follower of Jesus Christ. Acts tells this historic story. Saul came face to face with the Risen Christ in a mystical con-frontation. In the "red letter" Bibles (quot-ing Jesus in red letters) the reader, in our case, twenty-one centuries after the fact, cannot help but see the simple command of Christ to Saul: "Get up!" and "Go!" Saul got up. Saul followed the command. Saul became "Paul," the primary author of the New Testament, an Apostle of Christ, and a martyr for the faith.

Isn't it time for me to hear the com-mand of Christ, and just do it? Paul wrote, "Put on the mind of Christ." Einstein commanded a new mind set and action with the simple insight: "The problems we face cannot be solved at the same level of thinking we had that created the prob-lems." The new mind of Christ works that way. Love, not fear becomes our *modus operandi*—love in action. Albert Camus challenged Christians at the time of war in Europe against the tyranny of Hitler. "What the world expects of Christians is to speak out loud and clear, and that they should voice their condemnation in such a way that there is never a doubt. The grouping we need is a grouping of people resolved to speak out clearly and pay up personally."

I think the word that I hear in the Word of God today is this: Get up and go put the love and justice of Christ to work in the place you live.

Christ, help me to convert my convic-tion to conduct, for doubts in life are re-moved only through action. Amen

Simon Peter answered, "You are the Messiah, the Son of the living God." Jesus replied, "I tell you that you are Peter and on this rock I will build my church, and the gates of Hades will not overcome it." Matthew 16:16ff

We live in an empowering world of instant communication, Twitter, Facebook, Big Data, trillions of bits of information come at us 24/7. Nearly all people want to "change" something: political rulers, political parties, economic systems, social mores, or religious institutions. Massive instant communication reality makes us think we can.

The first step of change: Know where you are. Planning consultants love to use this story. A company was contracted to build a major freeway through what had been considered an impassable jungle. Engineers started surveying, heavy equipment operators started slashing through trees and moving huge rocks. HR managers set up systems to pay staff and schedule benefits. One lone entrepreneur scaled the tallest tree on the highest ground in the jungle, shot smart phone videos of the panorama, and came back to corporate headquarters and announced: "You are doing a lot of stuff quickly and effectively, however, one thing needs to be pointed out. *You Are In the Wrong Jungle.*"

How much of my time and effort 'to make a living and life' was spent in the wrong jungle? Act now, time is of the essence, but choose the right jungle for the life journey.

The second step of positive and creative change: Know Who you are following.

The scripture suggests Christ. His disciples are a "company of believers" we know as "the church." T. S. Eliot: "There shall always be the church and the world/ And the heart of man shivering and fluttering between them/ Choosing and Chosen./ Valiant, ignoble, dark and full of light./ Swinging between hellgate and heavengate/ And the gates of hell shall not prevail./ Darkness now, then light."

Thank you, God, for Christ, our Messiah, and for the church, His Body of faithful followers and thank you for the mission you have given us. Amen

Keep your heart with all vigilance, for from it flows the springs of life.
Proverbs 4:23 NRSV

Soren Kierkegaard told a story to answer the question, "What is it like to talk about the gospel to an unbelieving world?" This is a paraphrase of his answer. Once there was a village full of excited people because the circus was coming to town. On the day of arrival, everyone left the village and went to the top of the hill to watch for the caravan. When they saw the circus entourage approaching they began to cheer loudly. All laughed at the clowns leading the parade. The villagers, facing the caravan, did not notice what the clowns, facing the town, could see. The village was on fire. The clowns tried without success to warn the people. The more animated the clowns became, the more the villagers laughed. The clowns never convinced the villagers with their serious message. The town burned to the ground.

Paul, writing to the church at Corinth said, "I am a *fool* for Christ." The Greek word for 'fool', *paraphronia,* translates "madness." I cite a letter, with permission, from a nine year old: "Dear Mike, Please pray for my dad and mom. They fight a lot. The only time I hear them talking, they're fighting. I really like them and it hurts that they hate each other. I wish they went to church with me. I see other kids with their parents and I get jealous. Dad and mom don't listen to me."

This child is a man now. I have seen him regularly with his children at worship. He understands Kierkegaard's clowns. "That was myself, trying to talk to my parents," he told me. But, being a 'fool for Christ' that he was, he kept the faith and now from his heart today *flows the springs of life.* His children understand the message of the circus clowns. They believe Christ, and joy, like a circus brings, fills this family.

Thank you, Christ, for the messengers of faith who persistently spoke your truth. Amen

They all joined together constantly in prayer.
Acts 1:14

Just as we were about to begin a high school basketball game, a college football player whom most sports fans recognized, a Young Life leader, came from the stands to ask our coach, "Mind if I pray with the guys before the game?" Coach said, "H---, we've never done it that way before, and that's a good reason to do it now, the way these kids have been playing."

The scene in Acts takes place days after the resurrection. We know from scripture that "the disciples did not believe" the resurrection. When did they change their minds? Two things happened: after prayer, and after the gift of the Spirit of God.

It is the same today. You and I believe with integrity after we have sincerely prayed, and after we receive the gifts of the Spirit: love, joy, peace, kindness and patience...naming a few marks of character I need. What about you? We never out grow our egos. The superlative powers of 'self' can always distract us. Late in life, I still need to recommit each day to Christ aware that ego is a barrier to love, joy, and peace. Some scientists say there is no such thing as "ego," and Freud was wrong about the term. A neurologist once told me: "I did MRI's on the brain, micron by micron, and there is no 'ego.'" It would have been cruel to ask his wife if the scientist had an 'ego.' Even if you have not done it before, join me in a prayer composed by Martin Luther 458 years ago.

"Behold, Lord, an empty vessel that needs to be filled. My Lord, fill it. I am weak in faith; strengthen thou me. I am cold in love; warm me and make me fervent in love for others. I will remain with thee of whom I can receive but to whom I may not give." Amen

*Whoever serves me must follow me; and where
I am, my servant also will be. My Father will honor the one
who serves me. John 12:26*

Eternal God, help me to accept the projective power of believing. True belief opens doors. You, O Lord, are the source of my belief. You create new vistas for the eyes of faith. Let me doubt my doubts, and believe my beliefs, all the while thanking you that believing is a doorway to knowledge.

Believing hearts are courageous hearts. You have said that if I believe, even though I die, I shall live. Because I must put to death all things that steal life from me, I accept the power of the resurrection in your love that overcomes death.

What I believe, I become. Therefore, let me believe what is real, true, and just. I confess that when I refuse to believe something, I am prone to believe anything. Let me learn how to respond to my inner cynic, pessimist, and inquisitor. Forgive Lord, my unbelief that repels the gracious gifts of life.

You have said, "Choose this day who you will serve." I choose this day to believe in you, in your justice and providence in history. I choose not to believe in self-aggrandizing power, wealth, and the retributive morality of doing unto others as they have done unto me.

May I accept the simple belief taught by Jesus, that you care for all people of your creation even more than you care for the flowers of the fields. I see the beauty in your care for the whole creation's panoply of color, light, sound, and sight. I ask that seeking your kingdom in my life is my first priority, and all of your gifts of creative love and joy are added to this equation for human fulfillment and meaning in existence. Amen

*Be strong and courageous. Do not be afraid; do not be
discouraged, for the Lord God will be with you wherever you go.*
Joshua 1:9

Betty, my mother-in-law, has a lot of experience and stories to tell. History is more collapsed into a single life span than we sometimes calculate. It has been less than 200 decades since resurrection of Christ and the birth of the church. Betty has lived in all or parts of ten of those 200 decades. All of us have legacies, for better or worse, whether we want one or not. Consider how quickly the personal histories of disciples intertwine from the key turning point of the history of humankind, the life-teaching-death-resurrection of Christ, to the present day.

On a sleepless night sometimes I imagine the simple brief line of witness from Jesus to the present moment. For example, John wrote the gospel that emphasizes the love of God in Jesus Christ. John was later exiled but continued having a legacy effecting all of history to follow. John was a mentor of Polycarp; Polycarp's legacy included his mentorship of Irenaeus, whose theology influenced Augustine, Aquinas, Calvin, and Karl Barth in the 20th century. Irenaeus was a mentor of Hippolytus. Hippolytus was elected by the Christians of Rome to be their bishop. Under Maximinus Thrax (I love the name Maximinus, almost an oxymoron), Hippolytus was exiled to become a slave in the Roman mines on the island of Sardinia. There he died. But his legacy is carried on through the history of the centuries. The very word 'centuries' seems formidable. It's not. Ask my mother-in-law; she has lived in one twentieth of all the history from Jesus to the present.

From John through Hippolytus to each of us, the key to the legacy of life is love. E.E. Cummings had it correct: "Be of love a little more careful than of anything."

Thank you, God, for loving, not condemning the world, through Jesus Christ. Amen

Without me, you can do nothing. John 15:5
With faith, nothing can separate you from the love of God.
Romans 8:38

The best sermon I heard all year in 2010 was a movie. "The Blind Side" is the story of Michael Oher, the phenomenal NFL player who was a street person as a teenager, struggling to survive, to stay in school. Literally, Michael did not have a place to sleep, and often no food to eat.

God arranges rescues. The rescuer in this case was a suburbanite white housewife who saw Michael an African American on the street, took him home, fed him, and gave him a permanent residence. Her husband and children were part of the new opportunity that Michael seized. In February 2013, if you watched Super Bowl XLVII, you saw Michael and his team, the Baltimore Ravens, win over the San Francisco 49ers, 34-31.

Michael Oher describes his new life in these words: "I'll never ever wake up one day and get comfortable with my situation. It'll always be unbelievable. I'll always be a hard worker. I know that (my new life) is all God. Without God, I wouldn't be here. It's impossible. What I'm trying to do is…give back to kids that grew up kind of like the situation that I was in. I know there are thousands and thousands of Michael Ohers out there."

Michael responded to his redemption epic the way great examples of saints of Christ do. "I have received infinitive grace, now it is time to give back to others." I used to think the Noah story was a little too silly to take seriously—the boat, the animals on board, the drunkenness all added up to a comedic episode. I missed the point of the metaphor; it was not about the boat per se, it is about the flood. Some people are *inundated* with horrendous problems, and God does rescue them.

Thank you, God, for the witness of Michael Oher and the message of hope he lives. Amen

An argument started among the disciples as to which of them would be the greatest. Jesus, knowing their thoughts, took a little child and had him stand beside him. Then he said to them, "Whoever welcomes this little child in my name welcomes me; and whoever welcomes me welcomes the one who sent me. For it is the one who is least among you all who is the greatest." Luke 9:46-48

The gift of children in a family, school, church or community is quintessential to the adult search for meaning in life, because, we have so much to learn from children.

Christopher Morley's philosophy on this subject comes in poetry: "The greatest poem ever known / Is the one all poets have outgrown: / The poetry, innate untold/ Of being only four years old./ Still young enough to be a part/ Of Nature's great impulsive heart,/ And unselfconscious as the bee—/ And yet with lovely reason skilled / Each day new paradise to build / Elate explorer of each sense, / Without dismay, without pretense! / In your unstained transparent eyes / There is no conscience, no surprise: / Life's queer conundrums you accept, / Your strange Divinity still kept.../And Life, that sets all things in rhyme, / May make you poet, too, in time— / But there were days, O tender elf, / When you were Poetry itself!"

Jesus knew true greatness requires humility and wisdom to say, "I don't know. I don't have the answer, but let's find out." Children can do this because they are not burdened with false premises. Children are wise beyond their years discerning the most important virtue of another person, home, school, or church. Marc Chagall described this one great virtue this way: "In our life there is a single color, as on the artist's palette, which provides the meaning of life and art. It is the color of love." A child knows when he, or she, is loved.

Thank you, God, for children who teach lessons in love. Amen

*The heavens declare the glory of God; the skies proclaim the work of his hands…
May these words of my mouth and this meditation of my heart be pleasing in your sight,
Lord, my Rock, and my Redeemer. Psalm 19:1,14*

Dag Hammarskjöld provides an eloquent comment on 'wonder.' He said, "God does not die on the day when we cease to believe in the personal presence of God, but we die when our lives cease to be illumined by the steady radiance of wonder, the source of which is beyond all reason."

We have a small Kashmir rug on the reading room floor. It is The Chosen Rug, the rug that two generations of dogs chose to lie upon as we read. This rug has symbolic meaning. I bought it from a family in a mountain village between Islamabad and Srinagar. This geo-political region of contested Kashmir is picked by some experts as the place 'where the nuclear war of the future will start.' Pakistan and India are armed, angry, and ready. The rug came from a family who wove the patterns representing its tribal traditions. It was crafted with love. Kashmir is now the seedbed of old conflicts. The war of annihilation could escalate from this beautiful land sitting in the cool air drifting down from the Himalayans. Aussie, our dog, is asleep on the rug. Should I wake up Aussie and tell her the background story of the rug? Will anyone in the governments of world wake up to hear the story?

Yes, the creation is beautiful as the Psalmist declares. I pray for the family of rug makers. I pray that future generations will be able to see "the work of God's hands." The tapestry of life is God's handiwork. The backside of the tapestry is a collage of knots we don't understand; the front is a glorious story we believe.

May the brilliance of the sunrise, and the strength of your creation, be ours through your love. Amen

> *If Christ has not been raised, your faith is futile*
> *... If only for this life we have hope in Christ, we are of all people*
> *most to be pitied. I Corinthians 15:17,19*

Books on 'religious news' rarely get a gig on major media prime-time international news. Orthodox Rabbi Pinchas Lapide's *The Resurrection of Jesus: A Jewish Perspective,* scored a perfect ten for the media editors. It was published simultaneously in Hebrew, German, and English.

As a little backstory on the citation from Lapide that follows, we should mention the context of politics in the 1st century. The Pharisees comprised the strongest party in the coalition that ruled Judaism, and they believed in 'resurrection' theology. The Sadducees did not believe in the resurrection. Politically, all Jews were under Roman authority. Therefore, the Pharisees were very aware of the dangers of what could happen if the person they condemned to die was in fact raised from death. The resurrection of Jesus would be a threat to Jewish and Roman leaders. After all, the most cruel *coup de grace* the Romans could devise was death by crucifixion. The resurrection of Jesus threatened the Roman rulers and the rulers of Judaism.

Lapide said: "In regard to the future resurrection of the dead, I am and remain a Pharisee. Concerning the resurrection of Jesus on Easter Sunday, I was a Sadducee. I am no longer a Sadducee." The reaction to Lapide, a noted theologian and a diplomat for eighteen years, was like a tsunami in public opinion. He had more to say, "I cannot rid myself of the impression that some modern Christian theologians are ashamed of the material facticity of the resurrection. They are straining out a gnat and swallowing a camel."

For me, the resurrection of Christ is the central thesis of the gospel story. What is your belief?

Thank you, God, for the resurrection of Christ and our faith in a Living Lord. Amen

Greater love has no one than this:
to lay down one's life for one's friends. John 15:13

Rick Rescorla laid down his life for his friends. Rick is a 9/11/2001 hero, a date all who love a free nation remember. *History Channel*, books, and the San Francisco Opera have featured Rick's life story.

Born in Cornwall, England, Rescorla joined the British Army, and then joined the U.S. Army to served two tours in Vietnam. Rick received the Silver Star, Bronze Star with Oak Leaf Cluster, and the Purple Heart. He became a U.S. citizen, went to Oklahoma University, then onto Oklahoma City University Law School, receiving his law degree in 1975, the same time my wife was there. He wound up in NYC working for Dean Witter Reynolds, which became Morgan Stanley. In 1990 he warned authorities that the World Trade Center was vulnerable to a terrorist car bombing. In 1993 the WTC had a major bombing by Islamic terrorists. Rick warned the authorities that the WTC Towers were vulnerable to bombing by aircraft being flown into them. NYC authorities again rejected advice. Rick gave disaster training to the nearly 2,700 employees of Morgan Stanley who occupied floors 44 through 77 of WTC Tower Two.

9/11/2001. First the families and friends, soon the whole world, knew that the procedures these trained employees received from Rick saved 2,678 lives. The Port Authority's "official order" via the intercom after Tower Two was hit by an exploding aircraft was, "EVERYONE STAY AT YOUR DESK." Rick's group followed his command, "*Be calm. Be silent. Be calm,*" as they orderly filed down the steps to safety. Rick sang a Welsh Hymn with his rich baritone: "Tongues of fire on Idris flaring, /News of foeman near declaring./ To heroic deeds of daring, / Call ye Harlech men!" (Google "Men of Harlech" to hear this hymn)

Rick died, 9/11/2001, last seen going up the stairs at Tower Two.

Thank you, God, for Rick Rescorla and all who have died that freedom may be alive. Amen

I pray that the eyes of your heart may be enlightened
in order that you may know the hope to which he has called you, the riches
of his glorious inheritance. Ephesians 1:18

The Apostle Paul, to use a phrase from Barbara Tuchman, had a "distant mirror" into which he could look and see the far away future of Christian faith. I offer this paraphrased 'executive summary' of his startling address to the Ephesians.

"I thank God for you Ephesians who believe in Christ. Each day I pray that you may see with the eyes of the heart what God is doing now and for the future. A power that is immeasurable, a power greater than all intelligent imaginations or wildest dreams is already at work in you. This power raised Christ from the dead. This power is now in you and the church. Together, you are the body of Christ. You have the gift of eternal life through God's grace. You know this by faith. You cannot separate your faith from the impulse to serve others. The distant future and your destiny are directed by this power in you, the Spirit of God." (Ephesians chapters 1, 2)

Could any one in Rome see in the 'distant mirror' the complete demise of Rome's glory and the endless witness of Christ through believers in all centuries to come? Dom Gregory Dix, an expert on Roman history, wrote: "The empire was an awe-inspiring achievement, the apotheosis of human power. In the last analysis it represented nothing else but the lust of the flesh and the pride of life triumphant and organized to the point of stability." Does that critique sound familiar?

What do you and I see with the eyes of the heart about our selves, our families, our nation, and our world in the distant mirror. Look, if you dare. See the "glorious inheritance."

Lord of the future, give me ability to see with the eyes of the heart, my destiny. Amen

(This is the birthday of my grandson, Charles Michael Sandefer, who was age 11 when he wrote the following devotional thoughts, February 2013.) The Lord is my strength and shield; my heart trusts in him, and he helps me. My heart leaps for joy, and with my song I praise him." Psalm 28:7

Charlie wrote:

"Sometimes God seems non-existent but he is always there. No matter what it is, He is helping you. A lot of times, I wonder if God is not watching over me, especially when I am going through something hard. Then I open my eyes, and see how much God has given me, and how much God has helped me. I have come to realize how God is always blessing us. He is rooting for us all the way. God has loved us every second of every day. I hope we never forget that."

To Charlie's words of wisdom, we add those of a Founding Father. Benjamin Franklin understood something about children I hope we never forget. In 1749 he wrote "Proposals Relating to the Education of Youth in Pennsylvania." In his words, "It is inconceivable how many things children are capable of, if all the opportunities of instructing them were laid hold of, with which *they themselves supply us.*" The last four words stand out for me, "they themselves supply us." I have a debt of gratitude to my four daughters. Each has taught, loved, and persevered their dad. I am confident all four are now learning from nine grandchildren.

Today's prayer are phrases from Psalms 22 and 23.

My God, why are you so far from saving me, so far from cries of anguish. Do not be far from me, for trouble is near and there is no one to help. You are my strength; come quickly to help me. From you comes the theme of my praise in the great assembly. Even though I walk through the darkest valley, I will fear no evil for you are with me. Amen

Therefore, as God's chosen people, holy and dearly loved, clothe yourselves with compassion, kindness, humility, gentleness, and patience. Over all these virtues, put on love, which binds them all together in perfect unity. Colossians 3:12,14

God of the everlasting waters of forgiveness, wash me clean. You have demonstrated to all history your forgiving heart. Jesus taught us to pray daily that we shall be forgiven as we forgive. In Jesus we see the essence of the gospel is forgiveness.

I admit to stumbling on this rock of truth. Can I freely forgive others who have caused pain and suffering? 'Forgive us our sins as we forgive those who sin against us;' your words are a hard truth.

There is refreshing release in forgiveness. When I do forgive, I am released from the negative hold of another person on me. Accepting the fact that you accept me releases me from the burden of shameful regrets. If I forgive another, I feel the lightness of the new air that leads me outward on the wings of new and fresh vitality. When your love through forgiveness is present, life is reborn.

I admit my needs and shortcomings and all my failed attempts to live faithfully. Your mercy is from everlasting to everlasting. You forgive me forever. Thank you.

Lord, you have made forgiveness the strongest link in the golden chain of love. We take this journey of life through unfamiliar jungles of human entanglements. The most difficult obstacles, often, can only be surpassed by the detour of love that leads us back to the highway of faith.

When I am caught up with thoughts of vindictive blame of others, let me see two things more clearly. My incompleteness. Christ's forgiveness of me.

You have shown us, God, what is true. Forgiveness opens the door to freedom.

For freedom Christ set us free. Amen

Speaking the truth in love, we will grow to become in every respect the mature body of him who is the head, that is Christ. The whole body builds itself up in love as each part does its work. Ephesians 4:15-16

King James I of England, who was James VI of Scotland said, "Presbyterians are no gentlemen." (The King's English grammar) What I am sure he meant was true. Presbyterians took seriously the core philosophy of Protestant thought, namely, 'No authority has the divine right to stand between the human conscience and God.' Tough idea if your job depends on "The Divine Right of Kings." Protestants "protested" the Catholic and Monarchies' notion of the "Divine Right of Kings." Note: "protestant" was not yet an "ism." One sees this Protestant philosophy carried forward in English history.

The Royal Society is the first scientific society ever formed. It is remarkable that the science organization grew out of the meetings of the "invisibles." These were the meetings of Protestant scholars who quietly met in the home of Robert Boyle's sister, Katherine. She supported the "Parliamentarians" in a revolt against Charles I. The motto the Royal Society adopted was *nullius in verba,* "Take no one's word for it."

That is a good premise of science and faith. Boyle of course is the innovative chemist whose name is known to all first year General Science students, "Boyle's Law of Gases." Isaac Newton was a member of the Royal Society. Self-replicating scientific theory has deep roots in early Protestant theology.

Dr. Francis Collins is presently the Director of the National Institutes of Health, the greatest biomedical research body in the world. He said, "If faith has meaning it can't be off in one part of you. It has to be integrated. I think my faith (Christian) adds to the experience of being a scientist in the way that discovering something has more meaning, sort of glimpsing the mind of God."

Thank you, God, that there is no mere authority figure between truth and our self. Amen

Be strong in the Lord and in his mighty power. Peace to the
brothers and sisters, and love with faith from God the Father and the
Lord Jesus Christ. Ephesians 6:10, 23

In the midst of the sea of mediocrity flooding society where massive numbers of people have given up to achievement, given in to challenge, and given over to drugs, it is refreshing to see a victorious person overcome obstacles far greater than the bland majority can imagine.

Dr. Kellie Lim is a hero. She was a triple amputee at age eight, now she is a Doctor of Medicine, graduated from U.C.L.A. Medical School, and chose pediatrics, with a specialty in infectious diseases. Meningococcemia attacked her when she was eight. Retinitis pigmentosa attacked her mother and left her blind at age 20, further complicating Kellie's life.

After graduating from Northwestern University, Kellie took the GRE, the LSAT, and the MCAT "just to keep my options open."

Kellie has taken up surfing, and has done tandem skydiving. She uses the background of her illness and the subsequent challenges she faced as informed motivation to pass on to children she serves. She said, "Just having that experience of being someone so sick and how devastating that can be—not just for me but for my family too—gives me a perspective that other people don't necessarily have."

Kellie, now 42 years old, will have many years, God willing, of heroically mentoring children in her chosen field of medicine. The distinguishing feature of Kellie when she appeared on ABC's "Person of the Week" was not her prosthetic legs or her one-handedness. It was her beautiful smile. (Check her smile out on Facebook.)

Robert Downing, Jr.'s definition of a "hero" fits Dr. Lim perfectly: "'Hero' is not just a noun, it is a verb."

Lord, thank you for the life-lesson taught by Dr. Kellie Lim. We may not control our circumstances; we can choose our response. Thank you, God, for this choice. Amen

Christ's love compels us, because we are convinced that one died for all, and therefore all died. Therefore, if anyone is in Christ, the new creation has come. II Corinthians 5:14,17

"The Great Disproportion" is the phrase used by the Westminster Confession of Faith, written in revolutionary times in England in 1647. The original treatise is entitled "The Humble Advice of the Assembly of Divines, Now by Authority of Parliament Sitting at Westminster." The Reformed theologians and authors of the document wrote about the "great disproportion" between the reality of our best human thoughts, ethics, and efforts at goodness, and the reality of God's true infallible, ineffable love. The writers considered the Spirit of God to be the source of interpreting God's splendor to our broken humanity. T. S. Eliot wrote about this action of God's Holy Spirit encountering the human spirit. (From "The Four Quartets")

"The dove descending breaks the air / With flame of incandescent terror / Of which the tongues declare / The One discharged of sin and error. / The only hope or else despair /Lies in the choice of pyre or pyre? / To be redeemed from fire by fire./Who then devised the torment? Love. / Love is the unfamiliar Name / Behind the hands that wove / The intolerable shirt of flame. / Which human power cannot remove./ We only live, only suspire / Consumed be either fire or fire."

We will live and die "by fire or fire" metaphors of the fire of destruction that life without love creates. Or, we live by the purging fire of the Spirit that separates the gold of hope from the dross of empty despair.

The Great Disproportion between a life of self-destruction and a life of saving grace is reconciled only by *"Love, the unfamiliar Name,"* the love of God.

Thank you, God, for building a bridge of love over the great canyon of disproportion that separated our broken life from your New Creation in Christ. Amen

*The heart of the discerning acquires knowledge, for the
ears of the wise seek it out. Trust the Lord with all your heart and lean
not on your own understanding. Proverbs 18:15 and 3:5*

Proverbs, many of which are attributed to King Solomon, combines the roles of faith and reason. On the one hand, get all the knowledge you can; on the other hand, ultimately trust the Lord with your heart. The engineer and the poet, the scientist and theologian are welcomed to the community of God.

Jane Goodall saw the need for this balance of science and spirit. "Science does not have appropriate tools," she said, "for the dissection of the spirit. How sad it would be, I thought, if we humans ulti-mately were to lose all sense of mystery, all sense of awe, if our left brains were utterly to dominate the right so that logic and reason triumphed over intuition and alienated us absolutely from our innermost being, from our hearts, from our souls." (*A Reason for Hope*)

Aspen Institute's *Gig.U* project is a consortium of 37 university communities that has been discussing Smart Cities: access to abundant bandwidth, abundant human intellectual capital—Silicon Valley, Austin, Ann Arbor, Cambridge and Boulder. The web, social networks, and cloud computing provide *the new, new thing.* Two billion people on the Internet now with one trillion interconnections with *intelligent objects* (sensors and robots) produce the 'raw product' of the new Smart City and smart world. Big Data and content will increase 44X, or 35 zettabytes, by 2020 (1 zettabyte is "1" with 21 zeroes/bytes of data). The future belongs, *Gig.U* thinks, to those who mine, sift and analyze information. Collaboration and creativity are the human components of the Smart City. Will it work? Only insofar as we do not alienate our inner most heart and soul, and trust ultimately in God, not our intelligence.

I think Jane Goodall and King Solomon should be consultants to *Gig.U.*

Lord, we know so little about what we know. We trust in you with all our heart and soul. Amen

Come, all of you who are thirsty, come to the waters; and you who have no money, come, buy and eat! Come, buy wine and milk without money and without cost. Listen, that you may live. I will make an everlasting covenant with you, my faithful love promised to David. Isaiah 55:1, 3

Can you hear the voice, tune, and lyrics in your brain triggered by the mere thought of "Que Sera, Sera" ("Whatever Will Be, Will Be")? The voice belongs to Doris Day, the tune is a memorable jingle, and the lyrics are the philosophy of millions. There is an old repartee counterpoint: "When I was just a little boy, I asked my mother, what will I be? Will I be handsome? Will I be rich? Here's what she said to me." She said, "No!"

Is the history of our lives controlled by fate? The "what will be, will be" philosophy is depressing. It is not biblical. The Bible is clear: we have choices that determine destiny. Why? God's M.O is love. That means there is always a choice. Our lives are not controlled by fate; our basic choices—I mean by that "our decisions"—create our history. Think of the three great choices every young person can make that change the entire history of their adult lives. 1. The choice of faith, "In Whom will I put my trust?" 2. The choice of a partner for life, "Who will be my companion for life?" 3. The choice of vocation, "What calling will I follow?"

Edmund Burke is frequently quoted without credit for saying, "Those who don't know history are destined to repeat it." Those who don't know history may think "Que Sera, Sera" is immutable. Therefore, they will repeat the foibles of the past because they did not know the stunning freedom of choices God has put in our hands.

We may choose to trust God's "faithful love and everlasting covenant."

'Listen, that you may live.'

God, who is love, thank you for the choices you have placed in my journey of life. Amen

The life I now live in the body, I live by faith in the
Son of God, who loved me and gave himself for me. I do not set aside
the grace of God. Galatians 2:20

It's September. I apologize, for some reason my mind wandered to football. Last week Kenny Stills and Drew Brees were honored for their stellar performance in New Orleans' win over Atlanta. When Kenny left the University of Oklahoma for the NFL a year early, many critics voiced their doubts that Kenny Stills would be ready for the NFL. Since his high school days in Carlsbad California, Kenny has received ambiguous messages about his demeanor and appearance. He is an attraction: Mohawk, pierced, tattooed, and Tweeting, set records as a true Freshman, runs a '4.3s 40yd,' wears a strong theological statement (tattooed from wrist to elbow, on the inside of the arm so he can be reminded what the message is), and succeeds in performance... these types get hypes.

I would rather talk to Kenny about his faith statement-tattoo: "When God takes something from your grasp, he's not punishing you. He's merely opening our hands to receive something better. The will of God will not take you where the grace of God cannot protect you." St. Francis de Sales said, "Do not wish to be anything but what you are, and try to be that perfectly." I think Kenny Stills is a perfect Kenny Stills. And, from our old friend Kierkegaard, *"There is nothing with which every man is so afraid as getting to know how enormously much he is capable of doing, and becoming."*

Kenny catches the attention of people who are not hearing anything from the oracles of the pulpits. Kenny will talk to you about his faith. He may even Tweet you. Have you talked, Tweeted, tattooed, or texted anyone about your faith lately?

Eternal Christ, let me never, ever, 'set aside' your grace. Amen

Praise the Lord. How good it is to sing praises to our God, how pleasant and fitting to praise him! He heals the brokenhearted. The Lord delights in those who put their hope in his unfailing love. Psalm 147:1, 3,11

Have you ever had your heart broken? By a person you love, by heart disease, by a physical wound? Hearts heal remarkably. If you have a broken heart diagnosis, listen to this optimistic broken heart prognosis: "God heals the brokenhearted."

Major Sullivan Ballou wrote this letter to his wife, on July 14, 1861, a week before the Battle of Bull Run: "Dear Sarah, / The indications are very strong that we shall move...tomorrow. Unlest (sic) I should not be able to write you again I feel impelled to write a few lines...

"I have no misgivings about the cause in which I am engaged. My courage does not falter. Sarah, my love for you is deathless. It seems to bind me with mighty cables that nothing but omnipotence can break. And yet my love of country comes over me like a strong wind and bears me irresistible with all those chains to the battlefield.

"If I do not return, my dear Sarah, never forget how much I loved you, nor that when my last breath escapes me it will whisper your name...I shall always be with you in the brightest day and the darkest night. Always, always. And when the soft breeze fans your cheek, it shall be my breath, my spirit passing by.

"Sarah, do not mourn me dead. Think I am gone and wait for me, for we shall meet again."

Major Ballou was a 32-year-old attorney in Smithfield, Rhode Island and answered the call of President Lincoln in April of 1861 when Fort Sumter was bombarded. He was killed at the first Battle of Bull Run.

Have you put your hope in God's unfailing love?

Thank you for the challenging memories of Sarah and Sullivan and all witnesses to your omnipotent power to heal the broken heart. Amen

Do not boast about tomorrow;
for you know not what a day may bring. Proverbs 27:1

"**C**an you give one reason that you cannot make the good, and right decision now, today? You have already said it is a decision that affects all the days of the rest of your life." These were the words offered to a person in the crux (think: "crucible.") of making a tough but right decision.

"Get action. Seize the moment. Man was never intended to become an oyster."

I think Theodore Roosevelt was 'pretty cool' when he said this. The oyster is just sitting around in a *Waiting for Godot* mode of life, waiting for the environment around her to make a valuable "pearl." The polymath Johann Wolfgang von Goethe had it right. "Plunge boldly into the thick of life, and seize it where you will, it is always interesting." We can laugh with Robin Williams statement, "*Carpe per diem*—seize the check." It is fun, down right joyful, to make good and right decisions. The increased dopamine in our brains confirms us.

Kalidasa gets credit for a beautiful statement translated from Sanskrit: "Look to this day:/ For it is life, the very life of life./ In its brief course/ Lie all the verities and realities of your existence./ The bliss of growth,/ The glory of action,/ The splendor of achievement/ Are but experiences of time./ For yesterday is but a dream/ And tomorrow is only a vision;/ And today well-lived, makes/ Yesterday a dream of happiness/ And every tomorrow a vision of hope./ Look well therefore to this day; / Such is the salutation to the ever-new dawn!" (circa 399 A.D.)

You have shown me, O Lord, what is right. Today shall be a new beginning.

God, we are grateful that you give us opportunities this day, this moment, for new beginnings. We praise your great love, we humbly bow before your presence. Yours is the kingdom, and the power and the glory forever, world without end. Amen

"In your anger do not sin." Do not let the sun go down while you are still angry, and do not give the devil a foothold. Ephesians 4:26-27 (Paul, quoting Psalm 4:4 from the Septuagint, a Greek translation of the Hebrew Scriptures—Old Testament)

I make no apologies for using "golf" as a metaphor for the spiritual life. After all Jesus used unusual metaphors to describe spiritual integrity, such as a simple flower, "Consider the lilies of the field..." Today we look at an interview with Byron Nelson, an exemplary representative of the art of golf. (*Golf Magazine*) I see five axioms in golf as a metaphor of life:

1. Practice, practice, practice. *"In golf, practice builds confidence,"* Nelson said. I remember coach Abe Lemmon's view of practice. "One day of practice is like one day of clean living. It doesn't do any good."

2. Circumstances cannot be controlled—response to circumstances can be. "I *lived through the depression,"* Nelson said. *"It makes you stronger."*

3. Happiness is accepting who you are. *"My wife Louise and I were married twelve years before we could buy any furniture...one of the happiest times of my life."*

4. Forget the past—press on now. Everyone has seen a golfer melt down with anger for playing badly. It ruins his day, maybe others too. The Bible says get rid of anger before the sun goes down. Nelson says, get rid of it now: *"Forget the last bogey when you get to the next tee. Play one shot."* Press on now.

5. "Fortune favors the bold," according to a Latin proverb; Nelson says, *"By nature I'm conservative, but sometimes you have to step out boldly."*

One reason why metaphors work for describing faith: our belief in Christ is completely emerged in the reality of the world where we live. The spiritual world and the material world co-exist in Christian theology.

God, I learn about faith everywhere, even on a golf course. May I learn to honor you through all the activities and thoughts in my life. Amen

You have heard that it was said, 'Eye for eye, and tooth for tooth,' But I tell you, do not resist an evil person. If anyone slaps you on the right cheek, turn to them the other also. Matthew 5:38-40

Sometimes I muse, "Wish Jesus hadn't said that, or, hadn't done that." My dear mom and I had a little discussion on this subject. I was about 25 years old, living in Scotland, when I told her about my first taste of Port wine, in a Church of Scotland, the pastors' study, with all twelve elders present and participating. It was the custom of this Kirk's elders and pastors to enjoy a beverage ritual every Sunday after the last of the morning services. The pastor and elders briefly talked among themselves, then, standing in a circle, everyone was handed a beautiful *Port Sipper*. A bottle of *Fonseca Tawny Port* was passed, each filled the neighbor's glass, the pastor said some-thing, and we sipped Port and continued conversations. It was a quasi-sacramental moment.

Upon relating this to mom, she took exception. We had a nice discussion about wine, wine scenes from scripture, and I reminded mom that Jesus turned water to wine (John 2). Her classic response: *"I know he did, but I would have thought better of him if he hadn't."*

Jesus did and said ethical things we hesitate to do: forgive an enemy, accept persecution for beliefs, challenge authorities, and be a victim who "turned the other cheek." Today's scripture on 'turning the other cheek' is the text that Branch Rickey gave to Jackie Robinson. Ricky, the white President of the Dodgers, was mentoring the first black athlete to break the 'color barrier' in baseball. Both belonged to Methodist churches, both knew the teaching of Christ. Ricky quoted Jesus to Robinson who faced abusive situations numerous times. Robinson reminded Ricky, "I have only two cheeks." You know the story of the famous Robinson. Faith and perseverance won. The history of America changed.

Thank you, God, for Jackie Robinson and those saints who heard and obeyed Christ's words. Amen

I will sing to the Lord, for he is highly exalted. The Lord is my strength and my song*; he has become my salvation. Exodus 15:1-2 *(The word 'song' in this Hebrew text may be translated 'defense'.)

Eternal God, whose mystery is beyond the reach of all human minds, I thank you for the miracle of music. In many ways you unveil yourself to us, especially in the universal language of music. Music sooths the harsh edges of negativity. Music caresses the longing in my soul. Music pacifies anxiety. Music elevates the mind to majestic vistas. Your steadfast love and abounding grace make music in my heart.

You were the Lord of the Dance when Moses and his sister Miriam played the tambourine and danced to music praising you. God, thank you for the image of Moses and Miriam pirouetting to song in praise of you.

You gave your servant Deborah a song of victory. You gave Mary, the Mother of Jesus, music to "magnify" her soul. Lord, guide me to that humble place of hearing music that my soul may be magnified with love.

When the truth streams into my heart through music, I am filled with joy for the canticles of faith. "In distress I call upon you, and you hear my cry." Heavenly Father, with David I sing: "You are my rock and my fortress. The waves of death may encompass me and the torrents of perdition assail me." You are the redeemer who gives me a song of rejoicing.

Thank you for the image and imagined sound of the Apostle Paul singing in his prison cell during a terrible night of suffering. I delight in the image of Jesus singing in the night before his crucifixion. I confess my inability to sing along a road leading from Gethsemane to Golgotha. Without music from you, Lord God, I would be a body without a soul. Praise unto you, Christ, my strength and song, my mediator and music. Amen

*For I am not ashamed of the gospel, because it is the power
of God that brings salvation to everyone who believes...'The righteous will
live by faith.' Romans 1:16-17*

This text is the thesis for Romans; it is also the theme of the Protestant Reformation. To show the relevance of this theme for our times, I shall paraphrase a story told by Karl Barth, one of the greatest theologians in history. The story is a metaphor of his own life as a minister of the Word of God.

A pastor of a village church wrestled weekly for a sermon to give to his parishioners. One night he was fearfully alone, and his mind simply could not concoct one more sermon. He climbed up inside the bell tower to the top. It was midnight. Maybe he could get an inspiration in the cold night air. Still no idea came for a sermon. In his angst he lost his balance, stepped backwards, and began to fall to bottom of the bell tower. He saved his life by grabbing the only thing solid in the middle of that empty space—the rope to the great bell inside the bell tower. The frantic grasp saved the pastor's life, but it also began the tolling of the bell. The villagers awakened and ran to the church. Gathering inside the chapel they waited with impatient expectation for the pastor to give them an emergency message in the middle of the night. The disheveled preacher stood before them. He had no message. There was a long, long silence. The villagers went home.

That, Karl Barth said, is what the people of Europe were getting from the established church pulpits in time of war. Expectations to hear...the spokespersons for Christ are silent. In the time of World War I, Karl Barth transformed his own message about the Gospel of Christ. Romans 1:16-17 became his new theme.

Do you have a Bible text for the theme of your life?

Thank you, God, for the grace of Christ that we receive freely, only through faith. Amen

For I do not do the good I want to do, but the evil I do not want to do—this I keep on doing...What a wretched man I am! Who will rescue me? Thanks be to God, who delivers me through Jesus Christ our Lord. Romans 7:15ff

Paul is writing as a Christian. He knows himself, and is honest about himself. His life is a divided enterprise, a duality of intense interests pulling against each other. Adam Smith said, "On the road from the City of Skepticism, I had to pass through the valley of Ambiguity." Paul notes how deep and dark that valley is.

No one understood better than Paul, the experience of Christ's grace that touches us in the core of our personality and the center of our spirituality. In the words of Karl Barth, "No one can be saved—in virtue of what he can do. Everyone can be saved—in virtue of what God can do." The bridge of grace crosses over the canyon of our duality.

Do we not experience a little bit of Arthur Schopenhauer's widely known 'Parable of the Porcupines?" I briefly summarize: A group of porcupines are freezing one winter's night. They huddle together for shared warmth, but the closer they get to each other, the more they prick each other with their quills. So, they pull apart, and freeze, then come together again and irritate each other. Is there ever a balance between the need of dependent companionship and the feelings of aversion and independence?

In the Bible we see a love relationship with God that allows for the close companionship and independent choice. Independently, "Work out your salvation with fear and trembling." Dependently, "For God is at work within you both to will and do his good work." Solitude and community in the community of Christ is healthy, and required.

Lord, guide me in the choices of solitary experience of your love, and the community of your presence with love for others. Amen

Sing to the Lord a new song, for he has done marvelous things.
Shout for joy to the Lord, all the earth, burst into jubilant song with music.
Psalm 98:1,4

In one phase of my ministry I had the enjoyable and educational opportunity to visit Christians in their respective church homes in over sixty nations of the world. Because our international mission relationships dealt mostly with the people of greatest need, the persons I met were in the lower income levels of nations that were themselves in the lower income levels. There was a common denominator among these humble believers. Joy. Over and over again, in their homes, worship services, and community centers I heard laughter and expressions of resiliency best described as joy. I could imagine what it was like for Romans in cities like Athens or Ephesus to come across a group of Christians. Were they not impressed with the sense of authentic happiness and joy expressed by Christians? Why would a Christian be extraordinarily happy?

"Laughter is the closest thing to the grace of God," Karl Barth said; he added, "Joy is the simplest form of gratitude." I have seen this often enough to believe unquestionably the phenomenon. William Wordsworth in "Intimations of Immortality from Recollections of Early Childhood," reflects on the remembrance of joy. "O joy! That in our embers / Is something that doth live, / That nature yet remembers / What was so fugitive!"

Wordsworth's insightful analysis of the mood of joy: it is the 'fugitive' hiding in our hearts, and then it is found. When we find the 'fugitive joy' and release that positive energy in our lives, we will want to pray, "Thou has given so much to me, Give one thing more—a grateful heart... Such a heart whose pulse may be thy praise." (George Herbert, 17th century)

Lord God, I confess looking for vain forms of happiness; let me find the springs of joy that shall flood my heart with jubilant praise for you. Amen

What is mankind that you are mindful of them? Psalm 8:4
Set your minds on things above...your life is now hidden with Christ in God
...put on the new self. Colossians 3:2ff

What does it mean to be fully human? The New Testament does not minimize humanity. It elevates humanness. Scripture shows a cast of characters who found a greater sense of the value about themselves when they were motivated by the energy of God's love.

Ultimately, whom do we follow in faith? At the tertiary levels of faith, we follow people like John the Baptist, Mary the Mother of Jesus, Paul the Apostle, or modern representatives of faith. At the highest level of faith we follow the living Christ. Here's the difference between Christian faith and religions of the world. All religions have a *way* to follow. Christians follow a *person*. In Christian faith we hear Christ say, "I am the Way." We follow Christ, not a prescribed theology ensconced in ideology.

What then is the place of will power in this view of life that we follow Christ? Arthur Schopenhauer's thought is helpful and fits the scripture's view that we have will power, but it is limited, not omnipotent. His analogy: "Will power is to the mind like a strong blind man who carries on his shoulders a lame man who can see." For the follower of Christ, we choose to follow him. We choose him whose love is given to us and proved for us.

Abraham Lincoln understood the choice of humble faith. He wrote over a million words, but only one short paragraph about himself. In 1859 he was running for the office of President of the U.S.A., and a publisher asked for more bio data. He said, "There's not much to it because there's not much to me." Lincoln's humanity is a remarkable model. What does it mean to be human? Choose to follow Christ in what we say and do. Then, our true humanity is discovered.

Today I will commit my faith in you, Lord, and follow the Living Word, Jesus Christ. Amen

Let us then approach God's throne of grace with confidence,
so that we may receive mercy and find grace to help us in our time of need.
Hebrews 4:16

There is for me a high moment of exhilarating expectancy when I sit down (on time) in a theater seat prepared to enjoy a Broadway show in New York City. NYC guarantees that you will have a few anxious moments before one gets to the theater: crowds, gridlock, missed subway stops, pre-theater dinner waitpersons who don't care when the shows start, and oh yes, who has the tickets—wife, myself, which pocket? But we made it! There was time to read the Playbill. *Les Miserables* was the show, spectacular, scintillating, and a historically eloquent epic about the French Revolution. Quoting a note from the Playbill, Victor Hugo wrote, "Will the future ever arrive? Should we continue to look upward? Is the light we can see in the sky one of those which will presently be extinguished? The ideal is terrifying to behold, lost as it is in depths, small, isolated, a pinpoint, brilliant but threatened on all sides by the dark forces that surround it; nevertheless, no more in danger than a star in the jaws of the clouds."

To the 1st century persons seated with expectations in the theater of God's drama featuring Jesus Christ, did they see with confidence that brilliant pinpoint of light, The Light of the World, threatened on all sides by dark forces that surround it? Some saw, believed, and followed that light. That was the beginning of the Greatest Revolution in the history of the world.

We have a high moment of exhilarating expectance this day seeing with the eyes of faith the work of Christ in our lives, and in the world today.

Let us pray a prayer from St. Augustine:

"O God, you are the light of our minds to know you. You are the strength of our wills to serve you. You are the life of our souls to love you. Let me so know you that I may love you perfectly, and so love you that I may serve you fully, whom to serve is perfect freedom." Amen

In all their distress he too was distressed,
and the angel of his presence saved them. In his love and mercy
he redeemed them. Isaiah 63:9

My first over night hunting trip was with my dad and uncle. We were in the Selkirk Mountains near the confluence of the Pend Oreille and Columbia Rivers on the border of Washington State and British Columbia. Tired from the long drive I was embarrassed about my exhaustion. It would not be "manly" for a seven-year-old to complain. The first act of hunting was breakfast cooked in a black skillet and eaten on a tin plate. Thirsty? Drink from the creek flowing out of the shadows of spectacular mountains. Standard protocol. The hunt began.

"You follow the creek upstream," dad said, "Uncle Oliver will go to the ridge on the right, I'll be on the left." Dad handed me a .22 caliber rifle and they left. After following "orders" working my way through brush up the stream, I began to feel more and more isolated. Nothing to see, the rapids were all I could hear, and the sun disappeared in the shadows of the great pine trees. After a couple of hours I was sure that I was lost. Would never be found. Could not detect if I had taken the wrong branch of the stream that divided from its sources of two different canyons. Shouting, "Hello, is anyone there?" seemed futile. The water shouted louder than I.

Suddenly my fears stopped. Dad met me. "Think you were lost? From the ridge where I was standing, I could see you all the time."

"In their distress...his love and mercy saved them." I had a wonderful lesson about God; even though we feel lost, distressed, abandoned, we discover he never leaves us nor forsakes us. "Even when I walk through the valley of deep shadows, you are with me." God can see us all the time.

God, I have felt isolated from love, from your love, only to discover you have never separated your love through Christ from me. Amen

Jesus told them another parable: "The kingdom of heaven is like a mustard seed, which a man took and planted in his field. Though it is the smallest of all seeds, yet when it grows, it is the largest of garden plants and becomes a tree." Matthew 13:31

Dr. Wilfred Funk, famous for the *Funk and Wagnall Dictionary,* was asked, "What are the ten most expressive words in the dictionary?" He answered the intriguing question: "The most bitter word is 'alone.' The most tender word is 'mother.' The most tragic word is 'death.' The most beautiful word is 'love.' The most cruel word is 'revenge.' The most peaceful word is 'tranquil.' The saddest word is 'forgotten.' The warmest word is 'friendship.' The coldest word is 'no.' The most comforting word is 'faith.'"

What do you choose as the most expressive words of the New Testament? I would pick: "grace" "love" "peace" "forgiveness" "unrepentant" "heartless" "disbelief" and "trust." You may match your words with Funk's descriptive phrases such as, "most bitter" or "most tender." Consider the enduring influence of the words you choose. Often, after great nations die, after celebrated people pass away, after adorning audiences are silent, *words* remain as the imperishable foundations of human memory.

The parables of Jesus are the 'right words' for the condition of our humanity. For example, Dr. Funk said 'forgotten' is the saddest word. Jesus assured us that God has not forgotten us. "Look at the birds of the air, your heavenly Father feeds them. Are you not much more valuable than they?" As I write this, a humming bird is feeding outside the window; this bird's wings flap ninety times a second, it can fly up, down, backwards and forward with stunning agility, grace and speed; it's a long distance flyer too, migrating north to the Canadian Yukon, south to Panama.

Does not God care infinitely more for you and me?

Eternal heavenly Father, thank you for creating me and caring for me. Amen

I saw a new heaven and a new earth...Look! God's dwelling place is now among the people, and he will dwell with them. They will be his people, and God himself will be with them and be their God. Revelations 21:1ff

Please permit a recursion to an old fairy tale by George MacDonald entitled *The Golden Key*. Briefly paraphrased: Once upon a time a boy named Mossy and a girl name Tangle met a wise old woman in the forest simply named Grandmother. Mossy had found a Golden Key in the forest and Grandmother said it is their job to find the door it opens.

After a long time going deeper into the woods, Mossy and Tangle come to a grassy plain, or was it a great lake? They could not decide because "it was a sea of shadows." As they walked on they saw many shadows moving, "like groups of children," and there were shadows of "titanic shapes" and "wild horses." "Some of the shadows that pleased them most they never knew how to describe." They became tired from their long journey, sat down and cried: "We must find the country from which the shadows come," Mossy said. Tangle responded, "We must, dear Mossy, we must."

As the fable goes, the journey of Mossy and Tangle continues on for years until Mossy's hair is "streaked with gray and Tangle got wrinkles on her forehead." The fable is about you and me. Life's destiny is its journey. As Paul said, "Now we only see as if we are looking through a cloudy glass." On this journey we have a hunger for the "country from which the shadows come." Eternity, where God is "all and in all."

God, help me to continue in faith through the shadow-land to find fulfillment with you in eternity. Amen

Many people were coming and going...they did not even have a chance to eat. "How many loaves do you have?"...(The disciples) found out and said, "Five—and two fish." Taking the five loaves and two fish, he gave thanks and broke the loaves."... All ate and were satisfied...The number was five thousand. Mark 6:30ff

There are many levels of meaning in this story. For example, we learn that Jesus, the Son of God, practiced the power of prayer and expressed the essence of gratitude, and a miracle was done. In the same way, miracles of changed circumstances happen in our lives. Gratitude unlocks the fullness of life, it turns hunger into a satisfaction, a quick-meal into a ten course feast. We live in a *zeitgeist* of negativity. We transform our social and mental consciousness into positivity by the action of gratitude.

Saint Ambrose, a contemporary of Saint Augustine, taught ministers of Christ the significance of gratitude: "No duty is more urgent than that of returning thanks." Kierkegaard was a contemporary of Marx. His mental brilliance was acknowledged among the intelligentsia. He could have majored in erudite disputation, instead, he majored in spiritual formation. "To stand on one's legs and prove God's existence is a very different thing," he said, "from going on one's knees and thanking him."

Helen Keller, challenged in sight and hearing, never ceased to be thankful. "For three things I thank God every day of life: thanks that he has vouchsafed me knowledge of His works; deep thanks that He has set in my darkness the lamp of faith; deep, deepest thanks that I have another life to look forward to—a life joyous with light and flowers and heavenly song."

Lord, I stop now; stop all the fluttering dispassionate thoughts and worries about others, the world, and impoverished feelings about myself. I focus on you, your miracles of life that surround me. I thank you for faith, forgiveness, and new beginnings. Amen

Can you fathom the mysteries of God? Can you probe the limits of the Almighty? They are higher than the heavens above—what can you do? They are deeper than the depths below—what can you know? Job 11:7-8

Eternal God, Lord of all human-kind, I am unmasked by the test of history. Time will tell. If I am aware of history's lessons, I learn that I cannot live fully a self-determined life. Such a conceit about selfhood, for me, is like boating under full sail with no keel and no rudder. Without the ballast and balance of faith, without the wind power of your Spirit, I am lost at sea. Your wisdom helps me to understand the seas, the tides of time, and the destructive vortexes of the deep.

Without the leading of your truth I misunderstand even my own motivations. Rudeness and aggression may be an imitation of weakness and fear. Persistence may be disguised stubborn indecision. Obtuse profundity may be a shadow hiding the sense of lost understanding.

Without your truth about life, history, self, and community, I may even forget the simplest fact: with one exception, *the entire population of the world consists of others.* I am not the center of life or world history.

Is it true that other people mirror our selves? The power of choice in the attitude emanating from me surprises me. The attitude I project collects an environment I experience. If I live day by day with resentment, I collect about myself a coterie of unhappy people who are bitter about the direction of life and history. If I live with joy in my heart that Jesus had in his, I discover that cheerfulness is not a placebo but a reality.

Thank you, Lord God, for revealing to us the grace of Christ that is out of all proportion to the evil in the world. All wrongs do not compare to his right. Amen

You did not honor the God who holds in his hand your life and all your ways. Therefore he sent the hand that wrote the inscription: "MENE, MENE, TEKEL, UPHARSIN." Daniel 5:23-26

This text represents a dramatic scene in the stage of history. The time is the 6th century B.C. The place is Babylon (modern Iraq). The situation is the Jewish Babylonian Captivity and a feast that has been prepared by order of King Belshazzar. During the banquet a "hand not attached to an arm begins to write on the wall" these words, *"Mene, Mene, Tekel, Upharsin."* None present can interpret the meaning. A captive Jew, Daniel, is brought forward. (Recall Rembrandt's painting of this scene showing the horror and agitation on the faces of the patrons of the banquet.)

Daniel, guided by the Lord, gives the interpretation: "King Belshazzar, your days as a tyrant are *numbered,* you have been *weighed* in the scales of justice and found wanting. Your grand kingdom shall be *divided.*"

Historically, what did happen? That night Belshazzar was slain. In 539 B.C. Cyrus, King of Persia (modern Iran) brought down the Babylonian Empire. The Jews in captivity were set free to return to their homeland in Israel. The temple was rebuilt. The Medo-Persian Empire continued from 539 to 331 B.C. It was defeated by the armies of Alexander the Great; the Greek Empire continued from 331 to 146 B.C.; to be superseded by the Greco-Roman Empire that lasted from 146 B.C to 476 A.D.

History teaches us that the providence of God mysteriously endures the evils of the world. Ultimately, God's justice and mercy prevail.

The same paradigm of truth is at work in our lives. *Mene*= "numbered." *Tekel*= "weighed." *Upharsin*= "divided."

God, in the retrospect of my life, I thank you for teaching me that my days are numbered; you give justice and mercy; you divide from me what is not right. Amen

Rooted and established in love ... to know this love surpasses knowledge—that you may be filled to the measure of all the fullness of God.
Ephesians 1:17

More than once I had a person with sincere intentions, and facing a memorial service for a loved who had died, say words to this effect: "I want a service that is 'upbeat' and no mention of 'death.'" These good people are not an exception in our culture that has built itself from the dangling participles of technologies, and quick fixes for everything from diaper changes to funeral arrangements. (Yes, I read about a drive-in funeral home, "It Saves You Time, No Waiting in Line.")

The so-called "developed world" takes pride in speed and speed of change. Joel Swerdlow, Assistant Editor of *National Geographic* magazine, wrote a beautiful essay describing this adoration of speed, pointing out, "A billion hours ago human life appeared on earth ... a billion minutes ago Christianity emerged ... a billion Coca Colas ago was yesterday morning." Swerdlow then pointed out that some things don't change.

His good friend Bob Haggart, award winning writer for *The Post-Standard* of Syracuse N.Y., was dying of cancer, slowly, but heroically. Swerdlow asked Haggart as a person who knows death is real, "What is important and enduring?" The question was emailed and answered a few days before Valentine's Day in 1997. The last words of Haggart were to his wife: "This is my Valentine to Brenda. Unfortunately it will not taste as good as those 'hearts' that teachers in Kansas helped me paste on big pieces of red paper. It tasted almost as good as a peanut butter sandwich. The best words I have written in my life: *Bob Loves Brenda Forever.*" He died eleven days later and Swerdlow said, "I never got to see him or thank him for answering my question. The answer was *"Love Endures."*

Thank you, God, for the surprising places we see the evidence of your immutable love and enduring grace in Christ. Amen

*We had hoped that he was the one who was
going to redeem Israel...Then their eyes were opened. Luke 24:21,31*

God often meets us in the common events in our lives. Epiphanies can happen at bus stops. One of my colleagues, Jim, would ride the commuter bus from New Jersey to NYC via the Lincoln tunnel every day. After more than a year's experience on the same route, same time and place of boarding, he knew a few of his seat partners as 'friends.' One of his friends was an older businessman who left Lebanon during a period of pogroms to find freedom in America.

After many months of this casual relationship Jim began to miss his new Lebanese friend. Opening mail one morning in his NYC office, Jim picked up a hand written letter from his commuter bus 'friend.' It read: "I have come to regard you as a trusted Christian, and a reliable friend. Please use the enclosed gift to assist the needs of Christian brothers and sisters in Beirut. They are in dire need. Due to health problems, I will not be going to NYC anymore. I will miss you and our conversations." The enclosed check in cursive writing was the largest gift given to the United Presbyterian Church, U.S.A. in its history. Christ's mission work supported in Lebanon has continued for decades. A "chance meeting" in the common course of events creates the uncommon encounter of Christ with his followers.

Note that the two men who met the Risen Christ on the road to Emmaus were without hope, slow to believe, and finally startled by the epiphany of meeting Christ. It may work that way for you or me, now, in our time and place nearly twenty-one centuries later. Even at a bus stop.

Lord Christ, you surprise us in common meeting places of life with the majestic presence of eternal love. Thank you. Amen

Whoever tries to keep their life will lose it,
whoever loses their life will preserve it. Luke 17:33

Would you like to have abundant joy in your life? Would you like to experience serenity? Do you want more love in your life?

Yes, yes, and yes.

It was the inimitable Woody Allen who explained what it would take to become a believer. "If God would just suddenly reveal himself to me, I would believe." Some one asked, "What would that take?" "Well, I think a large deposit in a Swiss bank in my name would do it." I know that Woody is just being incorrigibly humorous, however, Woody's *deus ex machine* imagery of God and providence is not far from the quality of materialistic theological expectations that our culture produces. We want a 'god-out-of-the-machine' and at our convenience, like a vending machine god—put your money in and out comes god just in time to satisfy another self-centered need.

Regarding the leading questions, above, strangely we seem to answer "no, no and no." Why? Fear of involvement; the risk of love; and the desire to live life backwards through a mythology of a past that never really existed. The number one reason we fail to give a hearty "Yes" to God's offer of abundant life? It comes at the price of letting go. The wisdom of Jesus says, "Letting go of self is truly finding one's self."

Better than the Swiss bank account (beside the fact that our federal government is officially obtaining those records nowadays) is the gift of grace that allows us to accept "abundant life, serenity, and love" with no auto deductions from our personal accounts.

We can finally say, "Yes" to God, because Christ is God's "Yes" to us.

God, your love vastly exceeds all promises of this material world. Today, I choose to say 'yes' to your gift of life in Christ and follow his path of faith, justice, and love. Amen

A great and powerful wind tore the mountains apart and shattered the rocks before the Lord, but the Lord was not in the wind...the Lord was not in the earthquake...the Lord was not in the fire. And after the fire came a gentle whisper...Elijah went out and stood at the mouth of the cave. Then a voice said to him, "What are you doing here, Elijah?" I Kings 19: 11-13

Elijah is one of the heroes of faith, a prophetic leader of God's people, but Elijah was like you and me. Sometimes when the going gets tough we are not the tough who get going. Spiritually we run and hide in caves of denial. Elijah had given up on the providence of God.

I have had that experience. That is when the natural power of the created order surpasses our feebleness. Earthquakes, wind, fire, rocks splitting, the whole earth shaking. The power of the presence of God is incomparably greater than nature. Elijah met God, not "in" the natural terrible events, but as a voice independent of all circumstances. And it was personal, *"What are you doing here, Elijah?" Get back to the mission, with the people, where I, the Lord, am working with mercy and redemption. You may hide in a cave, but you can never hide from me.*

When the Word of God became flesh, the Voice of God is heard in the person of Jesus Christ. Then even the name for God becomes more personal in the timeline of biblical history. Through earlier scripture God is variously called, *Elohim, Elyon, Eloah, Yahweh, El Shaddai, Attiq yomin, Illaya Elyonin (Aramaic words) and Ehyeh ser eheyeh (Hebrew, 'I am who I am').* All of those names may connote "a far off God." Jesus called God, *Abba. Abba* translates from its Palestinian Aramaic source, the language of Jesus, as *Father, or Daddy.*

Thank you our dear and heavenly Father, for the personal words of faith, for revealing yourself as "Daddy" and making us "family." Amen

Whoever wants to be great among you must be your servant.
Matthew 20:26

In the New Testament Christians are called a "priesthood of believers" because a priest serves in the name of Christ and all members of Christ's church serve each other in his name. Bonhoeffer said, "The church is only the church when it exists for others." Emil Brunner wrote: "The church exists for service as a fire exists for burning."

In the 2nd century St. Irenaeus endured the persecutions of the Roman Emperor Marcus Aurelius. Irenaeus preached the good news of God's incarnation in Jesus Christ, the God who became human. Jesus set the standard for all humanity. "The Son of Man came to serve, not to be served." Irenaeus preached, "The glory of God is the human person fully alive."

It is a truism with historical evidence, that wherever genuine good is done the opposition of evil raises its ugly head. But it is not at first "ugly." A friend who is a wonderful sculptor created a great art piece depicting the temptation of Jesus by Satan. I asked Leonard McMurray about the way he sculptured Satan; he said, "I used the face of the most beautiful female model I knew." The artist complemented Irenaeus' idea. "Error," St. Irenaeus said, "never shows itself in its naked reality, in order not to be discovered. On the contrary, it dresses elegantly, so that the unaware may be led to believe that it is more truthful than truth itself." Seduction is often the introduction to the dark world.

The opposite is true. Service to others from a heart of love obliterates evil. And 'yes,' sacrifice may be involved.

There is a long, long lineage of Christian servants of Christ that connect the present day back through the generations of faith leading us to the foot of the cross.

God, I confess that you have shown me that the only thing in human life that really counts is love that serves others as Christ served us, without judgment, with grace and truth. Amen

*Forgive as the Lord forgave you. And over all these virtues
(compassion, kindness, humility, gentleness, and patience) put on love,
which binds them all in perfect unity. Colossians 3:12ff*

Some warning signs are not relevant. For example, there used to be a sign on a highway (maybe it's still there?) approaching Washington D.C. passing by Reagan National Airport. It read: "Beware of Low Flying Planes." I thought about that each time I saw it, but what do you do if you see a low flying plane coming at you?

Here's a relevant warning sign: "Put on Love Before It's Too Late." It is the only thing that endures in life. While living in the U.K. I would occasionally hear a British slang phrase, "Tickety-boo." Danny Kaye sang a Scottish song in the film, "Merry Andrew" that was entitled "Tickety-Boo." Loosely translated it means 'all is in order as it should be.' *Wouldn't life be wonderful if it were tickety-boo?*

In reality we encounter ambiguity, the shadow lands, the Dark Force, and 'barbarians at the city gates.' Life is not tickety-boo, for anyone. Thomas Wolfe describes a finality where love and destiny endure:

"Something has spoken to me in the night, burning the tapers of the waning year; something has spoken in the night, and told me I shall die, I know not where. Saying: 'To lose the earth you know, for greater knowing; To lose the life you have, for greater life; To leave the friends you loved, for greater loving; to find a land more kind than home, more large than earth.'"

"Love outlasts everything." "We love because he first loved us." "This day I will bless you," we recall from the Prophet Haggai. Why can this all be true? For one supremely clear, cogent, and concise reason: *"God is Love."* Now that's a warning sign I find relevant.

God of love, we humbly accept the gift of your love demonstrated in the life, teaching, death and resurrection of Jesus Christ. Amen

> *Let us hold unswervingly to the hope
> we profess, for he who promised is faithful. Hebrews 10:23*

Whether you are getting 'news of the world' the old fashioned way, reading more than one good newspaper each day, or checking 'Safari' on your iPhone, or looking over someone's shoulder at the establishment you frequent at 'attitudinal adjustment hour,' you are learning that many of the denizens of planet earth are in "A Descent into the Maelstrom." The short story with this title by Edgar Allan Poe is an allegory of life. It fits many people all the time, and is true for each of us at some time.

The story: three men on a fishing trip in the ocean are caught "in the most terrible hurricane that ever came out of the heavens." Their fishing boat was caught in a giant whirlpool, a maelstrom, that was awesome and devastating. Very large bodies of debris were drawn into the vortex and made a "rapid descent." The boat capsized, one survivor had studied the nightmarish scene and noticed only a few pieces of debris were not drawn into the vortex of death. He hangs on to pieces of carefully chosen debris. Those choices kept him alive. The American composer Philip Glass wrote "A Descent into the Maelstrom" in 1986. The music is so ingenious one can image being wet with ocean spray while sitting in the safety of a concert hall.

Have you experienced a deadly maelstrom in the storms of life when you were stranded in the high seas of anxiety? Do you know any one in this vortex of death?

Hear the good news: *I will never leave you or forsake you. Faith, HOPE, and love are the only things that last. Hold unswervingly to Christ who is our hope and you shall live.*

God, I have seen the depths of despair and the vortex of hopelessness. You have been with me, and saved me, again and again. I shall never forget. Thank you. Amen

The Advocate, the Holy Spirit, whom the
Father will send in my name, will teach you all things and will remind
you of everything I have said to you. John 14:26

This phenomenon has repeated itself several times. The setting is a serious discussion in a group of strong willed and accomplished people. The question is raised, "Who had the greatest influence for good on your life?" The answers invariably center on "*teachers*." Then, the discussion continues as one by one these individuals move from "stories of influence by teachers" to "stories of students and what I learned from them." The circle of influence is complete: *we learn as students from teachers, we learn as teachers from students.*

Is it any surprise that God sent his son into the world as a Rabbi, a Teacher? God also sent the Holy Spirit to us as a Teacher of "all things."

Carrie Underwood, a celebrity star, credits her success to teachers. This includes her mother, Carole, and two sisters, Stephanie and Shanna. All three are teachers. "Teaching was something that ran in my family," Carrie said. "I have always admired my mother and sisters for making a difference in the lives of so many." While Carrie has been #1 on the *Hot 100*, broke *Billboard* chart history, and #1 numerous times on country hits, in her own mind teachers and the faith she learned are the real number one priorities that count. (Carrie was salutatorian in high school and graduated magna cum laude from university.)

Some of the qualities I see in children who teach us: spontaneity in creative activity, unselfconscious exuberance, work and play are the same, and willing to ask "Why?" What traits would you add?

Hear Jesus say, 'become as a child when you enter the kingdom of heaven.'

I think God the Father, Christ the Son, and the Holy Spirit take delight in our childlike exuberance in faith and life.

Joyful, joyful, we adore Thee, God of glory, Lord of love. Amen

> *Above all, love each other deeply,*
> *because love covers over a multitude of sins. I Peter 4:8*

Consider the power of failure. The key idea for Paul is: "The just shall live by faith." His secondary thesis: "All have sinned and fall short of the glory of God." No exceptions, *all have failed.* What can we do except see the positive side of failure? The Greek word Paul uses for "sinned" is *hamartano,* meaning " missed the mark." It could be used in a Greek story of an archer aiming at a target, letting the arrow fly, and 'missing the mark.' This universal condition of humanity sets the stage for miraculous recovery from failure. *The just shall live by faith.* This is not a righteousness we earn, nor can a church give it to us. It is a free gift of God delivered in the person of Christ.

The first Christians knew about the power of failure, and the restoration of grace. They took risks. They were 'gamblers' risking their lives and property to tell the story of God's infinite love and grace. They risked disease, imprisonment, beatings, and death. Greek secular critics called them the *"Paraboluni,"* meaning "the Gamblers." They followed the example of Jesus who risked his life to heal lepers, forgive the condemned, and challenge the false authorities.

Tom Peters talks about the power of failure in the entrepreneurial world: "The essence to me of everything that one accomplishes is failure. That is the *only way to learn."* For the Christian, we fail and miss the mark of our best intentions, the enterprise of controlling our lives. Now we are ready for God's miracle of forgiveness and grace whereby we are controlled by his love.

Help me, God, to learn from my failures attempting to justify myself; I accept your free justification of me. Amen

(This day's devotion is by Ali Barr, my granddaughter, on her birthday, at age 14.) Honor your father and your mother, so that you may live long in the land the Lord God is giving you. Exodus 20:12

'Family' is a word that has a different meaning for every person. A family could have two people or twenty. The only thing that defines a family is the love that is shared with the people in it. Whether your family is related by blood or similarities no one is allowed to say that the family is qualified or not to be a family. Many people turn to the Bible to try to understand family. There are many stories and guidelines on how family members can best cooperate with each other. One of the most important rules is forgive your family no matter what the circumstances may be.

Dear Lord,
Please give me the knowledge to understand my father and mother. I know sometimes I question their motives, but in the end they always have had my best interests in mind. You tell me to love them indefinitely, and I always will. I thank you for my family. They will always be ready to help and love me, even when they are forced to 'turn the other cheek' to me, in Christ. Amen

"As, therefore, God's picked representatives of the new humanity, purified and beloved of God himself, be merciful in action, kindly in heart, humble in mind. Accept life, and be most patient and tolerant with one another, always ready to forgive if you have a difference with anyone. Forgive as freely as the Lord has forgiven you. And, above everything else, be truly loving, for love is the golden chain of all virtues. Let the peace of Christ rule in your hearts, remembering that as members of the one body you are called to live in harmony, and never forget to be thankful for what God has done for you." J.B. Phillips' paraphrase of Colossians 3:12-15

If God is for us, who can be against us?
He who did not spare his own Son, but gave him up
for us all—how will he not also, along with him, graciously
give us all things? Romans 8:31-32

Dietrich Bonhoeffer was a modern martyr of the Christian faith. He died in a Nazi concentration camp in 1945. His magnum opus was *The Cost of Discipleship.* Hundreds of thousands of Christians around the world have benefited from this seminal writing on the meaning of discipleship to Jesus Christ. The original German title of the book is *Nachfolge,* "to follow after" Christ. Bonhoeffer said that disciples of Christ will dare to do what is right. He adds, "Not in the flight of ideas, but only in action is there true freedom. Make up your mind and come out into the tempest of living. God's command and your faith are enough to sustain you."

Bonhoeffer wrote in another place that the disciple grows through four stages of faith experience: l. Self-discipline, putting faith into action. 2. Suffering, willingness to pay the price of one's convictions. 3. Joy: the pleasure of knowing one's life has irrepressible joy and meaning. 4. Death: the final destiny of resurrection through the power of God in the risen Christ.

More than a century ago, Thomas Carlyle noted the influence that action has over one's intellectual life. "Conviction, were it never so excellent, is worthless until it converts itself into conduct. Nay, properly, conviction is not possible until then...Doubt of any sort cannot be removed except by action." Charles Peguy was a French poet, Christian mystic, and a warrior for liberty. He died in the Battle of Marne, in World War I soon after he had written: "Everything begins in mysticism and ends in politics." His faith in action carried him into the tempest of living.

True faith leads to right actions.

God of all life, help me to hear, obey, and follow your Word. Amen

*The wise in heart are called discerning, and gracious words
promote instruction... Gracious words are a honeycomb, sweet to the
soul and healing to the bones. Proverbs 16:21*

I approached the entrance to New College Oxford for the first time with much timidity. I had already met with my Oxford 'Don' assigned as mentor whose credentials were somewhat awe-inspiring. Politely he informed me that 'no American student and no one who was married had ever finished the Ph.D. program he oversaw.' I was definitely American, and definitely married. Entering the college one may notice the motto, since the year 1379: "Manners Makyth Man." This motto in context of the 14th century was a bit revolutionary. In that era it was believed that "birth, wealth, or property makyth man." It was also revolutionary in that it was written in English. The language of all European universities was Latin.

When I stop and meditate for a moment on the text from Proverbs, "Gracious words promote instruction...gracious words are sweet to the soul" many thoughts come to mind. I truly don't remember the teachings of any boisterous, ball bearing jaw boned rapid-fire canon mouthed instructors. Probably like most students, I had my share of this type of instructor. All of the women and men whom I recall with love and gratitude for their 'gracious words' lived by the motto on the main entrance to New College.

Mother Teresa was noted for her wise and gracious words. She said, "We want to teach manners; a social community needs respect in order to overcome chaos."

The New Testament describes the most miraculous event in human history, the incarnation of the eternal Word in the flesh of a person, Jesus of Nazareth. He spoke the truth in love, and his words were like a 'honeycomb, sweet to the soul and healing to the bones.'

Are you looking for a spiritual mentor? Look for one "with a wise heart."

Thank you, God, for those whose manners reinforced good teaching of truths. Amen

When Christ came into the world, he said: "Sacrifices and offerings, burnt offerings and sin offerings you (God) did not desire, nor were you pleased with them." Then he said, "Here I am, I have come to do your will." Hebrews 10:8-9

No authority, power or person, can *forgive* what they cannot *give*. The sacrificial system of forgiving the community fell apart in ancient Israel centuries before Jesus. The elaborate festivals and offerings of Israel did not give life, love, and justice to the people, therefore, it could not forgive murder, hate, and injustice. All of the prophets taught this truth. "I hate, I abhor your festivals and burnt offerings: I require that you do justice, love kindness, and walk humbly with God." (Micah 6: 6-8) David was facing God with his confession of sin (Psalm 51). What does God require? "A contrite spirit."

There is no quid pro quo. No 'something for something.' There is nothing I can do to pay God back for what I have done. It is more than amusing how sophisticated we can be in trying to pay the mysterious power of deity for atonement. We cannot. There is no "something for something" that will make any difference for us, and if the prophet is correct, it irritates God ("Hear the word of the Lord, 'I have no pleasure in the blood of goats.'" Isaiah 1:11) I have not prepared *holokaustos* (burnt whole) offerings of animals for sacrifice, but I have made promises and attempted to change habits to appease God. I could no more appease God, than bribe God. God desires a contrite heart. The cross of Christ is the final word on forgiveness. God forgives all my sin, and all the judgment on sin. I can only accept that gift of love, thank Christ for his sacrificial love, and follow his love.

Lord, I confess my separation from you caused by my sin. I humbly receive your forgiveness through the costly grace of Jesus Christ. Amen

Repent, then, and turn to God, so that your sins may be wiped out, that times of refreshing may come from the Lord, and that he may send the Messiah, who has been appointed for you—even Jesus. Acts 3:19

Great omniscient God, you know all my thoughts and deeds. I pray for the insight of repenting. Repenting, the act of 'turning around,' will be the most intelligent and most moral act of my life.

I have pursued the false gods. They became illusory shadows of real life. False gods birthed stillborn relationships. Turning in a new direction onto a new road of life is my first and greatest need. I cannot take the first step on my own power. I am powerless until I find strength from you.

Thank you for the new way. I discover on my face the warm sun of a new day and the gentle wind of your Spirit at my back. You are a merciful God. You meet me with the most intriguing Companion of the way I have ever met—Jesus Christ. God, as I listen to Christ's words, as we walk together on this new path and new venture, I recall the ugly reality of my old style of thinking and acting. This truth is like hard rain in a storm. It hurts. It washes me clean.

Thank you, God, for the new companions of the way traveling in the same direction with Christ. Slowly I begin to see on the new highway of reality. Once I had to see in order to believe, now I know, believing is the first step to seeing.

Thank your for putting me on the right road. The trip is exciting.

For this I praise your name. Amen (*Credendo Vides*: 'by believing we see')

Rejoice always, pray continually, give thanks
in all circumstances; for this is God's will for you in Christ Jesus.
I Thessalonians 5:16-18

Could I give thanks to God if I had been in a Nazi concentration camp?

If you were there in Barracks 28 of the Ravensbruck Concentration Camp during WWII, you may have witnessed this extraordinary phenomenon of Corrie ten Boom and Betsie ten Boom. It is a story of 1,400 women inmates living in a filthy, flea infested, putrefied prison built for 400. The Nazi tormentors committed unspeakable crimes on these women. At Betsie's insistence, Corrie recalls, "We read I Thessalonians 5:18." Did Paul's admonition to give thanks in all circumstances, include a Nazi hellhole? Corrie thought Betsie was wrong when she said "yes" and that "includes the fleas."

The remarkable story told by Corrie ten Boom has been told to hundreds of thousands through all forms of media. It is a story of grace under fire, the ultimate form of courage. Betsie and Corrie found the window of hope in a seamless wall of despair—the Spirit of the Risen Christ.

Each of us has different experiences that catapult us into the prisons of fear. How did Paul find the courage, let alone the tune, to sing when imprisoned in Philippi? What words did Jesus sing as he made his way from Gethsemane to Golgotha? How can these courageous men and women have this much faith? Only through God who gives "not a spirit of fear" but one of hope and a "sound mind."

When we find ourselves in the incurable conditions, try the transformative power of gratitude: "God, I thank you for being with me and giving me your Spirit who can never be taken from me under any circumstances." Betsie ten Boom died on December 16, 1944; her last words: *"There is no pit so deep that God is not deeper still."*

Thank you, God, for your prevailing gifts of faith, hope, and love. If that is all I have, it is sufficient. Amen

I have come that they may have life, and have it to the full.
John 10:10

Let us think about faith for a moment. The scripture teaches in both the Old and New Testaments that we should love God with all our 'heart, soul and mind.' The New Testament Greek uses the word *psyche* for "mind." It also translates "soul." I do not believe God wanted us to believe only with our heart. If Christ's word is true, it applies to all of life, not a select part of life. Galileo paid a price for thinking as well as believing. He said, "I do not feel obliged to believe that the same God who has endowed us with sense, reason, and intellect has intended us to forgo their use."

Carl Jung was quoted often by the academics who taught the "Greatest Generation" and "The Baby Boomers." This citation likely missed many lecturers: Jung said, "Of all the people who consulted me since I was 35 years old, *there is not one whose problem in the last resort was not finding a religious outlook on life*. It is safe to say that everyone fell ill because they lost what living religion can give, and none were healed who did not regain a religious outlook."

It is true some proponents of faith may sound so heavenly minded that they are no earthly good. On the contrary, it seems to me that people who experience a mature faith have a healthy respect for the profound use of their God given intelligence. Faith, like all true science, lets the object of its investigation determine the method of investigation.

Do you want to know more about Jesus? Follow him; discipline is the doorway to freedom of both the heart and mind.

Thank you, God, for giving us hearts, souls, and minds to love you and one another. Amen

*The Son is the radiance of God's glory
and the exact representation of his being. Hebrews 1:3*

The legacy of Charles de Foucauld lives on in the lives of many Tuareg people in the Sahara Desert of Algeria. He was a military officer of the French Army, priest in the Catholic Church and missionary to the Tuaregs. He was assassinated during WWI, in 1916, while working on a project to keep the Tuaregs safe.

Charles de Foucauld lived a simple life with no income among the people he served. He had a meager hovel for a home, and a rich resource of joyful service for the poor. His writings are wise mediations honed by the austere backdrop of the great Sahara Desert. "Faith strips the mask from the world and reveals God in everything. It makes nothing impossible and renders meaningless such words as anxiety, danger, and fear, so that the believer goes through life calmly and peacefully, with profound joy—like a child hand in hand with its mother."

I learn from this desert missionary priest. The most significant possession we can have is free. It is the God-gifted joy of doing what God calls us to do, and becoming more Christ like in the search to find ourselves.

Maybe that's why God has given us deserts.

Let us pray a meditation from Charles de Foucauld:

"Father, I abandon myself into your hands; do with me what you will. Whatever you may do, I thank you; I am ready for all, I accept all. Let only your will be done in me, and in all your creatures—I wish no more than this, O Lord. Into your hands I commend my soul; I offer it to you with all the love of my heart, for I love you, Lord, and so need to give myself, to surrender myself into your hands without reserve, and with boundless confidence, for you are my Father." Amen

Now Thomas was not with the disciples when (the Risen Lord) Jesus came. So the other disciples told him, 'We have seen the Lord!' But he said to them, 'Unless I see the nail marks in his hands and put my finger where the nails were ... I will not believe."
John 20:24ff

Doubting Thomas got a bum rap and I just added to it; I called him "Doubting Thomas." He is actually a hero of our faith. All of us have doubted aspects of faith at sometime.

John is the only Gospel writer who gives us a bio sketch on Thomas. We learn things about Jesus we would never know without Thomas. I think Thomas represents many in our generation. Agnostic questions run deep in the spiritual tides and currents of thought today.

John tells us that Thomas was the one disciple to have courage to follow Jesus into Jerusalem just prior to the trial and crucifixion when Jesus warned, "I will die there." And he alerted the disciples not to go with him. Thomas alone stood up, "Let us go on. Let us die with the Lord."

A few days later the disciples were with the Lord who gave them private instructions of faith, words never delivered to the crowds. (Read the private discourses in John, chapters 14 through 17) When Jesus said, "You disciples know the truth and way." Thomas said, "No, I don't. Tell me what that means." Then we learn the great response of the Lord, "I am the way, the truth, and the life." Would we have that signal statement if Thomas had not questioned the Lord?

People of courage can be, like Thomas, also confused. He was honest in his not understanding the resurrection. Judge not. Luke makes it clear, "They all disbelieved." When the evidence of Christ's resurrection was given, Thomas made the first declaration in the history of humankind that Christ and God are One when he said: "My Lord and my God."

Thank you for teaching us about discipleship through the Apostle Thomas. Amen

> *One of them, when he saw he was healed, came back*
> *praising God in a loud voice. He threw himself at Jesus' feet*
> *and thanked him—and he was a Samaritan. Luke 17:15f*

There is a difference between religion and faith. When we study religious institutions including churches, we may find instances where religious trappings are simply accouterments added to the rest of culture. Here, the church becomes a club. God is not worshiped. God is a footnote in a eulogy.

Luke tells a story that clearly delineates the difference between religion and faith. Ten lepers come to the Lord, they need something from him. They have heard he may give them something, in their case, healing a disease. Only one was aware of what really happened. He may have come to the Lord for purely a personal need, but he experienced something he never sought, in fact, never knew existed. He received unconditional love. He returned to the Lord, humbly thanked Christ. He found faith. The others had religion, came to an institution that can solve a personal desire. And sometimes religion works, just that way. But religion does not answer the Great Need of our heart. We may have been so pent up in self-concerns that we denied the Great Need was there. The Great Need? To find and receive unconditional love.

All failure comes from our failed attempts to fill the void within us. The unconditional love of God in Christ can. It is free. It is grace. The one leper who found the truth that unlocks one's full humanity was a Samaritan—an outcast measured by the self-absorbed orthodox religious folks who thought the essence of life was performing, presenting, and preening. Can you imagine any thing like it?

Christ, thank you for helping me in a time of need, infinitely more thanks for your unconditional love. Amen

Jesus said to her, "I am the resurrection and the life.
The one who believes in me will live, even though they die; and whoever lives by
believing in me will never die. Do you believe this?" John 11:25

The first three generations of Christians suffered unspeakable atrocities; they were whipped, crucified, burned to death, and beheaded. Some were branded on their foreheads and forced into slavery. Scientists recently found evidence of the severity of the enslavement and the vitality of the Christians' faith. In the mines of New Medea in Africa, Christian slaves etched these words on the walls of stone. *"Bios"* and *"Christos."* The Greek words for "Life" and "Christ." These slaves died in their chains, but the stones testify to their undying faith in Christ who is the Resurrection and the Life. Can you hear Jesus say again, "even the stones cry out." (Luke 19: 40)

Could I leave a testimony of faith that scientists may discover nineteen centuries later?

My wife Lolly is a film aficionado; her rule is simple, "See all of them, except the ones with gratuitous violence." Therefore we saw *The Great Gatsby.* The film is a retrospective on the 1920's and 30's. My granddaddy told many stories about the "Roaring Twenties," "Prohibition" (1920-1933) and the "Great Depression." The real-life society leaders in the Great Gatsby era had a miserable legacy. If the Christians chiseled "Christ" and "Life" into their memory walls, the Great Gatsby gang left the whimper of "Despair" and "Death." Charles Schwab, president of the largest steel company in the nation, died penniless. Arthur Cutten, a grandee and financial speculator, died as a fugitive, insolvent. Jesse Livermore, one of the richest investors on Wall Street, committed suicide. The list of 'rich and famous' suicide accounts is encyclopedic. Can we learn from the past and not repeat it?

Each of us may ask, "What will the legacy of my days be?" What key "words" may I chisel in the stone walls of our age?

God, I choose Christ today who is the Resurrection and the Life. Amen

Do not be far from me...there is no one to help.
My heart has melted within me. My mouth is dried up like potsherd.
You lay me in the dust of death. Psalm 22:11f

William Langland is an obscure English writer from the 14th century whose dates of birth and death and the correct spelling of his name are disputed by experts. Yet, he gave us one line of poetry that I think will sink into your memory forever. Hear the poignant beauty and pristine clarity of Langland's (or, Langely's) 'psalm:'

But all the wickedness in the world, which man may do or think, is no more to the mercy of God, than a live coal dropped into the sea.

We can never underestimate the intelligence it takes to commit the atrocities we hear about everyday. We can never overestimate the deepest level of human depravity. I saw the hurt and suffering from a civil war in Mozambique. In one church the Christians were mutilated to death. The church lives today with a strong congregation witnessing to the Risen and Living Christ. As a symbol of the past, this congregation cut the hands and feet from terra cotta statues representing Christian heroes of faith and placed the statuary in a prominent exhibition that states: Cruelty will not defeat the mercy of God.

"All the wickedness in the world is no more to the mercy of God, than a live cool dropped into the sea."

I must awaken from my nightmare of negativities...most of them are of the 'niggling nabob' quality...and see the vision of the Risen Christ who squelches the heat of human rapacity in the wide cool sea of mercy.

O fathomless sea, O wisdom beyond measure, O forgiveness beyond belief, O joy in redemption, this day I thank you, the Eternal Living God of hope, mercy, and life forever. Amen

*Everyone who believes in him
receives forgiveness of sins through his name. Acts 10:43*

In the weird and wonderful dream of St. Peter recorded by Luke in his 'second volume' of the story of Christ and his disciples, Acts chapter 10, we witness a turning point in the life of Peter and the worldwide mission of the church. We see a bit of strangeness and notice the exhilaration of the effects of this dream. Maybe we can catch some of that emotive energy for our faith today. Here's the situation:

Peter, in a trance, sees a great sheet-like object dropped from heaven. In it is an assortment of animals and birds. God says, "Kill and eat." Peter says, "No, Lord." (What temerity saying "No" to the "Lord.") God gives Peter another chance to get the answer right, and Peter finally accepts.

The backstory: Peter was raised an orthodox Jew. Kosher diet is demanded. A new age, and a new set of circumstances exist. This is the work of God. "Anything I make is kosher," are the words, in effect, God directs to Peter. What is really taking place in this dream affects every Christian in the world in the 21st century. This faith in the Risen Christ as Lord is for all persons everywhere in all of time. Coincidentally it seemed, two strangers led Peter to a Gentile's home on the eve of his fantastical dream. Now he is getting the point of the juxtaposition of the visit and the dream. "My grace through Christ is for all persons, Jews and Gentiles, women and men, slaves and free." Christ is Lord of all, or not Lord at all.

Accident and providence may work in our lives too. That is no coincidence. Can you remember a "coincidence" (providence in disguise) that brought you the gift of grace?

God, today I surrender my preconceived conclusions about other people and accept your perfect will. Amen

*The message of the cross is foolishness to those who are perishing,
but to us who are being saved, it is the power of God...for the foolishness
of God is wiser than human wisdom. I Corinthians 1:18,25*

On the human scale we may think 'might makes right,' 'money follows money,' and 'intelligence leads to truth.' I took an old Mercedes bus trip with a few friends across the Sinai Desert in a day trip from Jerusalem to Cairo. The desert looked like deserts look, in photos. The surprises were the large number of old steel monuments, "dead military tanks," from the last war between Egypt and Israel. History is full of monuments proving that might, money, and intelligence don't prevail. These human scaled forces do build empires, but all empires fail. The Sinai belonged to the Egyptians, then the Persians, then the Greeks, then the Ottomans, then the British. None of these empires survived.

In this same territory the force known as the "foolishness of God's love" was unleashed twenty centuries ago. The kingdom of God's love centered in the humble love of Jesus Christ. His power of forgiveness and grace shall continue forever.

How else should it be? If God created us in order to love us, he created us to love him and all others he created. That is the foolishness of the love paradigm; he could not create us in love without giving us the choice, "Yes" we will love him, "Yes" we will love others, or, "No" we will not. That's the weakness or the foolishness of love. Can you think of a better design for creation? If God made us perfect, then there would be no choices. We would be perfect—perfect robots.

Thank you, God, Creator of all that is. You have given us the choice of accepting or rejecting your love. We are overwhelmed with gratitude for the wisdom of love. Amen

Jesus said to Simon Peter, "Simon son of John, do you love me?"
John 21:15

The Risen Christ asks The Tough Love Question of Peter. Peter was "hurt" (v. 17) by this question ... could Jesus not just have assumed "Yes" as the answer? No. He could not, not then, and not now for you or me. This "love of God" response in faith means a change in direction, motivation, discernment, and affiliation is going to take place in our lives.

This tough love question for those who follow Christ's love will be a life of purpose, joy, and peace. Strange, unexpected and difficult circumstances will happen to those who say, "Yes" to God's "Yes" given to us. The difference is this: bad stuff happens to everyone, but now we have the transformative energy of Christ to be our companion in all circumstances. By faith we do not merely acquiesce to new thought. We affirm a new companion and presence for the journey of life— the living Christ, the Lord of love.

Teilhard de Chardin, scientist and Christian theologian, said: "Someday, after we have mastered the winds, the waves and gravity, we shall harness for God the energies of love. Then, for the second time in the history of the world, man will have discovered fire." The Apostle Peter, and all the people since, who have responded to that tough love question from Christ, know the "power of love" that is greater than all the energies of earth, wind, water, and fire.

I hear the Risen Christ asking me, "Do you love me?" If I say, "Yes," I hear him say, "Follow me."

God, you revealed the mystery of creation in love. You manifested that love in Christ. I commit today to follow the mystery of love. Amen

Now I want you to know, brothers and sisters, that what has happened to me has actually served to advance the gospel...because of my chains, most of the brothers and sisters have become confident in the Lord and dare all the more to proclaim the gospel without fear. Philippians 1:12-14

There is a punctuated equilibrium in the saga of humanity sometimes called history. By and large, what you sow you reap, power rises up and falls, families continue for generations through change. That's the equilibrium. Unpredictably great persons come along who lead changes in everything, the punctuation points of history.

Martin Luther, on October 31st in 1517 nailed 95 Theses concerning the message of the Gospel of Christ to the door of All Saints' Church in Wittenberg and the Protestant Reformation exploded. Everything changed. With the new power of the printing press, the new reality of European universities, new questions about monarchies, and the power of scripture—putting Bibles in the hands of everyone, in their own tongue—the revolution began.

The Catholic Church imprisoned Luther. This gave him time to translate the Bible from Hebrew and Greek to German. That in turn released new energies for the Reformation. The value of reading the Bible in the vernacular produced the value of schools to teach Europeans how to read, write, and do the math. Schools sprang up in every church across Britain, Germany, and Holland. Authoritarian leaders found it much harder to control educated people.

Luther said, "Every person must do two things alone; one must do one's own believing, and one's own dying." He initiated new individual expressions of spiritual life through prayer and music. "Pray, and let God worry," he said. He wrote music and helped place a hymnal in the hands of all: "Beautiful music is the art of the prophets that can calm the agitations of the soul; it is one of the most magnificent and delightful presents God has given us."

God, thank you for education, the Bible, music, and individual freedoms. Amen

(After the crucifixion Jesus appears to his disciples) While they were still talking about this, Jesus himself stood among them and said to them, "Peace be with you." They were frightened, thinking they saw a ghost...He said, "Why are you troubled, and why do doubts rise in your minds?...Touch me and see." Luke 24:36ff

O Master of the tactile world, I praise your way of meeting us in the mystic of touch. You, Lord Jesus, said to the doubting disciples after your Resurrection, "Touch me and see."

Blind Isaac wanted to know that his beloved Esau was present. "Let me touch my son."

Lord, you know I prayed about near-death dreams as a child. I was scared, isolated in the deep fears of the somnolent mind. I awakened from my screaming to find the strong arm of my dad holding me. "It's O.K." I thank you, Lord, for your angels of mercy who touch us with love.

God our Father, thank you for the many times there have been healing touches of friends and family, in hospitals, after memorial services, during conversations about a miserable failure, in a 'family waiting room' when the doctor said, "I'm sorry—we did everything we could..." Indeed, the touch of the quiet embrace spoke silent words neither the doctor nor I could voice.

Lord, I can imagine seeing the woman crying out to Jesus in the midst of a noisy crowd, "If I can just touch his robe, I will be healed." She touches Jesus' garment, and I can hear the humming gasp of the crowd seeing that she was healed. God, you touch broken, empty, and lonely hearts. Thank you.

Christ of the incarnation, you said, "Bring the babies to me," and you picked them up, touched them. The Word became flesh in the touch of love and dwelt among us; you are the real Messiah in a real world. Thank you.

Spirit of God, you "teach us all things." Teach me to feel your transforming power touching my soul with truth. Amen

In Christ we, though many, form one body
...We have different gifts, according to the grace given to us.
Romans 12:5-6

"Invention is compounding an idea and transporting it from one field to another," philosopher David Hume said in the 18th century. As a student in Edinburgh I walked on "Hume Street" frequently. I'd ruminate, "If Hume were alive today he would exalt in the compounding of ideas taking place now. Hume knew that Guttenberg's "invention" of the printing press was a "compounding of ideas." In modern times, "compounding" and collaboration of ideas takes place at warp speed.

The first successful flight of the Wright Brothers is a perfect example of "compounding ideas" and "transporting them from one field to another," namely, from a bicycle shop to an airplane. Larry Page and Sergey Brin developed an algorithm suggested by "compounding the idea" how academics used a ranking method for the sprawl of data that are available in research articles, and, putting that next to the stunning volume of data that are available on the World Wide Web. Between "cataloguing and www." compounded ideas were transported via an algorithm creating Google. The old philosopher Hume was spot on; I don't believe the adage that "Philosophy bakes no bread."

The future of the church, the strength of the church shall be in the compounding of ideas from many followers of Christ who have different gifts. I believe the Apostle Paul's comments fit perfectly with Hume's proposition. The church as a whole is the body of Christ serving God's will for love and justice in the world. The church is a body of persons, each with different talents and gifts of the Spirit. The collaboration of all these resources "transported" to the place of need, the world. Though this world is painfully broken and desperately grasping for life, disciples of Christ collaboratively create a future with hope by *compounding their gifts and transporting them to good works of love.*

God in heaven, send me to work with others to do 'thy will on earth.' Amen

All authority in heaven and on earth has been given to me. Therefore go and make disciples of all nations...teaching them to obey everything I have commanded you. And surely I am with you always, to the very end of the age. Matthew 28:18-20

You can trust the future. Sounds implausible? It is not surprising that our Narcissistic Age has become a Cynical Era. Gazing at oneself as the singular reality that matters would naturally produce pessimistic cynicism.

Nevertheless, you can trust the future. Why, because you can trust the Lord of the future, he is Jesus Christ. "I am with you to the very end of the age," are the last words of the Risen Christ.

Moses packed lightly when he was fleeing from captivity in Egypt. The best of the Egyptian military were in fast pursuit in chariots. The Israelites travelled on foot and carried their baggage. In the hurried moments of preparation for the flight, Moses exhumed the "bones of Joseph" and carried the bones of Joseph, a hero of faith and leadership, on the "Exodus from Egypt." This strange gesture was a reminder to the Israelites: *You can trust the future.* You are following the same Lord God who guided and blessed Joseph. Joseph had been saved from the pit of despair and death to become a leader and savior. This Lord God is leading you now. Trust the future.

I know we look around and see a geo-political swamp. Yes, we may be up to our elbows in alligators and hear the shouting, "Why didn't someone drain the swamp?" But who is your god of the future? Is your hope for the future in a political authority like Merlin of King Arthur, Conan the Barbarian, Red Sonja the Vengeful, Jabberwocky the Hapless One, or Willow the Reluctant Dwarf?

Choose this day whom you will serve as Lord of the future. You may decide to follow Christ who is the Alpha and Omega, beginning and conclusion of faith.

Thank you, God, for Christ who has all authority to lead us to the future. Amen

*Therefore, if anyone is in Christ, the new creation
has come: The old has gone, the new is here! II Corinthians 5:17*

Change is inevitable, but some-times it is painful. When change becomes essential to survival we know 'it is for the greater good' but it never-theless may be fearful and impregnated with angst that we cannot escape. Do we have a choice between change or die? I say, change and overcome the fears com-mensurate with the transition. I have witnessed this costly grace, this painful change, and this period of vulnerability numerous times when persons "Twelve-Step" out of a life of addiction to sobriety.

Marine biologists discovered some-thing about lobsters that pertains to the art of transition. Lobsters depend on their shells to protect them from predators or being crushed by the surf against a rocky shore. However, in order to grow to matu-rity a lobster, we learn from the scientists, must shed its shell. It leaves the safety of its past life. For a time it is vulnerable to fish—predators for whom it was not prey when it was in its shell. Suddenly the lobster finds it can be a Bouillabaisse Provençale for many predators. Life in transition from the old to the new creation is not as easy as duck soup. The lobster waits as the new shell forms. If the lobster did not go through this transition, its old shell would cause its death. The old life would become a casket. *Transitory inse-curity is a necessity of maturity.*

What are the old shells around our old egos that needed to be shed, and if not, the old armor would become a casket in-stead: old prejudices, old paradigms of truths, old boundaries around our behav-iors, old parameters around attitudes of what is possible?

In Christ the new creation has come. The transition may make one feel vulner-able. The alternative may be soul-death.

Eternal God, thank you for invading this infinitesimal soul of mine and creat-ing the gift of the new creation. Amen

You are in error because you do not know
the Scriptures or the power of God. Matthew 22:29

In this text we meet Jesus upbraiding the Sadducees, expert lawyers, and charging them with ignorance of the law. Do you think some thought Jesus, an itinerate rabbi from Galilee, a wee bit impertinent?

I first met Reverend Dr. Benjamin Weir in Beirut before his kidnapping and imprisonment for seven years by Hezbollah. We became good friends. At the same time he was taken hostage so was Terry Anderson, a *New York Times* correspondent. After their release, *The Times* carried a story that referred to "Bible reading in a Muslim prison." The story was front-page news around the world. Anderson mentioned in their first press conference that one reason for surviving was "reading the Bible...I read it fifty times." Hezbollah allowed the hostages to have a copy of the Bible, and nothing else for reading. I asked Weir, "Is that true?" He said, "Yes, it's true and the number of readings Terry mentioned is reasonable." For both hostages, a journalist and a missionary, the Bible was a primary source for maintaining sanity.

I think this extraordinary scene of intensive focus on Bible reading takes place all over the world every day. As of December 31, 2011, the Bible had been translated into 2,454 languages and dialects of the world.

Some time ago, an assignment in my work for the church took me to a small village in the jungle of Java. There I met an Indonesian pastor noted for success in evangelism. I asked, "How do you do it?" He said, " I don't 'do' anything. I give the people a Bible in their own dialect, and a hymnbook, which essentially is the Bible set to music. The Spirit of God does the rest." His most recent startup church had 5,000 members in three years.

God, please direct my focus to seriously engage your Living Word, Christ, in the words of the Bible. Amen

I was shown mercy so that in me, the worst of sinners,
Christ Jesus might display his immense patience as an example for
those who would believe in him and receive eternal life.
I Timothy 1:16

"Do you think he will ever change?" This must have been the question in the minds of many first Christians who knew the real background of Paul (when he was Saul). He was a Pharisee, hated followers of Christ, and would stop at no extreme to remove them from this world. We may surmise that Paul was among the ruling council that put Jesus on trial and demanded his death. Pharisees saw the popularity of Jesus; "Look, the whole world has gone after him!" They plotted late into the night to kill Jesus. Paul had good reason to call himself, "The worst of sinners."

Paul changed. He gave his life for Christ's mission of love. Here are the steps of "change" that we see in Paul, and steps we could apply to ourselves.

First: I recognize the need for change. I can live behind walls of defensive mechanisms but life tends to break down the siege walls around my egocentric castle.

Dostoevsky said, "The only hell I know is the hell we build for ourselves." Life in that old self-absorbed castle is hell. Second: I accept the choice God gives. Jesus called it a choice between a wide gate and a narrow gate. The gate of destruction is wide because its pathway requires no discipline. The narrow gate invites us to follow One Lord, not many. Third: I am freed by forgiveness, now I can forgive. This cuts the vicious cycle of retribution that gets me nowhere. Fourth: I say "Yes" to the power of the kingdom of God within me.

We change the future by accepting God's change in us.

Spirit of the Living God, take me, change me, fill me, and use me in love's mission. Amen

I tell you, "All you need to say is simply 'Yes' or 'No';
anything beyond this comes from the evil one." Matthew 5:37

We live in a time of Equivocation. Listen to the pundits, the pulpits, politicians and all the people-pleasers. "Go not to the Elves for counsel," writes J.R.R. Tolkien, "for they will say both no and yes." A minister's wife called the bluff of her equivocating husband. "My dear, you are such a people-pleaser. I heard you tell one elder, who was against a pipe organ fundraiser, "You know, I think you're right." Minutes later another elder told you he wanted the fund drive and you said, "You know, I think you're right." Darling husband, you don't have conviction in your word. He said, "You know, darling, I think you're right." Yes, it is an 'oldie.' Unfortunately, it is still relevant.

The famous futurist Buckminster Fuller had these words put on his tombstone: "Just a Trim Tab." The trim tab is a humble device that can adjust the course of the mightiest ship. What is the humble device or action that can change the course of history of an organization, church, or nation? What would the trim tab be in our era of equivocation for yourself, your career, your family relationships, your church?

People of integrity who do not surrender to the goddess of Equivocation can change history. Say "Yes" to Christ. Say "No" to duplicitous deals. Say "Yes" to family. Say "No" to destructive addictions. Say "Yes," to empowering others. Say "No" to entitlements without service.

Gandhi said, "No one ever accomplishes a worthy end of life with unworthy means." None of us may be the primary cause of great change, but all can be willing agents of changes. We are like trim tabs, small and important, in the course of providential history.

Lord, today I want you, others, and my own inner mind to know where I stand. I say an unequivocal "Yes" to your perfect will. Amen

Then I saw "a new heaven and a new earth," for the first heaven and the first earth had passed away..."Look! God's dwelling place is now among the people, and he will dwell with them. They will be his people, and God himself will be with them and be their God. "I am making everything new!" Then he said, "Write this down, for these words are trustworthy and true." Revelation 21:1ff

If you listen to every word and envision every act of Jesus in the New Testament, you will in all cases find these two 'trustworthy' truths:

One, God's sovereign love is present in you. We have not always affirmed it, and we certainly have not always accepted it, but sovereign love is there for you. The Kingdom of God is in you.

Two, every single person you meet is, by nature, a person who needs forgiveness. That means the spouse, the child, the father, the mother, the employees, and the employer. It means all persons in positions of authority, in all nations. The need for forgiveness is the common ground of our humanity. The reality of God's sovereign love and grace is the foundation of all creation. "These words are trustworthy and true."

Standing in the presence of this sovereign love, we are in need of forgiveness. If we work on these two premises, we will find the renewing spirit of God working in our lives. It will change everything. It is the new creation.

Paul's convincing thought (II Corinthians 5:14ff) is based on the two truths: God's sovereign love, humanity's need of forgiveness: "For the love of Christ urges us on because we are convinced that he died and gave his life for all. From now on we regard no one from just a human point of view. Anyone who is in Christ is a new creation. The old has passed away. Everything has become new, and all of this is from God who reconciled himself to us."

Thank you, God, for your sovereign love and forgiveness in Christ. Amen

*The Lord said to Ananias, "Go! This man is my
chosen instrument to proclaim my name to the Gentiles and their kings,
and to the people of Israel." Acts 9:16*

Ananias could not have been pleased with this mandate from the Lord. The man he is sent to retrieve is Paul (then known as Saul). Ananias would have known that Paul came to do violence to Christians. He intended to put them in chains and haul them back to Jerusalem for trial and punishment, or death. The Spirit intervened. Paul was in the middle of a transformative conversion. There is no way Ananias could have known if Paul was now a good guy, or a baddie. But Ananias trusted, not his instinct, not the social media's opinions, but his inner spiritual insight. He knew and trusted the will of God.

Have you ever sensed what God's will is, but found yourself in a circumstance that it was hard to obey? Most of us identify with Ananias' trepidations.

When Agnes Gonxha Bojaxhiu was twelve years old she experienced a "calling," a sense of the Lord's will to become a nun. At eighteen years she thought the Lord was calling her to be a missionary. She asked a priest, "How can I be sure it is the right thing to do?" He told her, "Through your joy." Hemingway once defined the "ethical right" as "what feels good afterwards." Jesus pursued his calling from God "for the joy set before him."

Isn't the answer Agnes Bojaxhiu received from the wise priest the answer to our own calling? Christ has a mission, a purpose in life for each of us. Whatever it is, if we follow the calling, we shall know it is the right thing to do—"through your joy" your calling is confirmed.

Oh, yes. The whole world knows Agnes Bojaxhiu. She received the Noble Prize for her missionary work—a.k.a "Mother Teresa."

God, thank you for the calling and the joy, in Christ. Amen

Carry each other's burdens,
and in this way you will fulfill the law of Christ.
Galatians 6:2

In 1992, the Olympics were held in Barcelona. I clearly recall only one event, probably because it received repeat telecasts. Derek Redman, a U.K. runner in the 400m race pulled a hamstring about 300m into the event. That is a painful injury and it would be nearly impossible to continue a race. But Derek did not quit. In a few moments an older man jumped from the stands, ran onto the track, and threw an arm around Derek. Together they finished the race long after all the other athletes. The crowd went wild for Derek. The TV camera operators followed every step of the painful ordeal. In the post-race interviews Derek Redman got more face time on worldwide television than the men who received the medals. Of course he was asked, "Who was the guy that helped you? Did you know him?" "Yes, it was my father."

Lee Iacocca, a famous corporate leader, was fond of quoting Vince Lombardi, a famous coach, who told him what makes a great football team. "There are a lot of coaches with great players that don't win games. Discipline alone won't win games. Winners have great players, discipline, and they care for each other...The difference between mediocrity and greatness is the feeling these guys have for each other."

We reach the goal of life with the support of others around us. It works for sport-teams, companies, churches, and families. *We are saved by faith alone, but that faith is never alone.* The grace of God opens our eyes to someone who is hurting on the racetrack of life; someday it may be you or me. We are motivated to carry burdens of others by the Spirit of God, in this way fulfilling the law of Christ.

God, we know you care for us and strengthen us in times of our weakness. We choose this day to care for others fulfilling the law of Christ our Lord. Amen

Blessed are those who find wisdom, for she is more
profitable than silver and yields better returns than gold. Proverbs 3:15

The first Christmas catalogue arrived at our home on August 28. My wife said, "I didn't know anything started before football season; Christmas just did." Let's prepare for that dithering fast paced, party laced season ending on Christmas Day. I suggest *10 commandments for enjoying the true meaning of Christmas.*

1. Choose a significant purpose for the season. Write down and display it for all in the household to see. If you have the 'why' you can deal with any 'how." 2. Use time as your servant, not your master; make an Advent calendar that honors Christ. 3. Take a chance on your own creativity; don't insist on perfection—for any one or any thing. 4. Celebrate the symphony of the Christian Year. "Holiday" comes from "Holy-Day." Faith increases joy. 5. Include the whole family or your 'family of friends' in the plans for celebration. Little kids, big kids like grandpa/ma, need to participate in Christmas not merely 'be remembered.'

6. Consider inviting others into the tribal gathering. Christmas is a very lonely season for individuals outside a personal conclave. 7. Prepare food and drink with zest and symbolic ritual. See how many you can get involved. Variety in food can be fun. "You are what you eat," one nutrition expert proposed. 8. Expect the Lord to be present, invite Jesus to the celebration. The Lord loves a celebration, if in doubt read John chapter 2 again.

9. Demand for yourself a quiet time each day. Part of the holiday depression syndrome comes from too much human interaction. 10. Affirm with a thankful heart other persons, each day. Yes, affirm yourself too.

Contrary to widespread opinion, keeping commandments is enjoyable, especially if you endorse them in advance.

God, for three gifts I pray: Open my mind to learn more about Christ. Open my soul to receive a larger sense of your Spirit. Open my heart to receive and give love. Amen

I pray that you, being rooted and established in love, may have the power to grasp how wide and long and high and deep is the love of Christ, and to know this love that surpasses knowledge. Ephesians 3:17ff

The morning rays of sunlight filtered through a stained glass window. Select places in the chapel were bright with red, yellow, and blue colors from the window's pallet of hues. Other parts of the chapel were in shadows that seemed to move as one studied their shapes through the haze from the burning incense. The pipe organ's tones echoed off the stone walls and the high ceiling over the nave. Out from the shadows a priest stepped with a lively gait up to the lectern. I was surprised, his prayer was in English. We were in Prague. The priest explained to us after the worship that many of the services are done in English due to the cosmopolitan congregation. The priest read from Thomas à Kempis (1380-1471):

"Ah, Lord God, thou holy lover of my soul, when thou comest into my soul, all that is within me shall rejoice. Thou art my glory and the exultation of my heart; thou art my hope and refuge in the day of my trouble." After hearing the words "day of my trouble," thoughts flooded my mind about days of trouble the people of Prague have known in their lifetimes: occupation by Hitler's army, occupation by the Soviet Union's army with no day of peace between the two, from 1940 to 1989. Of course the stones in the chapel walls could tell their stories of the long nights of war and the short days of peace back to the 15th century when this chapel was built.

I learned from that worship...

Never let the moods of negativity overwhelm the glory and exultation of the heart because the power of Christ's love surpasses all knowledge.

(You are invited to pray the prayer of Thomas à Kempis, above.)

*I consider that our present sufferings are not worth
comparing with the glory that will be revealed in us. Romans 8:18*

"'Hope' is a thing with feathers—That perches in the soul—And sings the tune without words—And never stops—at all." These words of Emily Dickinson are not true for many of our compatriots on this earthly journey.

Ancient Greek mythology explained the problem of evil and human inadequacy by telling the story of Pandora's Box.

Prometheus defied Zeus by stealing fire from heaven and giving it to mankind. Zeus took revenge by sending all the gifts of Pandora (the name means 'all gifts') to humanity, good and evil gifts. Pandora's box of gifts was opened on earth and entered the flow of human history. The only gift that was not released was "hope." Churchill was a grand writer, a great political leader, however he never found the gifts of faith and hope. His last words were: "I am bored with it all."

I paraphrase the words of Paul about the power of hope: It appears to me that what any of us suffer in our darkest hours are dimly discerned shadows when compared to the radiance of the glory and wonder that God has prepared for us. It is as though all creation is standing on tiptoe longing to see an unforgettable vision. This present world does not know its end point. Hope is the gift to peer into the future and see the final victory of Christ subdue the murky machinations of evil. That hope is buried deeply in our hearts.

God, I confess that some days I have acted like one who had no hope, and maybe I was bored with the endless cycles of destruction in our world. Thank you for shaking the foundations of my faith; thank you for placing hope deep in my heart. Amen

I have called you friends, for everything
that I learned from my Father I have made known to you. John 15:15

Prejudice is the dislike of the un-like. It is a delight to meet people of vastly different cultural experiences and discover the commonality at the core of our humanity. Can you imagine Jesus a stranger to anyone? The familiar Gaelic Rune, "I Saw a Stranger," is based on Hebrews, chapter 13.

"I saw a stranger today; I put food in the eating-place, and drink in the drinking-place, and music in the listen-place. In the Holy Name of the Trinity, He blessed myself and my house, my goods and my family. And the lark said in her warble, 'Often, often, often…goes the Christ in the stranger's guise, O, oft and oft, and oft, goes Christ in the stranger's guise.'"

When my spiritual life is on the wane, when the springs of the spirit seem dry, when there is a paucity of peace in my mind, what causes this dis-ease, this disease? Is my spiritual mind fixed like words chiseled on a stone? An awakening of the soul has often come from meeting persons in the most unusual settings, persons some would label as strangers. I was the eccentric piece of the puzzle of truth. Someone I never expected became the force to bring me back to the centering place of love. God's angels in the "stranger's guise." (I project thoughts from Luke 24 as follows):

'Someone' is walking beside us, explaining scriptures to us, and vanishing from our sight. We are slow about rec-ognizing what happened because we are slow in trusting. We long to recognize Christ and refuse to trust the stranger he sends down our road. And so, we miss the blessing. We walk each day missing Christ in the companions of our journey. The journey is not ended. There is time to open our hearts to the message and the messengers along this road.

Our Father in heaven, thank you for the Companion of the Way, Christ our Lord. Amen

You are going to have the light just a little while longer.
Walk while you have the light, before the darkness overtakes you. John 12:35

God, you are teaching me year by year that joy is not found in how long I live, but in what roads I choose for the journey. I ask for guidance to choose the right roads.

Thank you for the choice to walk in the light.

Some days I walk in the dark hour before the sunrise. I cannot see what's ahead. Other times I walk in the last hours of the evening. My vision is impaired by weariness and a wandering mind; I focus too much on the concerns of the spent day. Some days I walk in the bright light of a sunrise filling the earth with splashing colors, first cobalt blues, then the light blues mixing with the cadmium reds, oranges, and yellows, also, the 'hints of pink and blue' moving in the drifting clouds and stretching out to all horizons. Lord, you know these 'walk-abouts' are symbols of my soul's journeys. Through choice, unknown causes both good and evil, I find my spiritual road wandering through dark hours, and hours of glorious light.

Thank you, God, for meeting me wherever I am in Jesus Christ who is the Light of the World. I choose this day to walk while there is light before the darkness overtakes me.

Lord, it is good to remember the forerunners of faith and their journeys with you as guide and Holy Presence. Sarah and Abraham wandered in the desert before they found you leading them to the chosen landscape. I reflect on the journey of Jesus, walking to the garden of prayer, walking to the city of Jerusalem, and walking, stumbling with a cross to Golgotha. Thank you, God, for all these journeys where you have been the inner force of infinite love. Your love is the 'lamp to our feet, and the light to our pathway.' Amen

*God did not send his Son into the world to
condemn the world, but to save the world through him. John 3:17*

In America we are heading into an era of increased skepticism. It is not new to the nation's psychological profile. The text for our meditation is pivotal in John's portrait of Christ. "Not condemning" is part of the theme of God's grace. However, that is not the experience of many regarding the message they heard before they left the church. (A 2013 poll shows the fastest growing denomination in the U.S.A. is "None," as in "What is your Religion?") Years ago Swiss psychiatrist Paul Tournier wrote: "One cannot deal with problems of guilt without raising the obvious and tragic fact that religion can crush instead of liberate."

C.S. Lewis has been one of the most prominent defenders of Christianity in the past hundred years. One time he listened to religious leaders debating "what is unique about Christianity that cannot be found in another religion?" "Incarnation" and "Resurrection" and "Predestination" are not unique. Lewis answered the question: "That's easy. It's grace."

God did not send his Son to condemn, but to offer the gift of grace. This is the core of the New Testament message. It is fundamental to the gospel of Christ. The gift of grace is the theme in the teaching of Jesus. The crowds said, "He teaches us with authority, not as the scribes and Pharisees teach." (Reaction to the Sermon on the Mount, see Matthew chapter 7.)

God does not condemn us. God gives his infinite love to us in the grace of Christ. *Christ's grace is the unyielding, unbounded, unfettered, astonishing acceptance of us, just as we are—weak humans in need of help.*

Can you accept that gift?

Lord, you know my thoughts before my words are spoken. I do not have words to describe the greatness of your love. Thank you for accepting my silence. Amen

Jesus said to the host (of a great feast), "When you give a banquet, invite the poor, the crippled, the lame and blind, and you will be blessed." When one of those at the table heard this, he said to Jesus, "Blessed is the one who will eat at the feast in the kingdom of God." Luke 14:12ff

The *Boston Globe* carried this story about a wedding feast a bride planned. She made a large deposit to the downtown Hyatt. The bill was projected to be about $15,000; a deposit of $6,500 secured the reservation. Fortuitously, the groom got cold feet and backed out of the marriage engagement on the day the invitations would have been mailed. The bride immediately went to the Hyatt and visited with the manager who said, "Because of commitments we have already paid for your banquet. We can only return part of the deposit."

The jilted bride maturely chose a creative alternative around circumstances she could not control. She went ahead with the full banquet. Food, drink, and music. Ten years earlier, the bride was a teenage cast away on the street because of runaway parents and no relatives to take her in. She not only survived, she succeeded. She recalled with gratitude the hospitality she received in Boston shelters for the homeless. These are the unseen lonely souls she invited to her banquet at the Hyatt. It was a picturesque *coup de theatre*, and an act of grace. And yes, among the sumptuous dishes on the menu the bride had the chef serve "Boneless Chicken" in memory of the ex-fiancé.

Have you noticed the varieties of people who have responded to the banquet feast of Jesus Christ down through the centuries? Jesus said, "Truly I tell you, that many will come from the East and West, and will take their places at the feast." (Matthew 8:11)

God, I am surprised by joy, love and exuberant celebrations in your grace. Amen

He took up our pain, and bore our suffering; he brought us peace.
Isaiah 53:4f

Mozart's *Requiem* has a line that causes me to pause, confess, and accept again God's forgiveness: *"Remember, merciful Jesus, that I am the cause of your journey."* I am "the cause of Christ's journey" from the peaceful hill country of Galilee to blood stained stones of Golgotha.

Soon after Bill Wilson and Dr. Bob Smith founded Alcoholics Anonymous, they went to visit prominent attorney "Bill D" who had flunked eight detox programs over a period of years. "Bill D" was strapped in a hospital bed because he had attacked two nurses. Remorsefully he shook his head confiding, "No, no it's too late for me. I still believe in God, but I know he doesn't believe in me any more."

Jesus told his disciples to forgive one another; one asked, "How often?" Jesus said, "Forgive them seven times seventy times."

I have a question for "Bill D" and for you and me: "Do you think Jesus could do that himself, seven times seventy times for me?"

We know the answer. Now what's stopping us from believing it?

Self-deprecation, regret, and despair are the toxins that thwart spiritual freedom in unforgiving hearts. George Herbert, a 17th century writer, used this memorable metaphor: *"He who cannot forgive another breaks the bridge over which he must pass."* Remember the scientific experiment called Biosphere 2 in the desert near Tucson? Four men and four women were carefully chosen to live in an environment designed as perfectly as possible. The "bionauts" were trying to develop reasonable criteria for long-term astronauts living in a space station. The earthlings never finished the experiment. They broke into two groups with an invisible wall of hostility between them.

Forgiveness is not only theological, it is practical, even in the biosphere.

Our Father, who art in heaven, forgive us our sins, as we forgive those who sin against us. Amen

"Then neither do I condemn you,"
Jesus declared; Go now and leave your life of sin." John 8:11

Not By the Sword is a true story by Kathryn Watterson. Larry Trapp of Lincoln Nebraska was a Grand Dragon of the Ku Klux Klan. Trapp made headlines by his conversion from a life of hatred to acceptance and understanding. His extreme and violent activities targeted Jews and others who rejected his principles of white supremacy and anti-Semitism. A particular target of this atrocious person was Cantor Michael Weisser of South Street Temple. After a long period of harassment by Trapp, Julie Weisser, the cantor's wife, suggested they "say something nice to Trapp." The cantor told Trapp, "I hear you are disabled and I thought you may need a ride to the grocery store."

This was the beginning of how hatred's power has an antidote in forgiveness. Because of the persistent congeniality and concern of the Weissers, Trapp broke from the old bonds of prejudice with a memorable question: "I want to get out of what I am doing," Trapp said to Weisser. "How can I?" The Weissers forgave Trapp and he accepted the forgiveness. The conversion began. Trapp gave his final years showing his contrition for his past, and affirming the very groups and individuals he previously hated.

Jesus said, "There will be more rejoicing in heaven over one sinner who repents than over ninety-nine righteous persons who do not need to repent." (Luke 15)

Do you hear the "rejoicing" singers from heaven?

Magnanimous forgiveness transforms life shackled in the web of fear, retribution, and self-revulsion. Forgiveness is the only power that finally breaks the cycle of the predicament of irreversibility—that cycle is hell. Forgiveness is greater than all the powers of evil, and that is why, in our Lord's words, "The gates of hell shall not prevail." (Matthew 16)

Thank you, God, for the rejoicing chorus in heaven witnessing sincere repentance on earth. Amen

The grace of the Lord Jesus be with God's people. Amen. Revelation 22:21
(The last eleven words of the 774,746 words in the Bible.)

Simone Weil's life passed through the bleak European politics of WWII like a bright meteorite full of light greater than herself. She died at age thirty-three. Offered the status and a chair in academia because she was widely regarded as a leading French intellectual, she chose instead to work in the factories and identify with non-elitists. When Hitler's armies rolled into France, she escaped to join the Free French movement. Her tuberculosis was complicated by malnutrition, causing her death. As her only legacy, Weil, a Jew who followed Jesus Christ, left scattered notes and journals. These comprise one of the finest records of spiritual formation ever written.

Weil wrote of two great forces at work in the universe—gravity and grace. Gravity causes one body to attract others and continually tries to increase its sphere of influence. Human beings do the same, Weil said, "Trying to be like gods with increasing influence over others." Adam and Eve are the prototypical humans. They desired all of the knowledge of God. *"All natural movements of the soul are controlled by laws analogous to those of physical gravity. Grace is the only exception."*

Isn't it true? We are drawn by the gravitational force of self-love toward ourselves. We attempt to draw others into the sphere of our self-love. Grace does the opposite. It is not a self-centered force.

The grace of Jesus is more astonishing than his miracles. Miracles broke what we thought were physical laws. Grace broke the death-force of evil. This free, unfettering, unrelenting, all pervading grace of Christ creates the greatest new reality you and I can ever see. C.S. Lewis described it: "Grace creates a full, childlike and delighted acceptance of our need, a joy of total dependence. We become jolly beggars."

God, 'beggar that I am, I am even poor in thanks,' nevertheless my love for you, my desire for your will, emanates from gratitude for the power of your grace in Christ. Amen

Where the Spirit of the Lord is, there is freedom. And we all,
who with unveiled faces contemplate the Lord's glory, are being transformed
into his image. II Corinthians 3:17ff

What is the "image" of Christ that comes to mind when you hear his name? When I was very young, the Bible given to fourth graders by the church had a picture of Jesus. His hair was long, soft, and highlighted. His eyes were blue. This Jesus had a hint of a smile, not unlike Mona Lisa's. I never believed that picture, not even as a fourth grader. Our church lessons from the Bible gave the backstory for a very different image: *Jesus said 'I have come to bring a sword'... Jesus drove the money changes from the Temple...Jesus called the established clergy 'a brood of snakes' and told them they 'knew nothing about God.'*

Italian filmmaker, Pier Paolo Pasolini was forced to stay in a hotel in Florence because of the gridlock of people outside cheering for the popular Pope John XXIII. He couldn't move his car. Sitting in the hotel he picked up a Bible and, for some reason he could not explain, read Matthew. He had never read a word of the Gospels before. Pasolini was a Marxist, and an agnostic. After the reading he put down the Bible, stunned. "I never had seen such an image of Jesus as portrayed in Matthew." Later this experience led to his award-winning film, "The Gospel According to Matthew." One critic said, "It had the power to hush scoffing crowds in theaters."

Norm Evans, a star for the Miami Dolphins, described Jesus, "I guarantee you, Christ would be the toughest guy who ever played the game." Martin Luther had this sense about seeing an image of Christ in action. *"Draw Christ as deep as possible into the flesh."*

This day, how do you see Jesus Christ in your mind's eye?

Lord, I contemplate the passion, the tears, the moment of anger, the compassion of your love revealed in Christ. Amen

> *Then he said to them, "The Sabbath was made*
> *for man, not man for the Sabbath. So the Son of Man is Lord even*
> *of the Sabbath." Mark 2:27*

Shabath (shaw-bath) is the Hebrew origin of "Sabbath." It means to "stop, cease, desist, repose." Regular time "to cease" each day, a special time each week, a period of time for a 'summer retreat' makes pure physiological and theological sense. The first time *"Shabath"* occurs in the first chapter of Genesis, God *'desists.'* Jesus reminds us that the Sabbath commandment is for the best intentions of persons created by God's love.

In the dawn of the Reformation in Scotland, Presbyterians were in ascendency. The new faith was interpreted by some as a legalistic control of society mandated from the pulpits. The Kirk leaders of St. Andrews, Scotland, record the first time in history that a man is arrested for playing golf on Sunday. That happened December 18, 1583. In 1613, in Fraserburgh, the sheriff arrested "John Burnet...and forced him to sit on the Maister's stool for correction." This was a high stool in the front of the congregation. We imagine the congregants quietly enjoyed watching John being reprimanded by the preacher while they noisily voiced their condemnations of this horrific sin. In 1900, Mrs. Darwin R. James, the leader of the Women's Sabbath Alliance, told an audience of *crusaders-to-save-the-Sabbath*, "Many golfers go out blowing horns, singing and flaunting their disregard for the *Sabbath*; caddies are forced to begin wrong by working on Sunday; all criminals start on the downward path by working on Sunday."

We are in the *laissez faire* era. We have the burden of free choice. Paul instructed the Galatians: "We were imprisoned and guarded under the law until Christ came...for freedom Christ set us free."

Yes. Amen.

Are we using, or abusing our freedom in Christ? You choose. *Tee Time* or *Time with Christ? (You can do both, in my opinion...and that is only an opinion.)*

Lord of the Sabbath, and all the days of our lives, thank you for the choice I have in using the time, days-months-years, you have given me. Amen

> (God) is not far from any one of us.
> For in him we live and move and have our being. Acts 17:27
> Pray always and do not lose heart. Luke 18:1 NRSV

Meditate for a moment on the universe(s) of all that is—God is the creator—progenitor of genes, designer of quarks, leptons, neurons and molecules, originator of exploding stars, dark energy, and glorious galaxies. Meditate for a moment on the immediacy of God—Spirit of the inner presence—instills life in consciousness, enlivens solitude, inspires the soul, infuses spirit in our innermost being.

Jesus said to "pray always and do not lose heart." I experience thoughts of remoteness, cynicism, self-pity, and negativity. Hear the good news: *there is a free antidote for these diseases of the soul. Jesus commended the remedy. It is prayer.*

We learn about prayer from the Galilean whose followers 'turned the world upside down.' Every sentence and paragraph in the narrative of Christ demonstrates the centrality of prayer. In Christ we see the proximity of holy presence. Prayer marks every step in the biography of Christ: birth, baptism, temptation in the desert, public teaching and ridicule, private mentoring of disciples, police courts, threats, beating, insane jealousy from men of power, rejection, hatred, execution, and resurrection.

Life has, in the lyrics of an old song, "loveliness everywhere." We can recapture the lost magic of childhood imagination, we gain sight to see with eyes of the heart, we gain quality of intelligence known as wisdom, we suffuse our senses with springtime joy, we learn to love our self creation, we enhance love for spouses, families, and friends—all of this comes from God through prayer.

Prayer is the antidote that cures the anorexia of the soul.

When we pray, we breathe the *wind-Spirit* of God. We pulsate with new songs, new ideas, and new life.

Ad majorem, Dei gloriam. 'For the greater glory of God' I bow in prayer to you, Father, Son, and Holy Spirit. Amen

You have searched me Lord, and you know me...
before a word is on my tongue you, Lord, know it completely. Psalm 139:1,4

Two essential facets of prayer: God hears prayer; God knows our thoughts before we think a word. *"Why pray then?"* someone may ask. *"Because."* Christ taught us to pray, Christ prayed, and God alone can fill the emptiness within us. Pray God's Presence.

Dr. Howard Rice was a seminary professor who possessed spiritual wisdom. Howard's life included an ever-present wheel chair to assist his physically challenged health. I knew him for thirty years and never heard a complaint about his affliction. The only reference to the wheel chair would be a humorous incidence related to the device. Regarding prayer he said, *"Some times we wake up at night and find monkeys swinging from tree to tree in the forest of our minds—monkey-brain night times."* How do we cure that? Watch late night television? Take a trip to the refrigerator? That doesn't work. *It only feeds the monkeys.*

Noteworthy people have a suggestion. The monkey-brain in the middle of the night disappears when prayer begins. The other witnesses to this truth: Mary the mother of Jesus, St. Francis, St. Teresa of Avila, Martin Luther, and Abraham Lincoln. Like you and I, these good souls experienced monkey-brain night times wrestling with fears and anxieties swinging, jumping, and screeching in the bramble bushes of the brain. Robert Burns light-heartedly said: "From ghoulies and ghosties and long legged beastyes and things that go bump in the dark, Good Lord, deliver us."

Let us pray *a prayer for thanksgiving.*

God, you have blessed our lives. For the nourishment of food, drink, laughter, conversations, and memories—we give you thanks. For strength to face challenge, for courage to overcome fear, for wills to choose what is right—we give you thanks. May we be mature enough to be as forgiving with the persons closest to the center of our lives, as you have been forgiving with us. The shadows of our small disappointments disappear in the radiant light of your love. For true love, life, and liberty—we give you Thanks. Amen

I come that they may have life, and have it more abundantly.
John 10:10 NRSV

This simple sentence of today's text is a great "opener." Writers and speakers are well advised to have a great opening sentence...that is where you lose or keep your audience. The best opener of the four Gospels is John's. *In the beginning was the Word, and the Word was with God, and the Word was God.*

Penguin Books published the "worst possible openers" for a book: e.g. "Just beyond the Narrows the river widens." First place for worst: "The sun oozed over the horizon, shoved aside darkness and with sickly fingers, pushed through the castle window, revealing the pillaged princess gaping in frenzied horror with a sodden amphibian lying beside her, disbelieving the magnitude of the frog's deception, screamed madly, 'You lied!'"

You may have life more abundantly. How many times have we considered faith a curtailment of life's most abundant and thrilling exploits? If you had the misfortune of having a Gestapo teacher or preacher of religion in your past, you may disbelieve this promise..."*Life more abundantly.*"

Saturday Night Live has entertained audiences for many years. Some will recall Chris Farley who died at 33 years, apparently from drug overdose. He launched his movie career from *SNL.* Farley said, "I used to think you could get a level of success where the laws of the universe don't apply. But they do...I still have to work on my weight, and other demons. But I'm a human being like everyone else. I'm not exempt." I'm sorry the demons won.

None of us is exempt from the reality that a deep center of our consciousness cries out, "It's not enough!" We have some choices how we fill the emptiness.

Would you consider the word of Christ?

Lord, thank you for the abundant joy and meaning for life that comes as a gift of grace. You have not exempted me from the fears and demons hovering around my frail humanity. You give your presence and your peace to fill my empty soul. Amen

All Scripture is God-breathed.
II Timothy 3:16

As we meditate on the text, consider the Greek word for "breathed" is the same word for "Spirit." When we say, "Scripture is *inspired*," we literally are saying "in-Spirited."

I think back on periods of introspective doubt and realize that picking up the Bible to look for textual inconsistencies—on which agnosticism chews its cud—is not *reading* the scripture. When I read with an open mind 'what the Living Word says through the written word,' then I feel the winds of the Spirit that lift the earthbound syntax to a sky of color and limitless horizons. My agnostic mind asks, "Why does John say that Jesus' ministry lasted three years, and the other three gospels say it lasted one year?" My open mind reads John and feels the power of the Spirit infused words, and my conscious presence listens to John: *The Word became flesh, and the Word was God. God sent his Son, the very glory of God, into the world, not to condemn but to save the world from its self-destruction.*

Franz Kafka describes the force of the written word: "A book must be the ax to break the frozen sea inside us." From the scriptures we learn about the providence of coincidence in the broad brush strokes of history. Two years before the U.S.A. was drawn into WWII, a Japanese diplomat named Chiune Sugihara was posted in Lithuania. The Germans had invaded neighboring Poland. Sugihara knew the atrocities of the Nazis against the Jews and began to give Jewish families visas to safe nations. He saved six thousand Jews. He did this on his own moral initiative disregarding his authorities and his own safety. In Israel today he is called the *"Japanese Schindler"* and a grove of cedar trees and a museum honor his name. Sugihara was listening to the words of people in need with an open mind and heart.

The scripture says, "Love one another, for love comes from God."

Open my mind to the scriptures, God, so that my mind may be opened. Amen

You may declare the praises of him
who called you out of darkness into his wonderful light. I Peter 2: 9

"Who is Christ for us today and what form should the church take?" These two questions from Bonhoeffer were among his last words before execution in a concentration camp in 1945. You and I may differ on our answers to the questions, but 'what form should the church take?' I believe an ounce of demonstration is worth a ton of speculation. I pray the church demonstrates Christ-like love.

In the center of Helsinki stands a new Lutheran Cathedral that is somewhat controversial because the architectural philosophy took seriously these questions—what form should a 21st century church take? Public complaints followed the grand opening. The church does not have a steeple, does not rise above the high rocks on the site where it was built. As my late wife and I entered the church, we knew our preconceptions of "cathedral" would be changed. We felt like we were entering a cave. Why not?

Our Lord Jesus was born in cave, tortured in a cave, imprisoned in a cave, and buried in a cave. The first Christians worshipped, hid, died and were buried in caves in the city of Rome.

We kept walking, entering that provocative cathedral. The worshipper moves into a large creative space of light. Isn't that what faith does? We walk through the darkness into the marvelous point of light from Jesus Christ. Bathed in the bountiful soft midmorning sunlight, we noticed the organ console was placed in the midst of people, not remote and above the people like most churches. We, the people, from nations around the world, sang a tune whose harmony was written by J.S. Bach in 1734. All sang in their native tongue. Ten Koreans standing next to us were singing. Their tears glistened in the sun rays on their smiling faces. Everyone knows the words, which are today's prayer:

"Break forth, O beauteous heavenly light, and usher in the morning." Amen

*"What no eye has seen, what no ear has heard,
and what no human mind has conceived"—the things God has prepared
for those who love him. I Corinthians 2:9*

It is beyond all the best minds of humankind combined: *The grace of God and his love for us is incomparable and incomprehensible. His grace heals the past, enlivens the present, and dreams the future.*

Martin Luther spoke of the grace of God in somewhat inexplicable words: "The atheist is God's dearest child." I take that to mean a right interpretation of the Shepherd who leaves the 'ninety and nine' in the sheepfold to go and find one lost sheep. Jesus said, "One lost sheep who is found brings the greatest joy to the shepherd."

Which reminds me of Lord Bertrand Russell. Lord Bertrand was a darling of the 'cultured despisers' and left of center intellectuals of his day. This group felt disenfranchised from the churches, but not from the universities. Lord Bertrand was very popular with American university crowds for books and lectures on such topics as, "The immorality of Jesus." Once he said, "The trouble with the world is that the stupid are cocksure and the intelligent are full of doubt." True on both accounts.

However, listen to Lord Bertrand toward the end of his life extol the essence of who Jesus is: "There are certain things that our age needs. (The Cold War was hot). Please forgive me for mentioning it—it is love, Christian love, or compassion. If you feel this, you have a motive for existence, a guide in action, a reason for courage, an imperative necessity for intellectual honesty." This statement in 1952 was a lightening bolt around the global community looking for visionary truth that *no eye has seen, nor mind has conceived.*

The dream of love that "fills mouths with laughter and tongues with songs of joy" is here, now, and for you.

Thank you, Christ, for superseding our best conceptions of the gift of perfect love. Amen

For I know the plans I have for you, declares the Lord,
plans to prosper you and not harm you, plans to give you hope and a future.
Jeremiah 29:11

Saul Bellow tells a story of a rabbi in the *shtetl*. He was famous for his lofty sermons. A mythology arose around the beloved leader of the synagogue. It was sincerely believed that the rabbi would vanish from the community the day before the Sabbath; he ascended to the gates of heaven. There he received words for the sermons the people loved.

A newcomer to the *shtetl* did not believe the story. Early one morning the newcomer stealthily followed the rabbi, and this is what he saw. Dressed in old clothes, armed with axe and saw, the rabbi went into the forest. He cut, gathered up the wood, and carried it on his back to the home of a poor old widow who was too feeble to get her own firewood. The rabbi had been doing this every week.

On the Sabbath, once again the beloved rabbi preached a lofty sermon. When a person spoke to the newcomer saying, "Our rabbi ascended all the way to heaven today." The newcomer said, "If not higher."

Jesus told his disciples, "Those who follow me will know the truth. The truth will set you free."

In obedience to the calling from God we receive "the plans" of God. This plan includes the gift of urgency for doing the perfect will of the Lord. Like the rabbi doing the work of compassionate love, we will find that God's plan will prosper us. We will be rich in measures infinitely beyond the value of diamonds and gold.

My Lord and my God, I prayed for money, you gave my life a mission; I prayed for painlessness, you gave me peace; I prayed to assuage my loneliness, you gave me love.

God, your plans give hope and a future. Amen

> *You must understand that no prophecy of Scripture*
> *came about by the prophet's own interpretation of things...though human,*
> *(they) spoke from God. II Peter 2: 20*

We learn about our faith from prisoners. Jesus, Paul, and Peter, among other founders of our faith, were tested in the crucible of unjust imprisonments. Part of our New Testament is 'Letters From Jail.' We are eagerly alert to the testimony of one who speaks through the pain and heartache of injustice and suffering. Consider the testimony of Commander Gerald Coffee, Reconnaissance Squadron 13, U.S.S. Kitty Hawk, 1960's.

The North Vietnamese shot down Coffee's RA5C Vigilante 'recon' aircraft. He was picked up from the sea and imprisoned by the Vietnamese for seven years. Coffee and his fellow prisoners were isolated from each other. They devised a code by which they could "tap" messages to each other. Every Sunday, for seven years, the American prisoners in "Heartbreak Hotel" tapped the 23rd Psalm to each other. Coffee said the most important words he heard in all those years were: "Even though I walk through the valley of the shadow of death, I will fear no evil, for Thou art with me. Thy rod and staff, they comfort me (even here). Thou preparest a table before me in the presence of my enemies. Thou anointest my head with oil, my cup runneth over." Coffee, a great motivational speaker, added to this story: "I knew my cup was running over in this situation because it was overfilled with joyful memories of a beautiful land and freedom, and the hope to return. That sustained me." Coffee was freed in 1973.

Jerry Coffee knew that his wife was pregnant when he left for Vietnam. When he was released from prison, the Commander learned that he was a dad of a seven-year-old son whom he never knew existed. The son's name is Jerry.

God of life and freedom, you have given us profound words of truth through men and women in prisons. We hear, and learn. Thank you for the final victory of freedom. Amen

If Christ has not been raised, your faith is futile.
If only for this life we have hope in Christ, we are of all people most
to be pitied. I Corinthians 15:17,19

I married a taphophile. This explains why visitations to *Pere Lachaise, St. Louis Cemetery No. 1,* and *Recoleta* have been on our travel itineraries. It is natural to inquire of a taphophile why this condition exists. My loving wife Lolly informed me: 'interest in people of the past,' 'curiosity about final statements of life purpose in epitaphs,' and, 'more importantly, signs of faith in life after death.' I was struck by these visitations to cemeteries: Paris, New Orleans, and Buenos Aires. Millions of people visit these sites every year.

The Bible has numerous stories about burials and the theologies attached to them. The high priests buried Judas' thirty pieces of silver *shame money* in the "Potter's Field," a cemetery for paupers, because they did not want to contaminate a Jewish burial ground. (Judas returned the betrayal money moments before his suicide). Christ was buried in a cave tomb given by a respected man of means in the Jewish community. Our word 'epitaph' comes from *epitaphium,* Latin for 'a speech made over a tomb.' King David's lament over the death of Absalom, some scholars believe, is the motive for several of the Psalms that are *epitaphium* type poems. I discovered one does not need to be a taphophile ('lover of trappings, including symbols of burials') to learn lessons of life from a cemetery.

Lucille Britt captured this interesting concept from a visit to a cemetery. Each tombstone had two dates, with a hyphen or dash between them: "It was the dash between the dates...the dates belonged to God, but that line is yours and mine."

My birth and death are in God's hands. The dash between the dates is the line representing my life. What am I doing with this priceless gift?

Our Father, you have revealed your love in Christ who is the Resurrection and the Life. Help me to use my gifted days faithfully. Amen

Since ancient times no one has heard, no ear has perceived, no eye has seen any God besides you, who acts on behalf of those who gladly do right, who remember your ways. Isaiah 64:3-5

Eternal God of all beings and all creation, you come to us as a soft echo in the morning mist across a sea in Galilee, in the voice of a prophet exiled in a friendless foreign land. *You come to us. Advent!* When we hear your voice, we find for the first time, the true source of ecstasy. Your presence *excites* us.

Thank you for giving us words from many languages to understand our selves, the universe, and the nature of faith. Thank you for the Greeks who gave us the word *ekstatikos.* You are the pure ecstasy of our souls. From you we have faith to get *out of the status quo* centered on self. This *ex—status—quo* is exciting. We are bored, diminished, and demented in self-worship.

God, I confess that the search for ecstasy has been a source of doom as well as divine rebirth. O God, you have shown me the inner void cannot be filled with false gods of ecstasy. You have forgiven me for accepting the vacuous attempts to excite my life.

Lord Christ, thank you for the true adventure of an exciting faith journey. You lead without coercion. You lead with love. You do not divide my soul from my intellect. You bind heart and mind in the passion for truth and justice. Thank you for the scintillating excitement that your leadership commands.

We see with a heart of faith your justice and mercy in the world. *You give us the delightful contemplation of divine displacement*: peace removes hatred, justice outweighs evil, and love overcomes fear.

Thank you for these ecstatic winds under our wings of our flight-paths through life. Amen

Don't you know that you yourselves
are God's temple and that God's Spirit dwells in your midst?
I Corinthians 3:16

"There are only two ways to live your life," Albert Einstein said, "One is as though nothing is a miracle. The other is as if everything is." Einstein chose the latter.

As I sat at the writing desk (allowed by museum officials) of Isak Dinesen a.k.a. Karen Blixen at the *Blixen House* in Kenya, I could imagine scenes from the movie "Out of Africa" that were based on Dinesen's book of the same title. I think she lived by Einstein's choice, 'everything is a miracle.'

Dinesen's *Babette's Feast* (the book on which the movie was based) also testifies to her belief in the miracle of God's grace. She said, "In our human foolishness and short-sightedness we imagine divine grace to be finite...But the moment comes when our eyes are opened and we see and realize that grace is infinite."

Personally, I cannot find "God" at the end of logical syllogisms, but I do experience God in everything. I believe if we are 'trying to find God,' we never will. God is not lost. We are. We are found by his infinite grace. That is the Gospel of Christ. God is familiar with our inner life. Our lives are his temple. Paul asks us in Corinthians,

"Don't you know that?"

Be, Lord Jesus, in the Sunrise of Hope, making Glad Mornings and new days.

Be, Lord Christ, in the Choice of Memories, welding strong links of Celebrated Tradition.

Be, Lord Jesus, in the present yearning, filling Love's cup with Thy Festal Wine.

Be, Lord Christ, in our election to enthrone Your Holy Spirit and Receive Your Grace.

Amen

(Today's devotion is based on a conversation with David Webb, my son-in-law, who is a farmer raising crops and cattle; this is his birthday.) Jesus told them this parable. "A farmer went to sow his seed...some fell on the path and the birds ate it; some fell on rocky ground and the plants withered; some fell among thorns and the thorns choked the plants; some fell on good soil, and it came up a hundred times more than was sown." Luke 8:5ff

"David, recall Brian Bosworth? He sounds like a farmer and theologian these days after his NFL and OU football career." "Yeah, what's he say?" "Bosworth said, 'You can create dreams; you plant seeds in people. God does it every day, and others come behind him and water the plants. A coach can plant a seed in a player.' What do you think David?" "I think Bosworth was a good football player, not sure about his farming."

"Jesus used a farming model in his parable of the seeds and soils," I said. "Did he get it right?" David said, "Yes, exactly right. And it was a short sermon. That's right too."

David and I mused a bit on the parable. The "seed" is the Word of God. Some people never get a plant of faith started; the seeds are destroyed. Some have their young plants wilt in the hot sun of life without spiritual nourishment. Others have the seed of faith choked out by destructive relationships. Some grow to maturity in the good soil of faith. Love, joy, and peace are the harvest.

Dr. Norman Borlaug, Nobel laureate and agronomist who invented the seeds that produced the Green Revolution, is credited with saving over one billion people from starvation. He said: "If you desire peace, cultivate justice, but at the same time cultivate the fields to produce more bread; otherwise there will be no peace."

God, you are the Lord of the Harvest; inspire us to sow seeds of love faithfully. Amen

We have been justified through faith; we have peace with God through our Lord Jesus Christ...We know that suffering produces perseverance; perseverance, character; and character, hope. Romans 5:1ff

Tommy Ventris was my high school football coach. His speeches mixed metaphors, deployed *non sequiturs*, and produced laughter (at the wrong time). The first half of a game we played like a confederacy of dunces. Ventris based his half-time speech on this memorable thought: "Let's learn from your stupid mistakes the first half and make new ones the second half." I can still identify with this kind of coaching.

What does make a world of difference between a winning and losing team, school, company, church, or, individuals? Paul got the formula right: choose the central theme of justification by faith, not works, and let the works that follow justify to the world around you what your faith means. Being a forgiven Christ follower does not diminish the value of *character and behaviors.*

Principal Rudy Bernardo gathered the teachers and students of a failing school that faced 'shut-down' in Dayton, Ohio. They discussed their future and what was necessary to succeed. They decided that *character* was missing, and it could be rehabilitated. The group decided on "Thirty-eight Character Traits that would Change the Future: Citizenship, Cooperation, Fairness, Honesty, Kindness, Patience, Promptness, Respectfulness, Self-Reliance, Truthfulness, Cleanliness, Courage, Generosity, Independence, Loyalty, Patriotism, Punctuality, Responsibility, Sportsmanship, Uniqueness, Confidence, Courtesy, Goodwill, Initiative, Neatness, Perseverance, Readiness, Self-Control, Thankfulness, Consideration, Dependability, Helpfulness, Joyfulness, Obedience, Politeness, Resourcefulness, Self-Discipline, and Tolerance."

The school used each word as a 'theme for the week' and concluded the week with a general assembly celebrating that week's "word" in plays, songs, and readings created by the students. The school moved from "failure" to nationally regarded success, transforming the students and the teachers. Seventy-eight percent of the homes represented in the school were below the poverty line.

Praise God from whom all blessings and character traits flow.

God, may I never judge another person's character with the thought he or she 'will never change.' First, change me. In Christ. Amen

Always be prepared to give an answer to everyone who
asks you to give the reason for the hope you have. But do this with gentleness
and respect. I Peter 3:15

How may times have I missed giving a 'reason' in response to a question concerning the 'hope' God has given me? O, let me count the ways. How many of my responses were without gentleness and respect? God, forgive me.

Our culture in America has the advantage of hard won liberty. Freedom misused and freedom abused shall be lost. I believe the church as the body of Christ lives always with this mandate to be prepared to defend the faith, and speak the truth in love. Paul said, "For freedom, Christ has set you free."

Is "silence" the besetting sin of our time? Of course we hear the cacophonies of politics and social engineers. That noise should never be a warrant for our silence. Jesus taught that the weightier matters of the law of God are justice and righteousness. Micah summed up the promise and purpose of the covenant of God with his people: "What does the Lord require of you but to do justice, love kindness, and walk humbly with God?"

God will free me from the burden of my regrets, but I shall never forget them. Today and in all tomorrows I commit to speak when asked for the 'reason of my hope in Christ.' I pray to God that wisdom, gentleness, and respect shall accompany my speech. My silence cannot be excused by timidity or fears, which are real. "The Spirit of God does not make us timid, but gives us power, love, and self-discipline. So do not be ashamed." (II Timothy 1: 6)

An old friend of the faith explained this to me. "There are times when God wants us to speak out, speak up, and then shut up."

Lord, my faith and liberties from you came through persons who defended these gifts. I remember my debt today. In Christ. Amen

For it is better, if it is God's will, to suffer for doing good than for doing evil. For Christ also suffered once for sins, the righteous for the unrighteous, to bring you to God. I Peter 3: 17

Boyhood memory has both sight and sound as I recall watching B-25 Mitchell bombers practicing low level approach runs to a target airfield three miles away. From my perch on top of the barn roof I saw the faces of the cockpit crews. Some years later, a WWII veteran who lived with us for several years told me what I had seen, the 16 medium weight bombers Lt. Colonel James Harold "Jimmy" Doolittle commanded. They were preparing for the daring 'Doolittle Raid' on Japan in 1942 several months after the Japanese attack on Pearl Harbor, December 7, 1941. Years later, General Doolittle said, "Democracy is stronger than terrorism, and we will not cower to the terrorists' campaign of fear." The "Raid" produced many individual stories of heroic survival. By plan, the bombers, who hit Tokyo, Kobe, Yokohama, and Osaka did not have enough fuel to return to the U.S.S. Hornet. They tried to land in China.

Jacob DeShazer was one of the pilots: shot down by the Japanese, tortured, imprisoned, and witnessed American prisoners beaten to death and starved to death. Jacob was an atheist but managed to get a Japanese guard to give him a Bible for a few days. He read the Bible, changed his beliefs, and became a transformed man after the war. In 1948, with his wife and baby son, DeShazer returned to Japan as a missionary for Christ.

WWII caused the U.S.A. to transform from a tertiary power in the world to a "super power." The war was instrumental in transforming the life of Jacob DeShazer. Suffering produced endurance, endurance produced character, in the Spirit of Christ.

Our Father in heaven, we ask your presence of strength for those suffering as they do your perfect will on earth. Amen

*Speaking the truth in love, we will grow to
become in every respect the mature body of him who is the head, that is,
Christ. Ephesians 4:15*

Every one may consider these two questions: "How many people are in the church because I am?" Alternatively, "How many people are not in the church because I am?" The leading pollster group for religion in America has data that illustrate an important point: "By far the number one reason new members join a church is from what they hear the members say about their church." Why do members speak up positively about their church? Ask them. Listen to the answers: "My faith is nurtured." "The mission serves people in need no one else sees." "I experience at worship the real presence of Christ."

Can anyone doubt the success of the early church in the decades following the death and resurrection of Christ? Historians, even harsh critics of Christianity, see a *nonpareil* phenomenon in the survival and growth of the church. It was not through power, elite family connections, wealth, or intelligence that the church became the strongest force in the Roman Empire. The strength of the church was the character of its members. The members of the church were inspired by one standard, Jesus Christ. In Christ the first disciples saw the irrepressible energy of *agape*, sacrificial love. When the hard human heart is changed in many people, history changes. God transforms individuals. A company of transformed people transforms the world around them.

There is a Gestalt axiom at work in this paradigm of change: when individuals are profoundly renewed by grace through faith, the group is infinitely greater than the sum of its parts.

God, praise and glory are yours: you first spoke the truth in love through Jesus Christ. Thank you, Christ. You are the head of the church. Amen

The only thing that counts is faith expressing itself through love. You were running a good race. Who cut in on you to keep you from obeying the truth? Galatians 5:6-7

W.H. Auden felt "cut in on" by the church when he was about thirteen. By the time he was thirty-three he had a 'reconversion' (his term) to Christian faith and joined the church. He had several mentors on the way back home to God: Reinhold Niebuhr, Dietrich Bonhoeffer, and Soren Kierkegaard. During these years Auden became an American citizen. He won the Pulitzer Prize for "The Age of Anxiety," a poem of seminal influence. You may remember Auden from popular movies, such as "Four Weddings and a Funeral." Of enduring love he wrote: "I'll love you, dear, I'll love you till China and Africa meet, and the river jumps over the mountain and the salmon sing in the street." Auden said, *"A real book is not one that we read, but one that reads us."* I pray for that 'reading' of myself when I open the Bible.

Niebuhr is quoted, in most cases unknowingly, by every member of Alcoholic Anonymous worldwide; he authored AA's universal prayer: *"God grant me the serenity to accept the things I cannot change, the courage to change the things I can, and the wisdom to know the difference."* Niebuhr defined the reason why Auden and many of us are drawn to the gospel. *"Forgiveness is the final form of love."* In Christ we receive this unmerited love. Faithful believers practice this unique love. It transforms despair, loneliness, and the dark spirits of rage and self-revulsion.

You may know someone who feels "cut in on" in the good race of life. You may also be the one who helps that person get back on track. The race ahead is pure joy and serenity.

Open my eyes and heart to the person I know who has felt they were 'cut in on' and then dropped out of the good race of faith. Amen

As God's co-workers we urge you not to receive God's grace in vain. For he says, "In the time of my favor I heard you, and in the day of salvation I helped you." I tell you, now is the time of God's favor, now is the day of salvation. II Corinthians 6:2

When the shadow of the wolf crosses your path, it is too late to run. This proverbial thought described the state of consciousness of a man who said to me, "I think it is too late to be asking questions about belief. I have neglected faith pretty much most of my life." He was 80 years old.

We talked about a couple of biblical characters who were somewhat 'aged' when enlightenment came. Then I gave my friend, who was keen on biographies, the names of five men, and said, "Sorry if this sounds like a school teacher's assignment, but would you check these people with your question, 'when is one too old to have a new experience of God?" The names were: T.S. Eliot, Evelyn Waugh, C.S. Lewis, Graham Greene, and Alexander Solzhenitsyn. The assignment was completed in about two weeks. My friend said, "I just became a Christian. I did not know about the 'grace of God' until I saw it in others from the pages of those biographies. The grace of God was the common crimson thread that ran through each of these lives who expressed a reconciliation with God late in life."

If we are breathing, it is never too late to meet God's grace revealed in Christ. My friend needed to live out his age of doubts until he discovered that his whole philosophy of life was nothing but dikes of negativisms holding back the sea of God's love. The dikes broke. The sea won. Lanza del Vasto said, "Between the marvels of the world and the distress of the human heart, the Spirit has fastened this bond named religion."

Search me, Lord, and know my doubts. I accept your love. Christ is my truth. Amen

(Today's devotion is written by my 18-year-old granddaughter, Kirstin Barr, on her birthday.) God is our refuge and strength, an ever present help in trouble. Therefore we will not fear, though the earth give way and the mountains fall into the heart of the sea, though its waters roar and foam and the mountains quake with their surging. Psalm 46:1-3

It is in times of deepest sorrow and suffering that we often come to doubt the power of the Lord. We often forget that there is something greater controlling the universe in ways we do not, we cannot understand. Our Lord is powerful in ways we cannot even comprehend. It is in the times of pain and fear that we must hold faith in Him, and we must try to understand that there is a higher order of things.

We search for the truth and still question at times. There comes a time when logic simply cannot explain why things are happening to us. This is the time when we must allow God to take over.

We have to realize that some things are out of our control. While it is a frightening idea that no matter how hard we try, we still cannot control all the things that happen in our lives. It should be an equally comforting thought that the Lord can and will take our pain, our fear, and our suffering away. He will help us during these times of trial, and will lead us into His light. Even when it seems that the Earth is collapsing all around us, our Lord will prevail and lead us along with Him. We are never alone. We just have to be willing to ask for help.

Dear Lord,
Please help me find You in times of pain. Help me to see Your light and allow it into my eyes. While it seems everything is falling apart, please take away my fear, pain, and anger. Help me to stand tall in these times and feel Your strength. Amen

Be still before the Lord and wait patiently for him.
Psalm 37:7

Eternal Christ our Risen Lord: Is time an illusion? You have given me a time to love, a time to laugh, a time to serve and a time to die. You have commanded me to do the Word and not merely speak the Word of your imperative truths. Strangely, you ask me to 'wait, and be still.' I confess my weakness to be still and hear nothing but the song of your joyous presence.

Help me to learn the fine art of waiting in stillness. I must wait for your will in the choices I make; Good Lord, help me. I must wait for the comforting presence of the Holy Spirit to overcome anguish and despair; Good Lord, help me. I must be still and wait for healing when love is lost, when death seems to have the victory; Good Lord, help me.

I wait for you, O Lord, as I step into the unknown tomorrow of illness and uncertainty. I shall wait for your presence when the present night is an impenetrable shadow of fear; Good Lord, help me.

You, Lord, have waited for us. Thank you. I have let the thoughtless currents of the world carry me in meaningless bays of discontent. You, Lord, waited for me to take hold of your saving grace. Lord, your mercy is from everlasting to everlasting; thank you for waiting for me when my impetuous self was fixated on gratification that cannot quench my thirst. Your mercy waited for me.

Take not your Spirit from me. Melt me in the crucible of life and love. Separate the dross of perversity and duplicity from my soul.

Like the Prodigal son, I return to you, the Waiting Father. Thank you for waiting for me. Amen

T.S. Eliot: *I said to my soul... the faith and the love and the hope are all in the waiting.*

You also, like living stones, are being built into
a spiritual house to be a holy priesthood, offering spiritual sacrifices
acceptable to God through Jesus Christ. I Peter 2:4

The world is a huge community *in search of personal community.* Kurt Vonnegut impressed many Baby Boomers. He lamented the world: "Here we are trapped in the amber of the moment. There is no why." His solution, "Find ways to inhabit primitive communities. That's my hope." Pope John Paul II said the "community needs a soul to become a true home for human beings. You, the people, must give it this soul." Aung San Suu Kyi, whom I call a martyr for democracy, spoke to all people yearning to be free: "We will surely get to our destination if we join hands." The cry is universal. We need a redeeming personal community to find personal liberty.

Sixty years have passed since Reinhold Niebuhr coined this phrase: "Man's capacity for justice makes democracy possible, but man's inclination to injustice makes democracy necessary." The whole world yearns for democracy. The word itself means "rule of the people." This can only come from a strong community where the integral value of life is shared.

Powerful individuals do not change the world. Christ called together the 'church.' In Greek *ekklesia (ek-klay-see-ah)* literally means 'the called out ones.' Called by Christ, each with a 'calling' and together, the 'Body of Christ.' Sandra Day O'Connor observed, "We don't accomplish anything in this world alone... and whatever happens is the result of the whole tapestry of one's life and all the weavings of individual threads from one to another that creates something." The mass of humanity longs for *community. But it must be a personal community.*

On this eve in which *This Day* begins *The Twelve Days of Christmas* leading to the birth of Jesus, we trust God who is the Lord of the future to bring to fruition the redemptive community of persons who, together, can change the world.

God, thank you for the 'promise' in your Promise through Jesus Christ. Amen

The Lord himself will give you a sign:
The virgin will conceive and give birth to a son, and will call him
Immanuel (meaning 'God with us.'). Isaiah 7:14

The condition of the world addressed by Isaiah was unadulterated chaos. The time is the last two decades of the 8th century before Christ. Assyria is the superpower *de jour.* In 722 B.C. ten of the twelve tribes of Israel were taken captive *never to be traced in history again.* Isaiah addresses 'Judah' which is the kingdom of two remaining tribes of Israel— Judah and Benjamin. God shall intervene in human history. Isaiah 'knows' this will happen because he believes in God's providence. He believes God is not remotely observing the world, but God 'so loves' the world he shall send The Messiah. The Messiah shall be born of a woman and born into the human community. The Messiah is not subtlety detached in the heavens like the Greeks' gods. This Messiah will be called *Immanuel,* 'God with us.'

Albert Camus spoke of a fundamental 'sin' in society: *"If there is a sin against life, it consists...in eluding the implacable grandeur of this life."* Can you and I behold the implacable grandeur of God's invasion into the human affairs of this wobbly world? *Immanuel* is the implacable gift of grandeur. He will teach us truth. If we hear, if we follow the truth of love, we shall be set free. Abraham Lincoln said, "In the end, it's not the years in your life that count. It's the life in your years." *Immanuel is truth and life.*

Immanuel, God with us, shall show us the power of forgiveness and love. No more cycles of vengeance. Retribution only causes a new round of violence against itself. Retributive justice is not just, because it doesn't create a better world. The new justice from *Immanuel* is love in action. "The Lord himself" will do this.

Thank you for fulfilling your promise of love, O God, in the advent of Immanuel in our world. Amen

Comfort, comfort my people, says your God...
"In the wilderness prepare the way for the Lord;...The glory of the Lord
will be revealed, and all the people will see it together." Isaiah 40.1ff

Christmas is for children. Christian faith is for all who have childlike openness of mind and heart. "I give you praise, Father, Lord of heaven and earth," said Jesus, "because you have hidden these things from the wise and the learned, you have revealed them to little children." (Luke 10:21) Dr. Seuss said 'adults are obsolete children' and that is why he preferred children for an audience.

Henri Nouwen discerned the quality of a message from God requiring child-like uncomplicated faith: "Many of us have become so serious and intense, so filled with preoccupations about the future of the world and the church, so burdened by our own lowliness and isolation, that our hearts are veiled by a dark sadness, preventing us from exuding the peace and joy of God's children."

We, adults in a world of wonder designed for childlike amazement, do not like to admit what are the most popular proclivities in the profile of adulthood. Just look at what we adults do and say. How do we spend our time, our money? What do we read and watch by choice? Here's the profile in four words: *power, revenge, attention-getting, feelings-of-inadequacy.* We have normalized the behaviors in our consciousness, and lionized these behaviors in celebrities. Casey Stengel saw the problem: *"The trick is growing up, not growing old."* Hang on to, reclaim the gift God gave to children: *curiosity, surprise, wonderment, and joy.*

Today's scripture speaks to my adult needs. I will listen to children sing and see the smile in their hearts. "Comfort those who sit in darkness...Peace waits for them...All flesh shall see the blessing...God's Word is never broken." (Genevan Psalter, 1551)

"Come, Thou long expected Jesus, born to set Thy people free; from our fears and sins release us; let us find our rest in Thee." Amen (Charles Wesley, 1744)

The Lord is in his holy temple; let all the earth be silent before him.
Habakkuk 2:20

Please for the sake of your mind and heart, let there be times of *holy silence* this Christmas.

"Let all mortal flesh keep silence, And with fear and trembling stand; Ponder nothing earthly minded, For with blessing in His hand, Christ our God to earth descendeth, Our full homage to demand." (Words from the Latin *Liturgy of Saint James,* 4th century, music from a French carol sung in American from *The English Hymnal.* Our faith today owes a debt of gratitude to people of many nations.)

In *This Day* we cite authors from around the world. Here are the words from an eighth grade girl in Oklahoma, Jordan Thompson: "God sent His tiny child/ To redeem our terrible sin./ Jesus came as a baby mild,/ But defeated the devil's grin./ For this present, God we thank./ At the time when it was most needed,/ He delivered a savior without rank,/ His gift we seldom heeded./ So when your gifts you receive,/ Or you admire Christmas lights,/ Remember God's love never leaves;/ Proof of this came the first Christmas night."

Was Oscar Wilde right? We are "people who know the price of everything and the value of nothing?" On the third of twelve nights of Christmas many people are looking at the receipts stacking up, "the prices of everything." We are checking prices in the Google ads, papers, and on store windows.

It's time to make Oscar Wilde's assessment wrong. "Let all mortal flesh keep silence," including my own, Lord. This day I will empathize with one of the Magi gazing at the starlight and hoping to find the Light of the World. I will listen with a shepherd's attention to sounds of the night, and imagine a song angels only could sing. With Mary and Joseph, I patiently wait.

In this silent moment, God, I thank you for the gift of Jesus Christ. Amen

*The earth is the Lord's, and everything in it, the world,
and all who live in it...Lift up your heads, you gates; be lifted up, you
ancient doors, that the King of Glory may come in. Psalm 24:1ff*

Only two days ago we cited Henri Nouwen, a world famous spiritual leader. Accomplished people, like all of us, need to renew the springs of nourishment to the taproot of their tree of faith. Nouwen did this with the wise and comforting counsel of Mother Teresa. When Nouwen, a teacher of theology at Notre Dame, Harvard, and Yale showed up in Calcutta, he said, "I am willing to spend six weeks" if necessary. I need the inner "wisdom" you have. Mother Teresa grabbed both of Nouwen's arms, looked into his eyes, paused, and said: "I can teach you Christian wisdom, not in six weeks, but in sixty seconds. *Give adoration to God, who alone is the Spirit of Love, for one hour each day. Then do everything that day that you think is right to do."*

I covenant with Christ this day to give focused time in Adoration to the Lord. Then, do what is right.

We get sidetracked on this railroad of Christmas commitments and may not get to the *main terminal* of this journey, *The Celebration of Jesus Christ.* Are we like the minions described by H.L. Mencken: "... people who go out to smell the roses and look around for a coffin." Negativities stack up like boxes in a department store backroom.

"Fling wide the portals of your heart; Make it a temple, set apart from earthly use for heaven's employ, adorned with prayer, and love, and joy." The King of Glory will come into the lives of all who lift up the ancient doors of fear, and let love in.

"Redeemer, come! I open wide my heart to Thee; here, Lord, abide. Let me Thy inner presence feel; Thy grace and love in me reveal." Amen (Georg Weissel, 1642)

The tender mercy of our God, by which the rising sun
will come to us from heaven to shine on those living in darkness and in the
shadow of death (shall) guide our feet into the path of peace. Luke 1:76

When I would ask my friend Don Nicholson, accomplished lawyer and cowboy at heart, "How ya doin'?" he would answer, "I'm running like a dog in tall grass."

Zechariah is the story of a priest 'running like a dog in tall grass.' Luke tells the story: A messenger from God told Zechariah that his wife Elizabeth would have a son, and this son would be a forerunner for the Messiah. Childless so far, Zechariah doubted the good news. The messenger said, "For doubting what God can do, you will not be able to speak, for a time."

Zechariah's turn had come to give the prayers and burn incense in the Temple. The great sanctuary was filled with a throng of people. Zechariah opened his mouth to speak, fear overcame him. He was totally mute. He returned home. Soon, however, his wife was pregnant. They had a son. The text we read today picks up the story, where Zechariah returned to the temple 'found his voice' and named his son John. (We know him as John the Baptist.) With his new voice Zechariah gives one of the most beautiful statements for *confidence in the future* ever declared: "The rising sun from God shall shine in the darkness of humanity. This Light of the World will guide our feet into the path of peace."

One of the miracles we may expect from Advent is the miracle of converting life's terrible extremities into God given opportunities. Like a dog running in tall grass, we break out into the light of Christ who will "guide our feet into the path of peace."

Thank you, God, for Zechariah and all your messengers of peace in Jesus Christ. Amen

John the Baptist came preaching in the wilderness of Judea saying, "Repent, for the kingdom of heaven has come near." This is he who was spoken of through the Prophet Isaiah: "A voice of one calling in the wilderness, Prepare the way for the Lord, make straight paths for him." Matthew 3:1ff

John the Baptist was like the town crier of Shakespeare's "Hamlet." Hamlet, in the narrative of the play, had written some lines for the actors to recite before the king. He instructed the actors to say the lines with passion, *"trippingly on the tongue."* Furthermore, Hamlet warned, if the actors cannot do this, he will give the role to the 'town-crier:' *"But if you mouth it as many of our players do, I had as lief the town-crier spoke my lines."* God did not wait for professional actors. He chose John the Baptist to be the 'town-crier' and awaken the people that the Messiah is coming to town. *"Prepare ye the way!"* The first task, even before you meet the Messiah, is 'repent.' The Greek word means 'turn around.'

We can do that today. *Turn around*: get new directions for life. Turn around from the wrong directions of celebrating. *Turn around*: Advent this year will focus on Christ, celebration of Christ on earth, restoring the miracle of Christmas. *Turn around*: Sing, "Prepare the way, Your Christ is drawing near!" We do not want to end life like Pilot Whales stranded on a barren beach because our moral guidance system failed.

Wayne Gretzky, one of the great stars in the history of the NHL, was spot-on when he said, "I missed all the shots I never took." Don't miss a shot at John the Baptist's message: "Turn around." Take the shot. Get new life-directions. The Lord is near. Awake! "Make straight the way for God within, and let us all our hearts prepare for Christ to come and enter there."

Thank you, God, for "coming" to our life and world. Your advent causes me to repent, turn around, and renew my faith in Christ. Amen.

(Christ) made himself nothing, by taking the very nature of a servant, being made in human likeness. Philippians 2:7

In humility there is strength. Followers of Christ have sung the words of this Latin hymn for twelve centuries: "Creator of the stars of night; Your people's everlasting light, O Christ, Redeemer of us all, we pray You, hear us when we call. When this old world drew on toward night, You came, but not in splendor bright, not as a monarch, but the child of Mary, blameless mother mild."

The grandest act of the Almighty is the humble advent of Jesus. The life of Jesus personified the strength of humility. "The Son of Man came to serve."

Once a European of supreme intelligence followed the course of many continentals, in the days of colonization, to Africa. This man had four doctoral degrees. He was not happy. One day he asked the "happiest person" he had ever met, a poor African village woman, "Would you tell me the reason you are always happy? I am not." She said, "Yes. Come in for tea." Inside the grass hut she offered him a cup of tea. She poured the cup full, and continued to pour as the tea spilled to the ground of the floorless home. "Now you see; you are filled with knowledge, ideas, and words. They are spilling over your full cup. To be happy, you must *first empty yourself.*" Albert Schweitzer thanked her.

"Christ made himself nothing..." comes from the Greek word *kenosis.* It means *"self emptying."*

Christmas is a feast of receiving and giving, and receiving and giving. This day, for the sake of true happiness, how can we empty ourselves? Are we too full of *things* to receive God's gift of *love?*

Lord Christ, you come to this gaudy, giddy world in the humility of a servant. Your Name has risen above all names through the power of love and grace. Amen

I am with you, declares the Lord Almighty.
This is what I covenanted with you when you came out of Egypt.
And my Spirit remains among you. Do not fear. Haggai 2:5

The Advent of Christ makes this promise delivered by the prophet come true. Christmas is a season to celebrate the real, incarnate presence of God; "my Spirit *remains among you. Do not fear."*

Our human habit reverts to ancient patterns unconsciously. Modern people have the same proclivities of the people of the covenant addressed by Haggai. We may become so fascinated with physical reminders of religion that the symbols become substitutes for the personal presence of God. The paradox is this: the symbol originated as a means to experience mystical presence, but an inversion takes place. The symbol becomes an end in itself, an idol. The Hebrew word for 'idol' translates 'no-god.'

The prophets unanimously warned the faith community of the dangers of idolatry. When the Jewish people were taken into the Babylonian Captivity, they lost the temple. A generation later the Persians defeated the Babylonians and allowed the Jews to return home, but without the sacred symbols of the Covenant. The Ark of the Covenant was a wooden box containing three sacred symbols of Judaism: 'stone tablets inscribed with the Ten Commandments,' 'a pot of manna' (miraculous food that kept the fleeing Israelites alive in the desert), and 'Aaron's rod.' The Ark of the Covenant was lost. Some believed faith was lost. The physical symbols were gone. (Note the 1981 movie "Raiders of the Lost Ark".)

Haggai: "No, you are wrong, *my Spirit remains among you."* The coming of Christ is the fulfillment of that promise. We hear this sung at Christmas in Handel's "Messiah:" *"I am sending my messenger to prepare the way before me...the messenger of the covenant in whom you delight—indeed, he is coming!"*

Thank you, God, for coming to us in Jesus Christ and giving us your Spirit. Amen

The angel went to (Mary the Nazarene) and said, "Greetings, you are highly favored! The Lord is with you." Mary was greatly troubled. The angel said, "Do not be afraid, Mary; you have found favor with God. You will conceive and give birth to a son, and you are to call him Jesus." "How will this be," Mary asked the angel, "since I am a virgin?" The angel answered, "The Holy Spirit will come on you, and the power of the Most High will overshadow you." Mary answered, "May your word to me be fulfilled." Luke 1:26-29

Two traits of Mary give us a key to our belief in God. One is *dubious reaction*; she had a personal encounter with the holy presence of God. She hears an invitation to a calling to serve God, and responds, (I paraphrase) "Moi? You can't be serious! LOL Just look at who, what, where I am!" The second trait is *prayerful acceptance*; Mary speaks seven words we prayerfully consider for ourselves: *"May your word to me be fulfilled."*

We learn from Mary. She had no money, no power, no privileged family lineage; add to this humble status, she was a woman in a male dominated world. In the 1st century society, Jewish men had a morning prayer: "Thank you, God, that I am not a Gentile, a slave, or a woman." The Greco-Roman world was organized in a male oriented hierarchical structure defined, among others, by Aristotle. He said in this hierarchy of the created order, angels are next to God, men next to angels, and women were between slaves and property. *The Lord Almighty disrupted this status quo.*

The incarnation of Jesus, the Son of God, the Word made flesh, shall come from a powerless woman who lives in an inconsequential outback province of the Roman Empire.

Lord, 'may your word to me be fulfilled' as you call me to follow Christ. Amen

357

The true light that gives light to everyone was coming into the world...All who receive him, to those who believed in his name, he gave the right to become children of God. John 1:9ff

"It's a Wonderful Life," starring James Stewart and Donna Reed is a Christmas classic and a 'parallel gospel.' George Bailey (Stewart) dreamed of being adventurous and successful. The Roaring Twenties quickly turned into the Great Depression. George gave up his dreams to help his dad run the Bailey Loan Company. His dad dies, the Depression hits. George took the money he saved for college and a honeymoon with his bride (Donna Reed) and gave money to customers who faced loan calls or foreclosures from the "baddie" banker, Henry Potter (Lionel Barrymore) "the richest and meanest man in town."

On Christmas Eve, George reached the end of the rope of confidence and hope. He thought he had lost everything, he felt totally worthless. Considering suicide, Clarence, an angel, intervened. Angel Clarence helps George find his true self. George Bailey simply discovered the true humanity of George Bailey. "I am the richest man in town—I have a beloved wife, family, and friends."

The movie is a parable of the Gospel. In God's gift of Jesus to the world, we meet the Word of God in the flesh. God encounters us at the deepest level and need of our human condition. We learn from Christ what it means 'to be fully human:' *To love, and to be loved.* Christ loves us and gives us his free gift of grace. That is the sublime present we can receive this Advent.

According to The Gospel of John, "The Word became flesh and made his dwelling among us. We have seen his glory, the glory of the one and only Son, who came from the Father, full of grace and truth."

Thank you, God, for the gift of Christ's love and the discovery of our true humanity. Amen

An angel of the Lord said, "Joseph, do not be afraid to take Mary home as your wife, because what is conceived in her is from the Holy Spirit. She will give birth to a son, and you are to give him the name Jesus. Matthew 1:20 In those days Caesar Augustus issued a decree that a census should be taken of the entire Roman world. So Joseph went to Bethlehem...to register with Mary...who was expecting a child. Luke 2:1ff

Christianity is the only living religion of the world with origins planted firmly in recorded history. Caesar Augustus had successfully united the Roman Empire after defeating competing generals, including Anthony and his Egyptian ally, Cleopatra. The birth of Jesus took place in the reign Augustus that lasted for fifty-seven years. The empire was never as large or as unified since Alexander the Great. The Roman world had legal, military, and transportation systems, and the common languages of Greek and Latin. That made possible the explosive expansion of the new faith centered in Jesus Christ.

Humble persons were vehicles of God's grace incarnated in Jesus Christ. Joseph is one of those heroes of our faith. He knew God and was obedient to the will of God beyond the limits of his understanding. St. Augustine said, "Faith is to believe what you do not see; the reward of this faith is to see what you believe." After the obedient act of trusting the integrity of God's will, Joseph saw the profound reason for God's miraculous works.

Imagine Joseph's stream of consciousness: *Lord, Bethlehem seems far away. Will we get there? As I hold Mary close and put my hand on her rounded stomach I feel the baby. In the dream you told me it was a boy. What will he look like, do, believe, and experience when he becomes a man? I am old, I may never know. I trust your mysterious ways.*

Our Father, thank you, for faith, on this eve of unimaginable expectation. Amen

The shepherds said, "Let's go to Bethlehem and see this thing that has happened, which the Lord has told us about." So they hurried off and found Mary and Joseph, and the baby, who was lying in the manger. When they had seen him, they spread the word...and all who heard it were amazed. Luke 2:15ff

The birth of Jesus turned the world upside down. The poor and common people were made strong, the sick were healed, the hungry were fed, outcasts were gathered in. A young woman without wealth or privilege became the most famous woman in history; millions of baby girls have been named after her— "Mary"— the mother of Jesus: "Maria," Spanish; "Malia," Hawaiian; "Maarja," Estonian; "Maliya," Mandarin Chinese. Her child grew up and "irresistibly became the center of history."

A Leo Tolstoy's Christmas story (paraphrased): Father Martin lived alone. His wife and children had died in a plague. He prayed to God, 'I do not want to live for one more Christmas. I am alone, and lonely.' An angel of the Lord answered in a dream, 'You shall not be alone, Christ will personally visit you, be prepared.' Father Martin prepared bread, tea, fruits, and cakes, and waited, and waited.

It was a cold Russian Christmas. Martin could see the street sweeper, frozen and hungry; Martin invited him in. Christ had not come as the angel promised, so Martin gave the sweeper bread, hot tea, and cakes. Looking out the window Father Martin saw the oldest and poorest widow in the village, selling apples. A boy had just stolen her basket of fruit and her money, pennies for Christmas. He helped the widow, gave her food, tea, and money. That night, again, alone, he prayed, 'Christ where were you?' The Lord answered, 'Martin, I was there with you, remember the street sweeper and the widow, inasmuch as you have loved the least, you have loved me, and I am with you always.'

God, thank you for the gift of Jesus Christ who brings love into our lives. Thank you for Mary, your chosen one, teaching us the power of humble obedience to your promises. Amen

There were shepherds living out in the fields nearby, keeping watch over their flocks at night. An angel of the Lord appeared to them, and the glory of the Lord shone around them, and they were terrified. But the angel said to them, "Do not be afraid. I bring you good news that will cause great joy for all the people. Today in the town of David a Savior has been born to you; he is the Messiah, the Lord." Luke 2:8

Why "shepherds?" This narrative of God's incarnation in the world of human affairs is stunning news, a miracle beyond miracles. I think the characters drawn into the gospel story are intentionally placed in the drama of revelation.

Shepherds were among the lowest common denominator of 1st century Judaism. They raised lambs for sacrifice in the great temple, one of the grandest architectural edifices of the world. The city walls surrounding the temple in Jerusalem had a "Sheep Gate," the only place the shepherds were allowed to enter. The priests needed the lambs raised by the shepherds, thousands of them. But the shepherds were not allowed into the temple area for worship. Because of their vocation, they were considered "unclean." It was impossible for the shepherds to follow the Kosher Laws for ceremonial washing.

Every shepherd knew the feeling of prejudicial rejection. The religious rulers wanted their lambs for the sacrifice, but not the people who raised the lambs. "Give us your sheep; you stay outside." This was not the first or last time in history that barriers were put up by elitists who demanded services of the very people they excluded.

The history of the gospel is the story of God's love in Christ breaking down the pretentious boundaries concocted by persons against persons.

From shepherds, we learn the paradox of providence: The meek shall inherit the earth. The last shall be first. Christ the Lord of all became a servant of all.

Lord, I thank you for teaching me how your love surprises everyone. Amen

After Jesus was born in Bethlehem in Judea, during the time of King Herod, Magi from the east came to Jerusalem and asked, "Where is the one who has been born king of the Jews? We saw his star when it rose and have come to worship him."
Matthew 2:1-2

The Magi (magician or wise person) from the East perhaps were Zoroastrians, an ethical monotheism that continues to the present time in Persia (Iran, parts of Iraq). The Magi were probably familiar with the Hebrew scriptures. Roman trade routes connected the East and West countries, and Jews lived in Babylon six centuries before the birth of Jesus. Perhaps the Magi knew about the Messiah passages in the Hebrew scripture. We know for certain, the gifts they presented were valuable. Frankincense and myrrh were equal to gold in trading value. Probably these gifts originated in *Arabia Felix*, a Roman term for the southern rim of the Arabian Peninsula. Myrrh is a clear resin from the *Commiphora* tree; when mixed with wine it has a narcotic affect, hence *"Arabia Felix,"* ('happy'). This is the mixture Christ refused during the crucifixion. The Magi were undoubtedly trained in astrology, a precursor to astronomy and widely studied by the Persians. Every 805 years there is an unusual alignment of Jupiter, Saturn, and Mars that gives the effect of a "bright star." Perhaps this happened at the time of Jesus' birth?

We know for certain: Christ was born, he taught, he was crucified, and raised from the dead. The first followers of Christ came from the nations of the world, East, West, North and South. Unlike any religion before, Christian faith included men and women, Jews and Gentiles, slaves and free persons.

When we meditate on the *visitation of the Magi*, we are immersed in the global consciousness and universal spiritual attributes of our faith. Christ is Lord of all, or not at all.

God, thank you for the gift of Christ, who is the Lord and Savior for the world. Amen

On the eighth day, when it was time to circumcise the child, he was named Jesus...
When the time came for the purification rites required by the Law of Moses, Joseph
and Mary took him to Jerusalem to present him to the Lord...and to offer a sacrifice:
"a pair of doves." Luke 2:21ff

Robert Browning wrote: "Life succeeds in that it seems to fail, a paradox which comforts as it mocks." The humble parents of Jesus followed the traditions handed down for generations. On that day they could not have known the paradox of failures and success for the future of Jesus. Mary saw his popularity as a teacher, and she saw the crowds turn on her son. She saw the malice of the same priests she knew from his childhood. She could never have imagined during that ritual of purification that later she would be a witness to his execution in the same city, Jerusalem.

God blesses us in not giving us a script, in advance, about the future. He does give us faith in his love. Our security is in knowing the love, not the details of our future successes or failures.

Judith Shea is a sculptor whose work, "Without Words," sits in my memory bank as if I saw it a minute ago. It is a life size bronze of a 'man' sitting on a bench. He is wearing a trench coat. Hands in pockets, slightly hunched forward, the figure has the feelings of...*tired, lonely, sorrowful, passive.* Wait, there is no man in the coat! The coat is totally empty. Aren't many of us, like Magi, like "Without Words", searching to fill our empty lives with love?

The paradox in the temple: Mary and Joseph handing baby Jesus to a priest, following tradition, who will sacrifice two doves for a human being. Unknown to parents or priest, this human being is the Son whose ultimate sacrifice frees us from the bondage of our sin, fear, and fate. Such a paradox! Such a glorious success!

God: your amazing grace sets us free, free at last, through Jesus Christ. Amen

An angel of the Lord appeared to Joseph in a dream. "Get up," he said, "take the child and his mother and escape to Egypt. Stay there until I tell you, for Herod is going to search for the child to kill him." Matthew 2:13

Envision yourself in Joseph or Mary's sandals. God, who led you in the past, is now saying, "Run! for your life." Could I trust my spiritual instincts, when such extraordinary commands were emitted? In jest it has been said: 'Science is looking for a black cat in a dark room and finding it. Philosophy is looking in a dark room for a black cat that is not there.

Theology is looking in a dark room for a black cat that is not there and finding it."

When I look at the faithful characters in the gospel's story, what I sense is that all three definitions are wrong. The New Testament confirms that we do not own a science, philosophy, or theology that "finds God." Our faith experience is this. *God finds us.* The New Testament narrative is more like a "divine romantic comedy." The people lost, like us, demonstrate expansive foibles. The people redeemed, like us, demonstrate love's joyful victory. *"God is love. God first loved us. I chose you."* What's amazing about God's grace is the way it initiates love. Our faith follows the divine initiative. Mary and Joseph were willing to follow the paranormal commands of an angel because they trusted the divine initiative of God's unvanquished love.

We learn from Mary and Joseph that destiny is not an outward conformity to the culture surrounding us. Destiny is created from an inward spirituality. To live by faith is to really believe God has a vested interest in your future, joy, and love.

Faith in the goodness of God enables us to let the past and the future co-exist in the present. It's a wonderful faith for ending an 'old' year and beginning a 'new' year.

Thank you, God, for all that is past, *Yes* to all of your future. Amen

The Son is the image of the invisible God
...He is before all things, and in him all things hold together.
Colossians 1:15,17

Charles Handy, Irish writer and philosopher, asked his family at an end of the year dinner party to 'list all the things that got better in the last decade.' Handy, a Christian, did not know what to expect. They agreed on one thing, "New Zealand wine."

In the last year, what 'got better' for you? Many today see a world in which 'all things are falling apart.' The research shows that among people who 'believe' in God there is a high rate of pessimism. Are we like Empedocles? Five centuries before the birth of Jesus, he defined "God" as "a circle whose center is everywhere and whose circumference is nowhere." That would include one's self. Indeed, Empedocles did believe he was 'god'; convinced, he jumped into Mount Etna's volcano. This *beau laid geste* does not impress. Christ gives us another definition of God: God came to us in Christ with the new cohesion of unconditional love. "In him all things hold together."

There is a beautiful illustration in the last book of the Bible. The Lord says, "To the one who is victorious, I will give a white stone with a new name written on it, known only to the one who receives it." (Revelations 2:17) In the Greco-Roman world of the New Testament era, white stones, as honors, were given to athletes with the abbreviation "SP" for *Spectatus* written on the stone. It was a sign of "proven valor."

The *name* you 'see' on your personal "white stone" shall be *the name by which you call on "Jesus Christ"* in whom "all things hold together." That's a future with hope. What name shall you see on your 'white stone?' This 'name' shall give you hope in a new year. Hold tight to your white stone.

Thank you, God, for the hope we have in Christ, for the future we hold in your will. Amen

If anyone acknowledges that Jesus is the Son of God, God lives in them and they in God. And so we know and rely on the love God has for us. God is love. Whoever lives in love lives in God, and God in them...There is no fear in love. But perfect love drives out fear. I John 4:15-18

It's New Year's Eve. This moment on the razor edge between 'this' and 'that' provides ample space to find what must be done now. *Express gratitude to God.*

Lord, hear our Prayers:

Thank you, God, for forgiveness.

Thank you, Christ, for unconditional love.

Thank you, Holy Spirit, for the 'gifts,' especially joy and peace.

We have already begun Resolution Lists for tomorrow morning. Tennyson said it poetically, "Hope/ Smiles from the threshold of the year to come,/ Whispering it will be happier." My list is not poetic: Courage enough to ask, "Who am I?" Curiosity enough to ask God, "How may I learn more about 'who you are?'" And, a Companion enough to ask a beloved one, "How may I be more loving?"

Learning an answer to any question is not merely being attentive to a voiceless universe of people. *Learning* includes knowing *where* to look. I think, believe, and hope that any answer to my three questions will come in the calculus of love.

With unyielding confidence we boldly take the journey to the future. We travel with Christ. Unexpected histories are being written. We see only a few words and pages at a time. We read on because we trust the Author of all history. We take this journey through the good and bad times, through all the New Years, knowing our destination is God. We are blessed, excited and filled with the abundant life given to all of us.

"Bon Voyage!"-French; "Yat louh pihng ngon!"-Catonese; "Goede reisil!"-Dutch; "Tanyan omani yo/ye po/pe!"-Sioux; "Safari njema!"-Swahili. "Have a Good Voyage!"-American.

O God of love, we know you have plans for our welfare and not our harm. Let us trust you to give us a future with hope, through Christ Jesus. Amen

About the Author

A Washington state native, Mike Anderson dribbled his way into the ministry as a basketball player at Whitworth University, found his voice at San Francisco Theological Seminary, and earned his Ph.D. at the University of Edinburgh.

Pastor of University Place in Tacoma, WA, then Managing Director of Interpretation and Stewardship for the World Mission, United Presbyterian Church, in the "God Box" in New York City, and later Senior Pastor at Westminster Presbyterian Church, Oklahoma City, Mike concluded his vocational calling as President and CEO of the Presbyterian Health Foundation, home to 36 bioscience companies.

Now happily retired, Mike lives with his wife, Lolly, also a writer, and their dog, Aussie, on a beautiful lake in Oklahoma. Father to four daughters and grandfather to nine grandchildren are joys beyond measure.

This Day is available through Amazon.com, Barnes & Noble.com, and your local bookstore. For discounted bulk orders, please contact Ionic Press at 405.478.2006.

IONIC
PRESS

CPSIA information can be obtained at www.ICGtesting.com
Printed in the USA
LVOW05*1341291113

363123LV00004B/7/P

Peace of the Lord!